MONEY IN BRITAIN
1959-1969

Money in Britain

Britain

1959-1969

THE PAPERS OF THE
RADCLIFFE REPORT - TEN YEARS AFTER
CONFERENCE AT HOVE, SUSSEX
OCTOBER, 1969

EDITED BY

DAVID R. CROOME

AND

HARRY G. JOHNSON

OXFORD UNIVERSITY PRESS

1970

Oxford University Press, Ely House, London W.1

GLASGOW NEW YORK TORONTO MELBOURNE WELLINGTON
CAPE TOWN SALISBURY IBADAN NAIROBI DAR ES SALAAM LUSAKA ADDIS ABABA
BOMBAY CALCUTTA MADRAS KARACHI LAHORE DACCA
KUALA LUMPUR SINGAPORE HONG KONG TOKYO

PRINTED IN GREAT BRITAIN BY
WILLIAM CLOWES AND SONS, LIMITED
LONDON AND BECCLES

PREFACE

This book contains the papers and proceedings of a conference of monetary economists working in British universities, banks, and government departments which was held in October 1969 to commemorate the tenth anniversary of the publication of the Report of the Radcliffe Committee into the working of the U.K. monetary system.

In the view of the organizers of the Conference, the tenth anniversary of Radcliffe not only constituted an appropriate point in time at which to review the Report, but might also mark the end of a historical epoch in the evolution of British monetary institutions. The Radcliffe Report was sceptical about the usefulness of monetary policy as an instrument for domestic economic stabilization, and its views probably contributed to the assignment of a relatively passive role to monetary policy from 1960 to 1968, as contrasted with the role it played from 1951 to 1959. The 1970s may well see a renewed emphasis on monetary policy in Britain, following the lead given by the revival of 'monetarism' in the United States and with the encouragement of the International Monetary Fund's prescription of control of the money supply as a means of improving Britain's balance-of-payments position. In parallel fashion, the 1960s may turn out to have been a period of once-for-all structural change in the British financial system, in response to the external pressures and internal economic policies experienced during the period, and the 1970s may witness a period of relatively stable financial growth.

In accordance with this view, the Conference had three major objectives. The first was to review developments in the areas about which the Radcliffe Committee had been especially concerned, and particularly changes in the country's financial structure and in knowledge of how the financial system works, in theory and in practice. It was unfortunately necessary to exclude external financial relations from the programme owing to limitation of time, but otherwise post-Radcliffe developments were fully explored. The second was to bring together economists from a variety of institutions concerned either practically or scholastically with the United Kingdom's monetary system, to pool their various special knowledge of and insights into the system's workings and problems. This meant, on the academic side, bringing together monetary historians, institutional specialists, econometricians, and monetary theorists; and, in the framework of the Conference, bringing together academic economists, bank economists, and economists from the Bank of England and the Treasury. To maximize the benefits of interchange, the authors of papers were selected from the experts in the relevant areas, bank economists analysing developments in monetary institutions, academic economists discussing theory, history, and empirical testing, and policymakers discussing the evolution of monetary policy. Discussants were so selected as to ensure the expression of official, commercial, and academic views on every question.

The third objective, related to the second, was to establish some common ground and the beginnings of a mutually understood frame of reference among economists customarily observing the monetary system from a particular institutional vantage point. The Conference was in fact the first of its kind ever held in this country; and both the formal sessions and the informal discussions that occurred revealed that, while participants were concerned about common problems, there were serious difficulties in finding a common language in which to discuss them. A particular example was the concept of 'liquidity', key to the philosophy of the Radcliffe Report, which turned out to mean quite different things to the econometrician intent on model-building, the theorist intent on analysis, the practical banker concerned with portfolio management, and the policy-maker responsible for monetary management. It is hoped that the Conference achieved some progress towards mutual understanding.

In editing the volume, we have reproduced the papers as they were delivered at the Conference. We feel that, while some topics are covered in more than one paper, it is preferable to retain the architectural intent of the authors, and that repetition of the same facts from different points of view may well be illuminating. We also feel that the differences in style among the papers will convey something of the interest and atmosphere of the Conference proceedings. To this end we have also included brief summaries of the informal discussions of the various papers, intended to record the more important points made, but without attributing views to particular participants.

In conclusion, we would like to record, on behalf of the participants in the Conference, our gratitude to the Committee of London Clearing Bankers for financial support, to *The Bankers' Magazine* for encouragement and hospitality, and to the Shell Company for advice and help in the technical organization of the Conference. We are also grateful to Prof. Richard Sayers for delivering an informal speech at the inaugural dinner of the Conference, on the subject of the work of the Radcliffe Committee.

DAVID R. CROOME
Queen Mary College

HARRY G. JOHNSON
*The London School of Economics
and Political Science*

London, November 1969

CONTENTS

I

THE RADCLIFFE REPORT IN THE TRADITION OF BRITISH OFFICIAL MONETARY DOCUMENTS

E. VICTOR MORGAN

Discussion Papers

(*a*) L. S. PRESSNELL
(*b*) W. T. NEWLYN

I

THE RADCLIFFE REPORT IN THE TRADITION OF BRITISH OFFICIAL MONETARY DOCUMENTS

E. Victor Morgan
(*Professor of Economics, University of Manchester*)

I. Introduction

THE history of monetary controversy in Britain begins in the Middle Ages, but in this paper I shall not attempt to go back further than the suspension of cash payments by the Bank of England in 1797. Since that time there have been twenty-one major enquiries into various aspects of the monetary and banking system, not counting several technical ones on the state of the coinage and on decimal currency (the first of these as long ago as 1857) and many concerned with industry, trade, or agriculture in which some reference was made to monetary matters.

The suspension, itself, was the subject of enquiry by both houses of Parliament; the Commons enquired into the currency and exchanges of Ireland (1804) and the high price of gold bullion (the famous Bullion Report of 1810); while both houses appointed committees on the resumption of cash payments in 1819. The forty years following the resumption of cash payments saw the rapid growth of joint stock banks, a number of very severe financial crises, and the controversy between the Currency and Banking schools. The Lords investigated the circulation of bank notes of less than £5 (1826–7) and the Commons enquired into the renewal of the Bank of England Charter (1831–2), joint stock banks (1836–8), and banks of issue (1840–1), while both houses appointed committees on each of the great commercial crises of 1848 and 1857. By contrast, the period from 1860 to 1914 was relatively calm; cyclical fluctuations in trade, employment, and prices continued and there were also secular upward and downward movements of prices, but financial crises became less severe and the period is still widely regarded as marking the height of monetary stability. Though there was a good deal of discussion of monetary matters in the press and among economists, there were only two official enquiries, into banks of issue (1875) and 'recent changes in the relative values of the precious metals' (the Gold and Silver Commission, 1888).

There are, of course, many other differences arising from the circumstances and climate of opinion in which different enquiries took place. Nevertheless there is enough common ground to amply justify the organizers of this conference referring to the 'tradition' of official monetary documents. There is an obvious continuity in the subjects covered, and the persons concerned (at least up to the Radcliffe Committee) shared a common heritage of theory which had been evolved in the fierce debates of the late seventeenth century and which was stated with great force and clarity by both Hume and Smith. The core of this theory was the quantity theory of money and its application to the international distribution of the precious metals, which was summed up by Hume as follows:

Suppose four-fifths of all the money in GREAT BRITAIN to be annihilated in one night, and the nation reduced to the same condition with regard to specie, as in the reigns of the HARRYS and EDWARDS, what would be the consequence? Must not the price of all labour and commodities sink in proportion, and everything be sold as cheap as they were in those ages? What nation could then dispute with us in any foreign market, or pretend to navigate or to sell manufactures at the same price, which to us would afford sufficient profit? In how little time, therefore, must this bring back the money which we had lost, and raise us to the level of all the neighbouring nations? Where, after we have arrived, we immediately lose the advantage of the cheapness of labour and commodities; and the further flowing in of money is stopped by our fulness and repletion.[1]

[1] David Hume, *Writings on Economics*, ed. E. Rotwein (Nelson, 1955), pp. 62–3.

A further logical consequence of the quantity theory which was also clearly seen by Hume is that money can have only a temporary influence upon the rate of interest which, in the long run, depends on the supply of and the demand for capital. These views never commanded universal assent as we shall see, but they were far more widely accepted and more influential than any of their competitors during the two centuries before the publication of the *General Theory*. The First World War and its immediate aftermath brought committees on bank amalgamations (1918), currency and foreign exchanges after the war (the Cunliffe Committee, 1918–19) and the amalgamation of the Treasury and Bank of England note issues (1924–5). To end the lengthy list we have the reports of the Macmillan Committee (1931) and the Radcliffe Committee (1959).[2]

It will be apparent from this summary that the earlier committees had fairly specific terms of reference, but those of more recent committees have been very broad. The Macmillan Committee was 'to inquire into banking, finance, and credit, paying regard to the factors both internal and international which govern their operation, and to make recommendations calculated to enable these agencies to promote the development of trade and commerce and the employment of labour',[3] while the Radcliffe Committee was simply charged 'to inquire into the working of the monetary and credit system and to make recommendations'.[4]

There has also been a change in the composition of the inquiring bodies. Until 1875 these were parliamentary committees and membership was, of course, drawn from members of the house concerned; more recently they have been either royal commissions or departmental committees composed mainly of officials, bankers, and businessmen with a small but influential sprinkling of academic economists. These changes are apparent in the reports; the earlier committees

[2] A full list of references is contained in A. Feavearyear, *The Pound Sterling*, 2nd edn. (Oxford, 1963), pp. 425–6.
[3] *Macmillan Report*, Cmnd. 3897, para. 1.
[4] *Radcliffe Report*, Cmnd. 827, para. 1.

often took voluminous evidence but their reports are usually brief, and they vary considerably in intellectual power; more recent reports, especially those of the Macmillan and Radcliffe committees, are both wider ranging and more detailed, and have a distinctly academic flavour.

The Radcliffe Committee, partly because of the influence of Keynes, departed from tradition in several important respects, though still following it in others. The rest of this paper will look at five areas: the objectives of policy and priorities among them; the relationship between money and prices; money and money substitutes; the operation of Bank rate; and the influence of government debt on the monetary system. In each case, I shall start with the ideas of the Radcliffe Report and then say a little about their historical pedigree.

II

The Radcliffe Report lays great emphasis on the contrast between the complexity of current objectives and the simplicity of those of the past. It lists the objectives of monetary measures as:

1. 'A high and stable level of employment'
2. 'Reasonable stability in the internal purchasing power of money'
3. 'Steady economic growth and improvement of the standard of living'
4. 'A margin in the balance of payments' to make some contribution to the development of other countries and to strengthen the reserves.[5]

The list of the Macmillan Committee was:

'Maintaining the parity of the foreign exchange without unnecessary disturbance to domestic business'
'the avoidance of the Credit Cycle'
'the stability of the price level', and
'the stability of output and employment at a high level'.[6]

The Radcliffe Committee omits the reference to the 'Credit Cycle' and adds growth and development. There are also

---

[5] Cmnd. 827, para. 69.   [6] Cmnd. 3897, paras. 280 and 282.

significant differences of emphasis; stability of the price level is not qualified by Macmillan as by Radcliffe, and when the two lists are read in their context it is clear that the Macmillan Committee attached a higher priority to international considerations and to the maintenance of exchange parity. Nevertheless, the Radcliffe Committee seems to exaggerate the difference between itself and its predecessors in this respect.

Of the nineteenth century, the Radcliffe Committee says, 'before 1914 the maintenance of convertibility at a fixed gold value of the pound was sufficient definition of the duty of the Bank of England'.[7] This view finds some support in the Cunliffe Report, which lays great stress on the automatic aspects of the gold standard. It is, however, both technically wrong and highly misleading as to the spirit that pervaded most of the nineteenth century. Technically, the maintenance of convertibility was not a duty but a legal obligation and, after 1844, the Bank's primary duty was to conduct its business under the law in such a manner as to preserve the solvency of the Banking Department. No one, however, believed that this was its whole duty, or that the monetary system did not have a powerful influence on prices, employment and the balance of payments. The Bullion Report is largely an analysis of the role of the monetary system in wartime inflation; the fall in prices that followed the resumption of cash payments produced a bitter debate in which the Bank was severely blamed; and all the committees in the long series between 1826 and 1858 devoted a large part of their time to the way in which the management of the currency and the activities of banks affected industry and trade. Even towards the end of the nineteenth century, when the gold standard was supposed to be at its most automatic, the Bank accepted the obligation of 'lender of last resort' and frequently allowed considerable fluctuations in reserve, thereby cushioning the domestic system against some of the effects of international gold movements.

The nineteenth century was more modest than the twentieth

[7] Cmnd. 827, para. 53.

in its view of how far official action, monetary or otherwise, can control events. Samuel Jones Lloyd (Lord Overstone), one of the leaders of the Currency School, wrote:

> The buoyant and sanguine character of the human mind; miscalculations as to the relative extent of supply and demand; changes of taste and fashion; legislative enactments and political events; excitement or depression in the condition of other countries connected with us by active trading intercourse; an endless variety of casualties acting upon those sympathies by which masses of men are often urged into a state of excitement or depression; all or some of them are generally the original exciting causes of those variations in the state of prices. . . . The management of the currency is a subsidiary agent; it seldom originates, but it may and often does exert an influence in restraining or augmenting the volume of commercial oscillations.[8]

Similar quotations can easily be found in his great adversary, Thomas Tooke, and in many other writers.

The nineteenth century was also clearer in its priorities than was the Radcliffe Committee. From the Bullion Report right through to Cunliffe, and indeed Macmillan, priority was given to convertibility and stable exchange rates. This was partly due to a recognition of the importance of a stable international currency to a nation so largely dependent on trade, but also to a belief that this was the best way of promoting the other objectives of stability in industry and trade and in the domestic value of the currency.

The likelihood of conflict between these objectives was less in the nineteenth century for several reasons: the average level of unemployment was much lower than that of the interwar period, though by no means as low as that which has prevailed since 1945; money wage rates were probably less rigid against downward movements; and the position of London as a short-term creditor enabled the Bank of England to replenish its reserve quickly and relatively painlessly by raising Bank rate. It was generally agreed, however, that if domestic prices were too high in relation to those of other countries, a reduction could only be brought about by means of a check to output and employment and a fall in money wages. There were differences of opinion as to the damage to

[8] *A letter to J. B. Smith*, p. 167.

output and employment, with the 'sound money' men of the Bullion Committee, the Currency School, and the Cunliffe Committee tending to minimize and their critics to exaggerate the difficulties of adjustment. Curiously, some of the more facile views occur in the later reports. For example, the Committee on the Currency and Bank of England Note Issue of 1825 (really a committee on the return to the gold standard) considered the alternatives of reducing British prices by ten to twelve per cent or waiting a few months before resuming convertibility and asked whether 'the substantial advantage of an immediate return to parity' were worth 'the inconveniences—temporary though possibly severe while they lasted—of the measures of "deflation" necessary to bring about the adjustment'.[9]

Finally, the nineteenth century differed from the Radcliffe (and to some extent Macmillan) Committee as to whether agreed objectives should be pursued by means of rules or discretion. The Bullion Committee put the case for rules; the restriction of cash payments had given the directors of the Bank the task of supplying, at their discretion, 'that quantity of circulating medium which is exactly proportioned to the wants and occasions of the Public. In the judgement of the Committee, that is a trust, which it is unreasonable to expect that the Directors of the Bank of England should ever be able to discharge. The most detailed knowledge of the actual trade of the Country combined with the profound science in all the principles of Money and Circulation, would not enable any man or set of men to adjust, and keep always adjusted, the right proportion of circulating medium in a country to the wants of trade.'[10]

The Bullion Committee believed that it had found a sufficient rule in convertibility; the Banking School argued in favour of convertibility plus discretion, but were overborne by the Currency School who found their rule in making the combined circulation of notes and coin behave as it would if

[9] Para. 16.
[10] The Bullion Report reprinted in E. Cannan, *The Paper Pound of 1797–1821* (London, 1919), p. 52.

it were wholly metallic. This rule was, of course, embodied in the fixed fiduciary issue of the 1844 Bank Charter Act. The Bank still had to use discretion but it was exercised in relation to the 'proportion' of the Banking Department, not the gold reserve. The rule was much criticized for having aggravated the crises of 1848 and 1857, but it earned growing respect later in the century and was defended by the Cunliffe Committee. The fixed fiduciary issue, the Committee argued, provided 'an automatic machinery by which the volume of purchasing power in the country was continuously adjusted to world prices of commodities in general. Domestic prices were automatically regulated so as to prevent excessive imports, and the creation of banking credit was so controlled that banking could be safely permitted a freedom from state interference which would not have been possible under a less rigid currency system'. Here is a good example of the tendency, mentioned above, of this Committee to stress the automatic aspects of the gold standard.

Though only twelve years separated the Cunliffe and Macmillan committees they had only one member (Lord Bradbury) in common, and the tone of the two reports, in this and many other matters, is very different. Of the fixed fiduciary issue, the Macmillan Committee said that, 'with the exclusion of gold coins from the domestic circulation . . . the old system has lost almost entirely its original meaning'.[11] From this it is only a short step to the Radcliffe Committee's dismissal of regulation of the note issue as 'otiose'. Neither committee was, of course, prepared to suggest a new rule in place of the old and the Radcliffe Report argues that, because of the complexity of modern policy objectives, 'it is no longer appropriate to charge the monetary authorities with unambiguous tasks that can be sharply differentiated from other government action.'[12]

III

In an oft-quoted passage the Radcliffe Committee states that, 'we cannot find any reason for supposing, or any experience

---

[11] Cmnd. 3897, para. 322.   [12] Cmnd. 827, para. 52.

in monetary history indicating, that there is any limit to the velocity of circulation.'[13] This would seem to imply a complete rejection of the quantity theory of money and the denial of any necessary causal connection or any stable and predictable relationship between the quantity of money and the price level. In other parts of the Report, it appears that some trace of causality may still remain insofar as changes in the quantity of money may affect the rate of interest or the liquidity, and hence the willingness to lend, of financial institutions.

Monetary measures are expected to work through 'the total pressure of demand', a conveniently vague phrase that occurs many times in the Report. Monetary action influences that pressure through its effects on interest and on liquidity. The interest effect is believed to be of little account, both because it is weak in itself and because the actions of non-bank intermediaries will minimize the effect on interest rates of a change in the quantity of money. The liquidity effect, operating mainly on the willingness of institutions to lend is claimed to be more powerful, though some passages in the report suggest a distinctly ambivalent attitude towards it.

It is very difficult to discern any coherent theory of how the pressure of demand affects prices, or indeed, of how the price level is determined. There are, apparently, different processes of adjustment in security markets and goods markets. In security markets, a decline in the quantity of money creates an excess demand for it and an excess supply of securities, and the market is cleared by a fall in security prices and a rise in the rate of interest. There is no trace, however, of any analogous process in goods markets; here, the effect on prices comes only when the 'pressure of demand' works through to production. There is an inconclusive discussion of the relationship between the level of employment and wage rates[14] and that is virtually all. It seems that, in the view of the Committee, there is no predictable relationship between changes in the quantity of money and changes in the price level and, furthermore, that any effect that might be brought about by a

---

[13] Cmnd. 827, para. 391. [14] Ibid., para. 64.

change in the quantity of money could equally well be brought about by any other circumstance affecting 'the total pressure of demand'.

The abandonment of the quantity theory without putting anything in its place is one of the most revolutionary and least satisfactory aspects of the Radcliffe Report. Having said this, however, one is bound to add that the version of the quantity theory that emerges from official documents is less refined and coherent than that of the textbooks.

None of the documents up to and including the Macmillan Report cast any doubt on the proposition that an increase in the quantity of money will tend to raise prices and vice versa. In general, the supporters of the Bullion Report and the members of the Currency School took a rather more rigid view than their opponents, and they were sometimes guilty of statements that suggests a strictly proportionate relationship between money and prices. It is unfair, however, to take these out of context. Reading their work as a whole, it is clear that they realized the importance of velocity and that they recognized both long-run changes associated with the evolution of financial institutions, and short-run changes due to fluctuations in business confidence.[15]

There was also general agreement that the price level can be affected by non-monetary as well as monetary influences, though there were many shades of opinion as to their relative importance and as to the power of sound monetary institutions to preserve stability by correcting disturbances arising from non-monetary forces. This is a matter which arose in many contexts—inflation during the French wars and depression after the resumption of cash payments; the sharp increases in commodity prices during booms and the disastrous falls which followed the financial crises of 1825, 1847, and 1857; and the secular downward movement from the mid-'seventies to the mid-'nineties; the inflation of World War I and the slump of 1929–31. The Macmillan Report summed up its view of this last event as follows: 'the recent world-wide

---

[15] A good example, too long to quote here, is in the Bullion Report. Cannan, op. cit., pp. 57–8.

fall of prices is best described as a monetary phenomenon which has occurred as a result of the monetary system failing to solve successfully a problem of unprecedented difficulty and complexity set by a conjunction of highly intractable non-monetary phenomena.'[16] This is a judgement with which most moderate opinion in the nineteenth century would have agreed.

One of the biggest difficulties faced by supporters of the quantity theory has always been to establish the precise means by which changes in the quantity of money are transmitted to the price level. Here, the tradition is one of broad agreement, though with many different shades of emphasis, and practically no empirical evidence. The broad agreement was to the proposition that the mechanism involved a temporary change of interest rates, which would then be reversed as soon as the equilibrium relationship between money and prices had been restored. Overstone describes the process thus: 'Contraction of the circulation acts first upon the rate of interest—then upon the price of securities—then upon the market for shares, etc.—then upon the negotiation of foreign securities—at a later period upon the tendency to enter into speculation in commodities—and lastly upon prices generally.'[17]

One of the areas of disagreement was the relative importance of short-term rates in relation to stocks of commodities and long-term rates in relation to fixed investment. Most writers in the early and middle years of the century would have concentrated more on 'speculation in commodities' and less on security prices than did Overstone. Later, however, opinion swung the other way. The Cunliffe Committee mentioned stocks of commodities 'carried largely with borrowed money', but its main argument was that, because of a general rise in interest rates, 'new enterprises were, therefore, postponed and the demand for constructional materials and other capital goods was lessened. The consequent slackening of employment also diminished the demand for

[16] Cmnd. 3897, para. 209.
[17] S. J. Lloyd (Lord Overstone), *Collected Tracts*, p. 253.

consumable goods.'[18] The account given by the Macmillan Committee is very similar.

Some writers argued that the availability of credit as well as its cost was important, and Henry Thornton (a member of the Bullion Committee) suggested that this had a direct effect on the demand for commodities: 'Every trader is encouraged, by the knowledge of this facility of borrowing, a little to enlarge his speculations; he is rendered, by the plenty of money, somewhat more ready to buy, and rather less eager to sell.'[19] However, such references to direct effects on goods markets are rare. I have been able to find no suggestion at all of any desired relationship between purchasing power and either income or assets; believers in 'Cambridge k' or the real balance effect will find no more support in the tradition than they will from Radcliffe.

IV

The Radcliffe Report is much concerned with non-banking financial institutions; their asset-creating activities are supposed largely to nullify the effect of a change in money supply on interest rates; their lending activities may frustrate any control that is exercised over the lending of the banking system; yet it is through its influence on their liquidity that monetary policy affects the 'total pressure of demand'.

Though some of the institutions with which the Radcliffe Report is concerned are of recent growth, the problem of money and money substitutes is a very old one. It involves the twin questions of how money should be defined and whether control over whatever may be defined as money can be rendered ineffective by changes in the supply of 'near monies'. These questions arose first in relation to metallic coin and Bank of England notes and, subsequently, in relation to country bank notes, bank deposits transferred by cheque, and bills of exchange.

With regard to the Bank of England notes, the Bullion

[18] Cmnd. 9182, para. 5.
[19] H. Thornton, *Paper Credit*, ed. F. A. Hayek (London, 1939), p. 195.

Committee argued that convertibility was a sufficient safeguard against excessive issues; if too many notes were issued their value would fall and the exchanges would become adverse; notes would be brought back to the Bank to be exchanged for gold for export, and the resulting loss of reserves would force the Bank to restrain its issues. The Currency School regarded convertibility as an inadequate safeguard mainly because of time lags, which might bring the Bank's reserve near to exhaustion and precipitate a financial crisis. Hence, their insistence on defining money as notes and coin, and on making the combined circulation behave as if it was wholly metallic.

The argument about country bank notes ran on very similar lines. Since country bank notes were normally payable in Bank of England notes, the country banks must keep a reserve of Bank notes or balances with their London agents which they could exchange for Bank notes. A country bank which over-issued would raise prices in its own locality, that locality would then develop an excess of payments over receipts with the rest of the country, and the bank would lose reserves. Again, the Currency School argued that this check was insufficient. Even though country banks might not be able to expand their issues indefinitely in face of a contraction by the Bank of England, they could do so for long enough to make the correct management of the Bank's own circulation impossible. They therefore contended that a single note issue, regulated according to their principles, was necessary.

When it came to bank deposits and bills of exchange the respective positions were somewhat different. The Currency School were confident that changes in the quantity of money, as they defined it, would quickly produce changes in the same direction in credit, so that the two would work together to restore equilibrium. The Banking School regarded only coin as money and included bank notes with deposits and bills of credit. They stressed both the large amount of credit outstanding and the variability of the volume of credit that could be sustained by any given amount of money. They did not, however, propose any regulation of credit, and Tooke's proposed remedies went no further than giving the Bank a monopoly of note issue and urging it to keep a larger reserve.

As the nineteenth century progressed, there was growing confidence in the power of the Bank of England to exercise the necessary degree of control over the rest of the monetary system. The view of the Cunliffe Committee has already been quoted. The Macmillan Committee referred to the inherent instability of credit, and to the difficulties of a central bank in maintaining stability, but these were difficulties of information, timing, international co-operation, and the response of investment to cheap money in conditions of depression; there was no suggestion that the Bank of England lacked the instruments necessary to control the creation of bank credit, or that such control was likely to be frustrated by the activities of other institutions.

V

There can be few greater contrasts than that between the Radcliffe view of Bank rate and that of the Macmillan Committee: 'There can be no doubt, in our judgement, that "bank rate policy" is an absolute necessity for the sound management of a currency and that it is a most delicate and beautiful instrument for the purpose.'[20]

The evolution of Bank rate over the past century and a half has been accompanied by many technical controversies which cannot be discussed here. There is no doubt, however, that the Macmillan view is in the tradition of British monetary documents, while the Radcliffe view is not, and there seem to be three main reasons for this.

One of the traditional virtues of Bank rate, and one which is supported by a great deal of evidence, is in replenishing the Bank's reserves by attracting gold from abroad. The Radcliffe Committee does not deny that this happened in the past, but it regards it as largely irrelevant to the present, partly because of obstacles to the movement of funds, but mainly because it found that short-term funds were now almost invariably

[20] Cmnd. 3897, para. 218.

'covered', so that any immediate gain to the reserves on spot transactions was matched by a forward liability.

Secondly, the traditional view of Bank rate gives an important role to the influence of short-term interest rates on the desire to hold stocks of commodities, and the Radcliffe Report emphatically denies that this effect has any importance under present conditions.

Finally, and perhaps most important, the Radcliffe Committee sees Bank rate in a role quite different from the traditional one in relation to the money supply. In the nineteenth century, Bank rate was normally used as a means of regulating the Bank's lending and, hence, the money supply. When money was tight, market rates were edging up towards Bank rate and the Bank was faced with an increasing demand for loans, Bank rate was raised in order to check that demand. Occasionally, Bank rate was raised when the money market was well supplied and, in such cases, the Bank usually engaged in open market operations in order to take money directly from the market and so make its rate 'effective'. According to the Radcliffe Report, 'if there is less money to go round . . . rates of interest will rise. But they will not, unaided, rise by much because . . . there are many highly liquid assets which are close substitutes for money.'[21] Bank rate, together with operations in the gilt-edged market are seen as the aids by means of which interest rates may be hoisted above the level which would otherwise have prevailed. This use of Bank rate as an instrument for maintaining rates out of line with money market conditions is quite foreign to the tradition.

VI

The Radcliffe Report is unique among official documents in its treatment of the public debt; two long chapters are devoted to 'The Financing of the Public Sector' and 'The Management of the National Debt', and the constraints imposed and the opportunities provided by the Debt are a pervasive theme of the whole report. By complete contrast,

[21] Cmnd. 827, para. 392.

the Macmillan Report has only two references to the subject—one to the effect of falling prices on the burden of the Debt, and one to the large volume of Treasury bills as a factor attracting foreign short-term funds to London.

The Radcliffe Report rightly draws attention to the fact that the British government had never before been a large and regular borrower in peacetime. However, the situation with which the Committee had to deal was also influenced by official attitudes and beliefs. Of particular importance was the view that the size of the Treasury bill issue precluded any attempt to influence the commercial banks through operation on their cash base, the belief that official intervention was necessary to maintain orderly conditions in the gilt-edged market, and the conviction that it was impractical to sell stock on a falling market.

The report gives qualified approval to the first of these. It points out the potential conflict between control of the bill rate and control of the volume of cash and concludes that, 'The Bank of England has chosen stability of the Treasury bill rate, and so cannot impose a fixed relationship between the amount of cash held and the amount of Treasury bills held by the private sector. . . .' The Committee does not, however, give any support to the extreme view in this controversy, that control by the cash base would be impossible even if the Bank were prepared to relinquish the attempt to maintain a stable Treasury bill rate.[22]

In their treatment of the gilt-edged market, the Committee are less ready to accept the official view. They acknowledge that a sharp fall in prices may give rise to speculation of a kind that will diminish rather than stimulate the demand for stock, but they suggest that this would be less likely to happen, 'If the intentions of the authorities could be more generally understood'; and they also point out that, 'It is equally possible that if the authorities half-heartedly follow market trends, gradually and reluctantly raising interest rates, the prolonged downward drag of bond prices will in the end do permanent damage to the market's appetite for Government

[22] Cmnd. 827, para. 376.

bonds.'[23] The Committee's own prescription is that the authorities should regard the National Debt as providing them with an instrument of great power for influencing the level and pattern of interest rates; that they should take a view as to the level of rates that is appropriate to long-term economic needs; that they should take a bold initiative in establishing such a level; and that they should then use their influence to maintain stability until there is a change in the economic situation calling for a 'change of gear'. This is one of the most revolutionary, and most controversial, proposals of the report, and a full discussion of it would take us a long way from the main theme of this paper.

Because of the fact that large-scale government borrowing has, until recently, been confined to major wars, its problems figure largely in documents written during the French Wars of 1793–1815 and during World War I, but very little in others.

The Bank of England complained in its evidence to the 1797 committees of the government's demands for advances, and it was generally agreed that these were a major factor leading to the suspension of cash payments. Throughout the Restriction Period, the Bank drew a distinction between advances to the government, which it consistently disliked, and advances to meet the legitimate needs of trade, which it maintained could never lead to an over-issue of notes however freely they were made. Even those, including the authors of the Bullion Report, who rejected this last proposition, agreed on the evils of advances to the government. The matter was raised again before the committees on the resumption of cash payments in 1819 and at the time of the Resumption Act the government undertook to repay £10 million of its loans from the Bank and passed further legislation to prohibit the Bank from lending to the government for a term of more than three months without the approval of Parliament.

During World War I, the government borrowed very heavily on Ways and Means Advances from the Bank of England and also sold large quantities of stock and Treasury

[23] Cmnd. 827, paras. 565 and 566.

bills to the commercial banks. Borrowing from the central bank was regarded as specially inflationary, but borrowing from the commercial banks was also believed to have an inflationary effect insofar as it led to an expansion of deposits. The Cunliffe Committee pointed out that a large part of wartime credit expansion arose, 'from the fact that the expenditure of the Government during the war has exceeded the amounts which they have been able to raise by taxation or by loans from the actual savings of the people. They have been obliged, therefore, to obtain money through the creation of credits by the Bank of England and by the joint stock banks, with the result that the growth of purchasing power has exceeded that of purchasable goods and services.' They concluded that, 'A primary condition for the restoration of a sound credit position is the repayment of a large portion of the enormous amount of Government securities now held by the Banks.'[24]

A particular source of concern in the early post-war years was the large volume of the floating debt—Treasury bills and Ways and Means Advances. The problem of renewing this debt was a cause of great anxiety and was widely believed to be the reason why a seven per cent Bank rate was maintained for many months after the collapse of the post-war boom and the onset of the very severe depression of 1921. This episode left a deep impression on officials of the Treasury and the Bank of England and helps to explain the strong penchant towards funding which these institutions still display.

During the Second World War, the government kept down its borrowing on Treasury bills and Ways and Means Advances by energetic sales of stock and by resorting to Treasury Deposit Receipts. Nevertheless, the war and early post-war years brought a very large expansion of credit which was essentially similar to that of the First World War. It is an indication of how far the thinking of the Radcliffe Committee departed from tradition that it shows so little interest either in

[24] Cmnd. 9182, paras 16 and 17.

funding or in the inflationary influence of government borrowing from the banking system.

VII

This paper has tried to show that the problems studied by the Radcliffe Committee were not different in kind from those which faced the twenty other committees that have examined the British monetary system since 1797. The objectives of monetary policy—the maintenance of the exchange value and the domestic purchasing power of the currency, the avoidance of trade depression and unemployment, and the creation of conditions favourable to the growth of industry and commerce —have remained much the same, though the language in which they have been expressed and the order of priority in which they are held has changed from time to time. The Radcliffe Committee was, however, writing in a much more interventionist climate and showed much more confidence that the wisdom of public officials unfettered by rules will shape economic events for the public good.

The most fundamental break with tradition is the rejection by the Radcliffe Committee of the quantity theory of money. It rejected this theory because it could no longer believe in the transmission mechanism that had been accepted, on a basis of wide experience but little empirical evidence, for two hundred years, but it was unable to substitute any other coherent and general theory. The central theme of previous documents had been the relationship between money and prices; in the Radcliffe Report, both fade into the background, and the centre of the stage is held by 'total pressure of demand' and 'general liquidity'. Looking at things from this point of view it is easy to understand how the Committee took the views that it did on non-bank intermediaries, Bank rate and the public debt; whether these views form the basis for a new theory or a sensible guide to policy is a matter for controversy.

Discussion Papers

(a) L. S. PRESSNELL
(*Reader in Economics, London School of Economics*)

I

I ENJOYED Professor Morgan's paper immensely. Its achitecture is superb and elegant, and his special skill in weaving together theory and history is enviable. However, the more I disaggregate the paper, the more I disagree with it.

I shall adopt a vice common amongst readers of thrillers and turn first to the end to see who really did the murder. The end results of my reflections on Professor Morgan's paper revolve around his two questions about traditions.

The first question is whether Radcliffe is in the tradition of the major reports in broadening our views of monetary fundamentals. Undoubtedly it is, and this is why there can be a 'Radcliffe—Ten Years After' conference. Moreover, it is far less one-track minded than the Bullion Report of 1810. Unlike the Cunliffe Report of 1918, it does not turn its back on past experience. It blends fact and theory more intensively than the Macmillan Report of 1931, and it extends the Macmillan Report's probings for enlightened monetary management.

The second question is whether the Radcliffe Committee strayed like lost sheep from the virtuous paths of quantity theory and of Bank rate tradition. I ask: *what* quantity theory? *what* Bank rate tradition?

Professor Morgan further finds Radcliffe's views on debt management and on long-term interest rates 'revolutionary'. Arguably, Radcliffe's views here are not so much revolutionary as an up-dating of policies with an ancient pedigree.

If these quite substantial corrections of Professor Morgan's propositions are justified, we might begin to give Radcliffe its due place in our historical perspectives.

The most helpful procedure, particularly for those whose monetary history is rusty, seems to be to scan the relevant history first, referring to Professor Morgan's points where appropriate. Then I shall focus my criticisms one by one on the five areas into which he has usefully arranged the main issues.

II

Three traditions have held together some three hundred years of our monetary history in a far from seamless garment, and the greatest of these is convertibility. The other two have been the need to regulate the supply of money in the short run, and the search to do this by an appropriate mix of rules and discretion.

For the significance of convertibility, we must go back a century earlier than Professor Morgan's starting date of 1797. The great monetary debate of 1695–6, the Locke-Lowndes controversy, resulted eventually in a fixed sterling price of gold which governed the supply of coins, then the principal means of everyday payment. The founding fathers of classical economics, Locke and Hume, regarded convertibility as sufficient to ensure, not stability of prices, but harmony of prices with those of other countries. Hume's treatment of the relatively novel topics of bank money and of money in relation to economic growth was notoriously unsatisfactory and vexing to his successors. Here as elsewhere, non-theoretical factors, such as monetary disasters, probably shaped classical views. Adam Smith tried to deal with banking by adding to convertibility discretionary management in the form of the real bills theory.

During the Napoleonic Wars Britain had for a time a Radcliffe-style monetary system. Uniquely, Henry Thornton saw its problems clearly and he justified discretionary management with or without convertibility. His apparent repudiation of this advanced theory when he signed the Bullion Report of 1810, which advocated a strict convertibility rule, illustrated the nineteenth century's concern less with the power of financial institutions to create liquidity than with their power to destroy solvency. This preoccupation, which will be well understood by anyone who has read the Bankruptcy Court records of perished banks and brokers, culminated in the straitjacket of the 1844 Bank Charter Act, the grandfather of D.C.E.

The appalling Cunliffe Report of 1918 canonized the rule-makers of 1844. This was a massive distortion of history and gave a spurious harmony to nineteenth century theory and policy. Its chief prophet, Ricardo, had not promised that convertibility would produce stable prices, only internationally compatible prices. His Currency School successors asserted a crude theory, but their aim, and achievement, of strict control of note issues did not reflect a faith in stable velocity. As Professor Morgan points out, the 1844 regulation of note issues was based upon their uncertain lag on changes in gold reserves. It seems to follow that, by thus touching only the fringe of 'money substitutes', the rule-makers were inconsistent. The Bank of England was to spend the next seventy years struggling with their error.

The opponents of the monetary puritans, John Stuart Mill in particular, cannot be excluded from the classical tradition, for they accepted long-run quantity theory. Mill, however, emphasizes in near-Radcliffe style, the significance for 'immediate and temporary prices' of the quantity of credit widely defined rather than 'money' narrowly defined.[1] The problem of money substitutes is indeed an old one, as Professor Morgan recognizes. It does, however, seem to involve more than one quantity theory. From which quantity theory is Radcliffe a renegade?

The strict 1844 rule crumbled in infancy. Subsequent developments suggest some qualifications to Professor

[1] J. S. Mill, *Principles of Political Economy*, Ashley ed. (London: Longmans, Green & Co., 1917), p. 523.

Morgan's impressions of continuity and of broad approbation of the Bank. Once again, the major continuing thread was really the gold standard determinant of basic reserves, but even that trembled in the deflationary 1880s. The Royal Commission on Gold and Silver nearly pushed sterling towards bimetallism, and the governors of the Bank of England privately polled the Bank directors on the subject.[2]

The Bank of England's concern was with the price of gold and the price of money. Stabilization of general prices was a novel concept as recently as the 1920s when it was resisted as a definite obligation by Benjamin Strong, America's pioneer central banker.[3] In Britain, the Macmillan Report of 1931 was quite explicit about the novelty of recommending that influence over prices 'be accepted as the guiding aim of monetary policy' (para. 276).

Before 1914, the Bank of England did not seek to obstruct the long term trends of prices or of interest rates. Its *shorter* run policy of Bank rate, etc. has sometimes attracted veneration, it is true. Like the veneration of Queen Victoria, it characterized the later years of the Bank's great reign, but Professor Morgan streamlines the trends overmuch. The Bank, like the Queen, went into semi-retirement and re-emerged about the same time, roughly between Albert's death and the Golden Jubilee of 1887. Like Queen Victoria, too, the Old Lady experienced desperate unpopularity. Much opinion never progressed beyond the *Punch* cartoon in the 1847 crisis, which portrayed the Bank as guarding a hoard of gold to rescue delinquent merchants and bankers. Even the overrated Walter Bagehot yearned for a pile of gold, ample to meet swings in domestic or overseas confidence without active intervention by the Bank. There were contrasting pressures for flexibility in note issues, but the super-reserve men won, with

[2] Two directors favoured the arguments of two other directors for bimetallism, twenty were against, and three were undecided. I am grateful to the Bank for allowing me to consult and to quote these records (Secretary's Department, p. 206.02).

[3] L. V. Chandler, *Benjamin Strong, Central Banker* (Washington D.C.: The Brookings Institution, 1958), pp. 199–201, 202–4, 355.

the effective elimination of the fiduciary issues well before 1914.[4]

Bank rate was certainly the Bank's distinctive policy but this point needs to be cleared of moth and myth. As a leader of market rates, Bank rate backed by open market operations dates from the 1870s. It no doubt had some cost effect on commercial bills. Increasingly, however, it operated on institutional liquidity and on the availability of lending. It influenced domestic money flows until bank amalgamation reduced the stickiness of domestic interest rates. It influenced international gold flows particularly in the last years before 1914.

The Cunliffe Committee of 1918 gazed right past this as though nothing had happened since 1844 and a high Treasury official could drily tell Lord Cunliffe in 1917, when he still ruled the Bank, 'Mr. Governor, I fear that you are obsolete.'[5]

The Macmillan Report's views on Bank rate differed from those of earlier reports and do not offer the great contrast with Radcliffe that Professor Morgan alleges. Almost always those bewitching words about the beauty of Bank rate in Macmillan resemble Macduff, who was 'from his mother's womb untimely ripped'.

Macmillan did indeed affirm that 'Bank rate policy . . . is a most delicate and beautiful instrument' but as a prelude to its immediate downgrading. The Report wanted active monetary management, insulated from the exchange rate and from Bank rate. It particularly favoured open market operations, both of the traditional variety and in a form akin to Radcliffe debt management, although it stressed interest rates rather than liquidity.

The 1931 crisis swamped Macmillan, but subsequent policy reflected its teaching. A major addition was the abandonment of the fixed parity, and then in 1936 came acquiescence in the adjustable peg system.

[4] See my study of 'Gold Reserves, Banking Reserves and the Banking Crisis of 1890' in C. R. Whittlesey and J. S. G. Wilson (eds.) *Essays in Money and Banking* (Oxford: Clarendon Press, 1968), esp. pp. 224–6.

[5] R. Rhode James (compiler), *Memoirs of a Conservative* (London: Weidenfeld & Nicolson, 1969), p. 61.

Four further developments bring us to Radcliffe. One was that the National Debt became better managed and became a smaller fiscal headache despite a major war. Second, American monetary debate in the 1950s featured debt management and money substitutes. The Radcliffe Committee mistakenly thought that its readers were as educated as its members were in these matters. The unfortunate result was that early comment on the Report sometimes smacked, in a classical economist's phrase, of all the arrogance of ignorance. Third, and possibly of major importance in Radcliffe thinking, the commitment to full employment opened an uncertain gap between Radcliffe and quantity theories old and new. Radcliffe's acceptance of the high-pressure economy might perhaps be seen in the context of the dismissal, before the Committee reported, of the Chancellor of the Exchequer who had appointed it. He had wished to reduce the pressure on the economy. The fourth development, as Professor Morgan notes, was that of the interventionist climate. This has involved the familiar official influences on interest rates and the consequent weakening of control over the money supply.

III

I have tried to show that there have been several monetary traditions. It is by no means clear that Radcliffe departed from them so radically as Professor Morgan sometimes suggests. We can now check that by following Professor Morgan through his five areas of discussion.

The first area concerns policies and priorities. There is more than a difference of degree from Macmillan which accepted, whereas Radcliffe does not, a gold standard constraint. Further, Radcliffe stresses not just the *mixture* of modern policy objectives, but also the shifting priority amongst them as an obstacle to the pursuit of relatively non-contentious goals.

We can take together the second and third areas. These concern the relationship between money and prices, and the question of money and money substitutes. Here, in Radcliffe's rejection of quantity theory, Professor Morgan finds its most fundamental break with tradition. I confess to finding a certain charm, contrasting with the assertiveness of some earlier Reports, in Radcliffe's recognition that we do not yet know the answers about the quantity of money. This apart, and apart too from the range of possible quantity theories, does not Radcliffe have something like a quantity theory of assets? If it is as woolly as some find it, does this stem from the volatility of expectations in an underlying inflation that is sometimes repressed, sometimes not, in an economy that, as R. C. O. Matthews[6] seems to suggest, is under a strong secular pressure of expansion?

Radcliffe's treatment of velocity is a problem. Can velocity be uncontrollable if, as Professor Morgan argues, Radcliffe advocates control of the liquidity of creators of money substitutes? Canadian experience invites study here. The Porter Commission of 1964 argued in effect that non-bank intermediaries simply interposed a lag in the eventual efficacy of interest rates, and I suppose that this was one consideration in the subsequent relaxation of constraints on rate competition. Before long, however, both money and interest rates threatened to go through the roof and dampened earlier hopes. Is the ultimate answer to money substitutes a higher level of rates and a more competitive banking system?

Can we rationalize these problems by stressing again—as I fear Professor Morgan does not do sufficiently—the distinction between the short run and the long run? Does not Radcliffe, like John Stuart Mill and like Macmillan, say that the regulation of the supply of money must be related to the *longer* term trend of the economy? This would seem to fit with Radcliffe's Wicksell-type proposal for the monetary authorities to operate an interest rate policy in line with profit expectations.

This leads one naturally to the fourth area, the operation of Bank rate. I have already noted the non-continuity of the

---

[6] R. C. O. Matthews, 'Why has Britain had Full Employment Since the War?' *Economic Journal*, Sept. 1968.

tradition. The crucial point is that, like Macmillan, Radcliffe did not regard Bank rate as a short-term wonder worker.

This brings us to the fifth and final area. This is the influence of the national debt upon the monetary system. Many of us, with John Hampden our hero, have chafed at Radcliffe's tenderness for the public sector, reaching as it does even to its case for a Post Office Giro. Arguably Radcliffe muffed this one by implying support for the cheap government financing that has been a costly plague of the monetary system for half a century. But we can pass to the heart of the matter. Radcliffe debt management is an up-dating of the Bank's 275 years of support of government debt and of its traditional influence over private sector liquidity. Professor Morgan views as revolutionary the proposal for a positive view and policy on long rates. Was not a long term view implicit in the gold standard and in the narrow Hume quantity theory? It also sounds Thorntonian and Wicksellian. Nearer home, the Macmillan Report half anticipated Radcliffe in urging that on changing Bank rate the Bank should be ready 'to inform the money market, and the joint stock banks, whenever it can, as to its views of the situation' (para. 218).

On funding Professor Morgan is right in noting the greater concern of some earlier Committees, but was Radcliffe wrong? The Second World War was the first major war for some 200 years not to be followed by massive funding. It was also the first major war not to be followed by a massive slump. One may go a little further and ask what sort of burden the debt is anyway, particularly if the electorate opts for a large public sector.

IV

There are two traditions left on which, in conclusion, I shall comment briefly. The first is the inadequacy of the empirical evidence in Radcliffe and its predecessors. This is a criticism of the failure of those responsible for not responding to the Macmillan Report's recommendations for the collection of more information to permit 'a more complete knowledge, both scientific and statistical' of the economy (para. 219). It is also a comment on, or condemnation of, the state of economics, including its historical side, in England—but, I cannot resist pleading, do have a heart. Carl Christ, whom I understand to be an authority on the subject, claims that developments in econometrics 'are not so great that they cannot be comprehended by an able economist of 25, or 65, if he has the proper training in economic theory, mathematics and statistics'.[7]

When we add to this little list the not inconsiderable skills of the historian who needs time to read as well as to count, I foresee a need for great patience.

The second tradition may not have been noticed. The major inquiries of 1810, 1918, and 1931 were initiated or published—or both—in conditions unpropitious for careful inquiry or for careful consideration of their reports. The vital Bradbury Report of 1925, which recommended the return to gold, was withheld from publication until *after* the decision to return had been announced. Alone, Radcliffe has been given a chance; this unique conference is surely the clearest sign of that.

[7] Carl F. Christ, 'Econometrics in Economics: Some Achievements and Challenges', *Australian Economic Papers*, 6 (9), Dec. 1967, p. 170.

Discussion Papers

(b) W. T. NEWLYN
(Chairman of the Department of Economics, University of Leeds)

PROFESSOR Victor Morgan has skilfully juxtaposed the Radcliffe Report with the rich historical tradition of British monetary enquiries. He has stressed the similarity of objectives on which I would only comment that any difference appears to me to lie in the greater complexity of reconciling the objectives. He has pointed out the major change in the doctrine about Bank rate which is a reflection of the changed structure of international finance and its mode of operation. He has selected two aspects as marking the distinctive character of the Radcliffe analysis. It is with these two aspects of the matter that I would like to deal.

Firstly Victor Morgan says that Radcliffe is unique among the official documents in its treatment of government debt. Secondly he says that the 'fundamental break with tradition is the rejection of the quantity theory of money', and he chastises the Radcliffe Committee for not putting anything in its place.

The paper argues that the traditional documents offer hardly any explicit coherent statement of the quantity theory of money. Nor is there any explicit coherent counter-theory offered by Radcliffe. Indeed its refutation of the quantity theory is not all that explicit. All I can find is one passage in which the Radcliffe Report contradicts the view of money as 'constituting a very powerful pressure of demand' (para. 388) and the famous flamboyant statement that there is no evidence of *any* limit to velocity. Had the fundamental break with tradition been simply the rejection of the quantity theory of money, the Radcliffe Report would not have been the controversial and stimulating document that it was. I would therefore put a different emphasis on this than did Victor Morgan: the Radcliffe Committee did not merely reject the quantity theory of money, it rejected money itself in a significant sense. The really distinctive feature of the Radcliffe Report is not that it emphasized that exclusive concentration on the quantity of money was wrong but that in doing so it denied that money had any special significance at all. '. . . we view it as only part of the wider structure of liquidity' (para. 389). It is this view, reflected right through the Report, that justifies the complaint that Radcliffe threw out the baby with the bath water or, to adapt the metaphor, drowned the baby with an excess of liquidity.

The Radcliffe Committee was so concerned with the situation of post-war excess liquidity, and particularly with the volume of close substitutes for money as an asset, that it dismissed altogether the unique significance attaching to money as a means of payment. Fortunately the baby has been resuscitated during the ensuing ten years and the dramatic impact of near tragedy has had the very desirable effect of warning us of the danger of neglecting the water.

Here there is danger of trespassing into the area of discussion of Harry Johnson's paper; but in commenting on Victor Morgan's way of putting the matter, I think it is important to distinguish between two things: the unique importance of money as a means of payment on the one hand, and its significance as an asset in the argument of an expenditure function on the other. Radcliffe failed to make this distinction. I think Victor Morgan also has failed to do so, as has the recent discussion in the press about British monetary policy in which both these aspects are merged as if it were an argument between the wicked Chicago quantity theory supporters and the rival upholders of good Keynesian doctrine.

The crude quantity theory is reflected in the quotation from Hume in Victor Morgan's paper in which Hume concludes that a reduction of four-fifths in the means of payment (specie, which is unmistakably outside money) results in reducing all prices in the same ratio, which implicitly assumes 'Cambridge

k'. This was probably not such a gross error in the days when the means of payment formed a large proportion of net worth. The wealth effect of halving the quantity of the means of payment might well have had an effect upon expenditure of that order of magnitude *ceteris paribus*. But what one has to ask in these crude examples of increases and decreases in the quantity of money is how they come about. It is impossible for the supply of money to change *ceteris paribus*. It can only change either by changing someone's income or by being exchanged for some existing asset already included in net worth. The analysis of both effects in traditional Keynesian terms is not inconsistent with an emphasis upon the importance of controlling the quantity of money. The significance of an increase in the money supply is that it permits deficit expenditure without any monetary constraint.

To argue the importance of the control of the supply of money does not make one a quantity theory advocate. On the other hand this argument should not exclude recognition of the significance of 'the whole liquidity position'. The great contribution which Radcliffe made was to focus our attention on this quantity, especially upon its most important constituent, government debt. Radcliffe's emphasis on government debt (the other peculiarity which Victor Morgan distinguishes) was absolutely right. Right not only because of its effect on the overall liquidity position but right because the attitude of the monetary authorities to the management of the national debt in the post-war period has made monetary policy in the terms of traditional literature quite impossible. This is only too clear in the excellent paper presented by the Bank of England. If the authorities hold themselves ready to convert government debt into money at all times then there is no question of controlling the supply of money. I would therefore cap Victor Morgan's comment on this aspect of the Radcliffe Report and say that the other distinctive feature of the Report was that the implications of its analysis meant that government debt management excluded monetary policy.

SUMMARY OF THE GENERAL DISCUSSION

THE discussion about the place of the Radcliffe Report in the tradition of United Kingdom monetary documents centred on whether the Report had abandoned the quantity theory approach of previous inquiries. It was noted that the authors of the Report had been forced to take a view about the relevance of the quantity theory since they had been appointed when the political atmosphere was influenced by a Chancellor of the Exchequer who held quantity theory views.

The theory which underlay the Report, and which had never been satisfactorily expounded, was a weak version of the $MV = PT$ relation, which extended some of the traditional relationships and commented on the predictability of others. The Report had replaced M, the money stock, with the wider concept of 'the liquidity stock'. There was an extended discussion about this, with general agreement that the nature and importance of M must depend on the institutions supplying money-like liabilities, and the size and composition of the National Debt.

The Report's concentration on the relation between types of liquid assets was seen to be in the tradition of the nineteenth century Banking School. In the early nineteenth century the Banking School writers had been concerned with the relation between the notes and coin of the money stock and the bank deposits and commercial bills which were then treated as 'near-money'. As the use of inland bills declined and bank deposits became an accepted part of the money supply in the later part of the century, the problem of money-substitutes diminished, but was revived again in the Radcliffe Report's discussion of the growth of the liabilities of non-bank financial intermediaries relative to bank deposits.

There were several opinions about the Radcliffe Report's

view of the relevant quantity for its version of the quantity theory. At one extreme, the uniqueness of money as a transactions medium and as providing the 'ability to pay' must make the money stock an important economic variable. Other discussants challenged this by suggesting that the Report was right in emphasizing the institutional linkages in modern credit markets which make the potential credit supply rather than the money supply the important quantity.

The distinction was linked with the question of the Report's treatment of the predictability and stability of velocity. The 'extended quantity theory' approach had many parallels with the work of Professor Milton Friedman, especially in rejecting the money stock as an adequate mechanism for 'fine tuning' in the economy, and in emphasizing the long-run importance of real variables in determining trends.

However, the existence of liquidity substitutes made the link between the money stock and prices very complex and, under the conditions of the 1950s, very weak. Because of this, policy needed to be aimed at controlling financial intermediaries' lending rather than at regulating the growth of their liabilities. Similarly, long-term economic trends should be influenced by policies which change the structure of interest rates, rather than by changing the supply of money. The Committee's quantity theory views could be seen in its recommendations about debt management, which stressed the need to control additions to the liquidity stock from debt operations.

In this connection there was a discussion about the tradition summarized by the 'Cambridge k', a stable link between money and income. It was claimed that the stability of 'k' was always assumed to be subject to the qualifications implied by A. G. Pigou in his 1917 *Economic Journal* discussion of possible changes in the velocity of money, but that these qualifications had tended to remain within the Cambridge oral tradition.

It was also suggested that the Report lacked historical perspective in failing to anticipate the development of the Euro-dollar market and the revival of the commercial bill in the 1960s. In reply it was argued that the Report had mis-judged the economic climate of the 1960s and had not anti-cipated that abnormal crisis conditions leading to credit stringency and high international interest rates would be such a regular feature of the decade. It was these conditions which had led to the revival of bill finance. Relating to this, the Committee had realized that it was basing its conclusions on poor data and, like most other inquiries, had made an important point of asking for more and better statistics.

The discussion also brought out the changing nature of official committees. Radcliffe, like its predecessors, had been expected to report on the basis of evidence untested by empirical research and quantitative studies. This approach could no longer be relied on, even though it was remarked that the Commission on Money and Credit study in the U.S.A., which had been published about the same time as the Radcliffe Report and which had massive research support, had been largely forgotten, while Radcliffe was still being extensively discussed ten years after.

II

THE RADCLIFFE REPORT—
TEN YEARS AFTER
A SURVEY OF EMPIRICAL EVIDENCE

A. A. WALTERS

Discussion Papers

(*a*) L. DICKS-MIREAUX
(*b*) M. PARKIN

II

THE RADCLIFFE REPORT—
TEN YEARS AFTER
A SURVEY OF EMPIRICAL EVIDENCE

A. A. WALTERS
(*Cassel Professor of Money and Banking at the London School of Economics*)

I. INTRODUCTION

SOME ten years ago I began a survey of statistical cost and production functions. A simple technical non-controversial topic, I thought, with well-defined problems. Ten years later I find that I am quite unable to keep up with the massive volume of papers that are being churned out by the profession —92 in 1967–8 according to one count! No one can claim that the field has been empirically fallow.

At that same time (in 1959) at Northwestern University I first saw the Radcliffe Report. And as I read it my amazement and curiosity steadily increased. For many years I had thought that economics had been steadily accumulating evidence, and had been using such data critically to examine theoretical propositions. This had certainly occurred in the theory of production and, although I know less about the analysis of consumer behaviour, I suspect that even more work has been done on the empirical foundations of demand and consumption functions. Yet it was clear that Radcliffe had not even regarded the empirical testing of hypotheses as an appropriate methodology! (This may be considered even more remarkable in view of the recent burgeoning of interest in the United

States, resulting in the publication in 1956—the year before Radcliffe was set up—of the splendid *Studies in the Quantity Theory of Money* in Chicago.[1])

The methodology of Radcliffe, although never discussed or justified in the Report, was one of 'institutional insight' instead of testing on the empirical side, and of an uncritical acceptance of neo-Keynesianism as a theoretical basis for monetary policy.[2]

The Radcliffe Committee listened to opinion rather than analysed data. For example, it was apparently content with the view of big industrialists that of all the factors that influenced their decision to spend, the rate of interest was the least important. No tests were conducted and no data were surveyed to examine the validity of this contention. A more important example of casual interpretations of evidence was the Committee's attitude to the quantity of money (paras. 389 et seq.). Control over the supply of money is merely 'incidental to interest rate policy' (para. 397)—but only 'very limited reliance can be placed on this' (interest incentive) (para. 397). The level of demand is influenced by 'liquidity'.

'Liquidity' however is an eternally elusive concept—a will-o'-the-wisp of monetary economics. Liquidity is 'the amount of money which people *think* they can get hold of . . .' (para. 390) or 'the lending behaviour of an *indefinitely* wide range of financial institutions' (para. 394), (my italics). It is impossible to grasp such a concept. Liquidity is a state of mind relative to an indefinite range of institutions. But even if one's intuition were to penetrate the mists to meaning it is clearly quite impossible *in principle* to measure 'liquidity'. No refutable theoretical propositions can be formulated in terms of liquidity. The pure Radcliffe theory can never be tested.

This puts the positive economist on the spot, and he has not been slow to complain. But of course Radcliffe did give us an enormous number of statements, distilled from the volumi-

---

[1] Edited by Milton Friedman, Chicago University Press, 1956.
[2] These views on theory were expounded with great effect by R. F. Kahn and Nicholas Kaldor; see *Principal Memoranda of Evidence*, Vol. 3 (H.M.S.O., 1960), pp. 138–53.

nous evidence of important persons, about the operations of the monetary mechanism. The Committee made no overt attempt to test any of these propositions.[3] These have been the subject of much of the quantitive analysis over the last ten years. Radcliffe did a very valuable job in setting up a battery of Aunt Sallys, derived from Bank of England and Treasury lore, Oxbridge common rooms and City offices. How well have they stood up to quantitative criticism?

II

One can determine the Committee's view on the dominant problem of the stability of the demand for money only by inference. The Committee dismissed any idea of a stable demand function in para. 391. 'We have not made use of this concept (the velocity of circulation) because we cannot find any reason for supposing, or any experience in monetary history indicating, that *there is any limit* to the velocity of circulation . . .' (my italics). The Committee clearly denied that any stable demand function exists or indeed has existed historically.[4]

Empirical studies of the demand for money have come thick and fast in the 1960s. And the periods covered have spanned almost a century. The results however have not by any means stilled all controversy. Probably the most serious disagreements are about the specification of the model and the identification of the parameters.

The simplest models have been single equation demand functions of the linear or log-linear type. A wide variety of independent variables has been used in the demand functions; it is convenient, however, to restrict this preliminary discussion to two, income, and the long-term rate of interest. If one begins with the individual (i), then the demand for money

[3] And, I think one should add that most of the witnesses did not appear to have much evidence to back their judgement. One notable exception was Frank Paish (p. 185 of Vol. 3, *Memoranda*) but the Committee apparently ignored his evidence on the velocity of circulation and interest rates (see para. 391).

[4] This statement is all the more remarkable since one will search the Report in vain for a long time series representing the quantity of money.

is represented by the following equation (omitting the disturbance term):

$$m_i = a_0 + b_1 y_i + b_2 r. \tag{1}$$

The individual takes the rate of interest and the level of his nominal income as given and he adjusts his nominal money balances. For the individual, therefore, nominal cash balances are the dependent variable. Very few studies, however, have used individual observations on households or firms. Most empirical works have used time series of aggregates for all transactions in the United Kingdom. The consequences of aggregation must be faced. Clearly, for the economy as a whole the quantity of money cannot be considered as the dependent variable. Let us for the time being ignore the rate of interest effect on the holding of money balances. Then the normal aggregate monetary theory would argue that the aggregate quantity of money is determined by the monetary authorities and that the level of nominal aggregate income is the dependent variable. Formally, therefore, the aggregate relationship is derived as follows:

$$\sum m_i = a_0^* + b_1^* \sum y_i \tag{2}$$

so that $m = a_0^* + b_1^* y$, with $m = \sum m_i y = \sum y_i$ and writing the levels of aggregate income as the dependent variables:

$$y = -\frac{a_0^*}{b_1^*} + \frac{m}{b_1^*}. \tag{3}$$

This is a reversal of the old quantity theory equation. It represents the reaction of real income and prices to an exogenous money supply.

The correlation or regression analysis of measures of contemporaneous money and income might be thought to identify this monetary multiplier $(1/b_1^*)$. But such a hope hinges on several suppositions of fact. It might be alleged that, instead of the micro-demand-for-money/macro-monetary-multiplier relationship we have simply measured the reaction of the monetary authorities to current income levels. Equation

3 assumes that the causal effect is from money to nominal income, not the other way around. If one were convinced, however, that money as such had little effect on income and that the authorities were passively supplying money for the 'needs of trade', then the measure of $b*$ would give information only about the reactions of the Bank of England to current or expected economic conditions. Two features of the model may be used to save us from such a mistaken identification. First there are very likely to be lags in the adjustment of the economy to new monetary conditions. Provided that the lag is sufficiently long, relative to the period of observation, it is possible to sort out the two effects.

Second and less obviously, there is a presupposition that the government's monetary policy does not in fact have the characteristic 'leaning against the wind' feature that is claimed—or at least that they 'do not know which way the wind is blowing'. This needs some explaining. Suppose that income were subject to shocks which, in the absence of action by the monetary authority, would be transmitted in the form of price and employment changes. Suppose that the Bank of England were a perfect forecaster and that its monetary instruments were precise and had exactly predictable effects; then the Bank would always be completely successful in offsetting the shocks. Income would proceed on a steady course whereas money would oscillate considerably. The monetary multiplier is perfect but the analysis of the time series will not reveal it. It is indeed possible to conceive of a case where one would actually observe a *negative* correlation between money and income. For example, one might suppose that the monetary authority, although blessed with perfect foresight, reacts too little, perhaps because of an innate conservatism or because it believes that the monetary multiplier is lower than it actually is. Then the exogenous forces acting on income will be only partly offset. The observed series will then show an increase in money stock associated with a decrease in income. The correlation is negative. This is of course merely an example of the old problem that crops up so often in the social sciences—one never knows what would have happened if there had been no intervention. The record of the system without intervention is never available.[5]

Much of the statistical analysis of monetary multipliers (or of the parameters of the demand for money) hinges on the assumption that monetary policy has not reflected the perfection of foresight discussed above, nor has it followed a Friedman rule. Most observers (may I risk *all* observers) would agree that perfect foresight and Friedmanian policies have not been characteristic of Britain's monetary behaviour. Fortunately, one needs to be less restrictive about the policy actually pursued by the authorities. Very little systematic empirical work in categorizing the behaviour of the Bank has been even attempted. But there is no need to doubt that the general policy in the post-war years at least has been concerned with 'maximizing the long term demand for government debt'. The stabilization of the price of gilt-edged has been the main tactical task of the government's broker. The strategy, however, is more difficult to elucidate. Appropriate interest rate levels are set by the Treasury, in consultation with the Bank, which are thought to achieve many objectives—dampening down home demand and attracting foreign funds to London are clearly two main aims of raising interest rates. Clearly this may well be related to the state of the balance of payments or of the stock of foreign exchange reserves—and in fact one can show that monetary policy in the years from 1955 to 1962 was partly determined by the state of the balance of trade in the immediately preceding quarter.[6] At least it is plausible to suppose that the monetary authorities react to the current indicators of conditions of the immediate past.[7]

---

[5] Yet another example—and the opposite of the first example above—occurs when a monetary authority follows a Friedman rule of expanding the money stock at a certain fixed percentage per annum (say 4 per cent). Income would vary as exogenous forces impinged on its growth whereas the money stock would grow at a constant rate. In this case there is no variability in the independent variable and so the statistics will not reveal the monetary multiplier.

[6] See Fisher (1968*b*), Walters (1966*b*).

[7] An associated problem is to determine whether the government fixes the quantity of money or the rate of interest or some combination of regulations on advances, ceilings on deposits, and so on. These are very important issues, and the instrumental role of the rate of interest is examined below.

Let us summarize the argument. The simplest possible appropriate analysis of the effects of monetary policy is to measure the regression of income on lagged values of the money stock (or advances or credit etc.). Even though the government takes account of current or past economic conditions and its expectation of future conditions it is unlikely to vitiate the measurement of the multiplier. The lags and the imperfections of monetary policy save us.

It is interesting that many studies of the demand for money (including my own!) regress the money stock on an interest rate (usually one of the measures of yield on long term or irredeemable bonds) and money income. The first question is whether there are good grounds for formulating the equation in this way for the United Kingdom. As we have described the behaviour of the monetary authorities in the U.K., the rate of interest does seem to be the prime instrumental variable; it is a fair caricature to suppose that the authorities fix the interest rate and supply the market with the quantity of money needed to sustain that rate. Thus a regression of the logarithm of money on the logarithm of interest rate might be thought to measure the interest elasticity of the demand for money. In particular, it might be used to shed light on the springs of the 'liquidity trap'.

There are some reservations to be made on this sort of study, however. First, and probably most important, measured interest rates are particularly deficient for the purposes of liquidity analysis. They are *money* rates of return whereas the Keynesian theory is concerned with *real* rates of return; and price change expectations are notoriously difficult to measure.[8] Owing to 'understandings' about borrowers retaining compensating balances, one may wonder whether the market rate reflects the loan rate. Many doubts exist about the appropriate interest rate to be used—the coupon maturity composition and so on. And one cannot apply the model in

---

[8] Some progress is at present being made by comparing rates of return denominated in money terms with those contracted in real terms; this seems to me to be a great improvement over the simple extrapolative model.

periods which have fixed interest rates—such as the war-time and immediate post-war years in the U.K.

Second, the role of income in such models tends to be both dominant and not simple. The demand function does not appear to be linear and homogeneous with respect to income so one cannot normally use the simple technique of analysing velocity and eliminating income as a separate variable. Past incomes and future expectations of income enter the function. Furthermore, the price and real components of income might be expected to have different effects especially in their expectational context. Third, it measures one of the structural equations rather than the reduced form of the monetary multiplier. Even if one treated the rate of interest as an instrumental variable independent of current income,[9] the rate of interest effect on money demand and supply does not record the effect of the money supply (and the rate of interest) on the level of money income. This is normally recognized implicitly by the fact that in the demand for money equation the levels of current and *past* incomes enter as independent variables. The contrast is

between a *Monetary Multiplier*[10]
$$M \quad \text{or} \quad r \rightarrow Y$$
(lagged)

and a *Demand for Money* equation
$$r \quad \text{and} \quad Y \rightarrow M.$$
(lagged)

III

Now is the time to survey the numerical results that have been obtained from these studies. The first point to be made is that the velocity of circulation is relatively unstable. Although the

[9] And it is clear that one cannot. The government increases Bank rate when prices start or are likely to start rising too rapidly.

[10] In many simple models of the monetary multiplier process it is possible to exclude the interest rate since the final form of equation eliminates this variable and incorporates the effects in the multiplier coefficients. If, for example, the liquidity trap was operating one would observe low coefficients in the monetary multiplier equation.

coefficient of variation is between 6 and 22 per cent according to the period chosen, this is much too large to be useful for policy purposes.[11] It is very important to stress that the *naïve version of the quantity theory is discredited by the data*. The reason for the emphasis is not because any economist believes in the naïve quantity theory hypothesis of constant velocity, but because of the use of this naïve theory as an Aunt Sally by those who are convinced *a priori* that the quantity of money is an irrelevant magnitude (the money-does-not-matter school).

Attempts to save the stability of the velocity concepts have taken the form of redefining the numerator or denominator— by excluding government transactions and cash holdings, by including all encashable assets in the denominator ('the amount of money that people think they can get hold of'?), and by suitably redefining the moment of observation of money compared with the period of money income. No significant improvements in stability were to be found in the redefined coefficients of variation. Similarly, there was no tendency for the velocity to become stable over time; on the contrary, it seems that much more instability occurred after 1913 than in the previous forty years.[12]

Nearly all economists, even quantity theorists, have admitted that some measure of the rate of interest is a determinant of the velocity. In the Radcliffe *Memoranda 3*,[13] Professor Frank Paish showed that over the period 1913–57 the reciprocal velocity (clearing bank deposits: net national income) was negatively related to the yield on consols. Results of a similar kind have been observed for more extensive periods.[14] Before the First World War the correlation is rarely high and occasionally in certain short sub-periods perverse. But for the period from 1920 onwards, excluding the war years, the

[11] Sheppard (1969), Chaps. 3 and 5; Kavanagh and Walters (1966).

[12] It is very important to emphasize that the results before 1913 depend on very poor statistics of the quantity of money, although these are being improved by the patient research of Charles Goodhart.

[13] *Principal Memoranda of Evidence*, Vol. 3 (H.M.S.O., 1960), pp. 184–5.

[14] Sheppard (1969); Kavanagh and Walters (1966); J. C. R. Dow (1964), Chap. VII, Ball Table 9.

elasticity of velocity with respect to the yield on consols has been between 0·19 and 0·55 (with 't' coefficients exceeding 6). So far as the existing studies go, there is no dramatic evidence of a liquidity trap.[15] Periods of low interest rates and rapidly declining velocity such as 1941–6 have been associated with wartime rationing and controls rather than with unemployment and deflation; and the 1920s and 1930s exhibited one of the most inelastic liquidity preference schedules of the whole period.[16]

While the period from 1929 to 1933 saw no drastic fall in the quantity of money, such as occurred in the United States, there was no rapid and substantial monetary expansion; and even the increases that occurred in 1934–6 were quite modest.[17] In short, expansion in the U.K. in the early 'thirties was not inhibited by a liquidity trap, but since the increase in the money supply was not large enough to test the trap hypothesis one cannot, from this evidence, dismiss it as a practical but as yet unrealized possibility.

For the post-war years, more reliable statistics, and in particular the availability of quarterly series for income, have enabled much more sensitive models to be tested. In particular one can identify the short run adjustment of the actual stock to the desired stock of money. Fisher's results for the period 1955 I to 1967 II show that, even in these monetarily chaotic years, there appears to have been a stable demand for money with long-run interest (consol) elasticities up to a maximum of 0·31 and long-run income elasticities up to 0·74. These are quite similar to those which one finds over the longer periods with annual data.[18] As far as a stable *demand* for money is concerned, the results for the late 'fifties and 'sixties were not

[15] With log-log formulations there is always an asymptote as velocity decreases so as a matter of arithmetic there is always a liquidity trap. But the observations cluster around the middle of the range and do not enable us to say with any degree of certainty what will happen at the extremes.

[16] Sheppard's (1969) figures show an elasticity of 0·19 for 1920–39. See also the graph on p. 306 of Dow (1964).

[17] These comments on the quantity of money also apply to the reciprocal of velocity (the Cambridge 'k').

[18] See, for example, Kavanagh and Walters (1966), Table II D1 first equation.

noticeably different from those of the previous 75 years.[19] Such stability in the coefficients of the demand function is unlikely to be explained by chance. One may well conclude therefore, that empirical research has uncovered a stable demand for money.

There are some further results of interest but there are also certain issues, however, that are outstanding. In this short survey they must be stated in a summary form:

(a) Different definitions of the money variable (from narrow money including only cash and the deposits of clearing banks to the very broad definitions including even shares of building societies) do not appear critically to affect the demand function, although the numerical values of the coefficient are changed, particularly for the 1955–67 period.

(b) Different but equally plausible specifications of the demand function do not drastically affect the main results. There is, however, a marked numerical difference between the short-run and the long-run income elasticities—as one would expect the short-run elasticities are much smaller than the long-run values.

(c) The role of expected price changes has been explored in a preliminary way using past price changes. Unfortunately, there is no obvious way of sorting out the effect of higher levels of prices on the quantity of money required and the effect of the increased cost of holding money balances due to the expected *increase* in price. The results suggest a 1 per cent change in price is associated with a 0·5 per cent change in the quantity of money. Further research incorporating more sophisticated accounts of expectations (such as the difference between real and monetary rates of return) would be most valuable.

(d) The lack of a linear homogeneous relationship between money stock and money income suggests that velocity is not a useful measure to use in the analysis of the demand for

[19] Explorations of the demand for money using quarterly data by Laidler and Parkin (1969) for 1955–67 have emphasized the important role of income and have shown that the nominal interest rate, although giving a negative sign, is much less important as a determinant of money holdings.

money. It is best to work in terms of the two separate components.

(e) Alternative measures of income and wealth have not been extensively explored—partly because of the lack of data. What evidence is available suggests that permanent income may have some slight preference over current measured income.[20]

(f) Most investigators have followed Keynes and used the *long*-term interest rate as the cost of holding cash. The use of Treasury bill rate, a short-term interest measure, shows that different components of the money stock respond to different rates—and it might be argued that one can thus dichotomize cash into the L_1 and L_2 of the *General Theory*.[21] But more work needs to be done here.

The existence of such a stable demand function does not necessarily imply that there exist also stable monetary multipliers. It does not follow that the quantity of money is an important determinant of the level of activity. At the simplest level one could write a model such as:

$$M(t) = ar(t) + bY(t - 1),$$
$$Y(t) = f \text{ ('animal spirits of entrepreneurs').}$$

Even though there is a stable demand function for money, with a lag in the income term, there is no monetary multiplier in this system. The level of money income is determined by investment which is exogenous and in turn is determined by Mrs. Joan Robinson's 'animal spirits'.[22] Many other models could be constructed with similar characteristics. For example one may argue that in Britain the Bank has always responded to the 'needs of trade' in supplying cash to the market. One could therefore measure a demand-for-money parameter from the aggregate statistics. But the stock of money may have no

[20] See Fisher (1968a), p. 337 et seq. Kavanah and Walters (1966), Table II D1, 7th equation.

[21] See Fisher (1968a), Walters (1968). This ties in with the work on term structure, see below.

[22] In all these and similar systems the lag in the demand function plays an important role. A minute lag in the demand function is sufficient to make money follow the exogenous income.

effect on income which may be determined by autonomous expenditure.

The best way to test the existence of a monetary multiplier is to measure the parameters directly in some version of the reduced (or final) form.[23] Extensive discussion has taken place in the United States on the efficacy of monetary multipliers, and on their relative stability compared with those of Keynesian autonomous expenditure models.[24]

Very little work has been done in the United Kingdom and the few available results have not been adequately challenged and tested. The general issues are: (a) can the money stock (or rate of interest, or 'credit', or 'advances', or some other monetary variable) be used efficiently to predict the level (or rate of change) of money income—perhaps decomposed into real and price changes; and (b) is the monetary multiplier a better (more stable and reliable) way of predicting income (or consumption) than the autonomous expenditure multiplier?

From the annual data for the period 1888 to 1962, the general approach has been to divide the period into:

(1) pre-World War I (1914),
(2) 1920 or 1922 to 1939,
(3) post-World War II (sometimes from 1955 onwards).

The war years have normally been excluded for obvious reasons. The results for the logarithmic first difference equations are summarized in Table II.1. One is perhaps not surprised to find a relatively good fit for the years before the First World War—and the R^2 does seem to be high in view of the very large errors in the basic data. The most unexpected result—at least to British economists—is the high coefficient of

---

[23] The rate of interest is not included among the independent variables in a monetary multiplier equation; the effect of interest rates is to modify the coefficient of the money stock and will be estimated as such. Note that one could work with a reduced form incorporating the interest rate as the independent variable instead of money; but because of the great difficulty of obtaining an appropriate measure and for other reasons, this has not been done.

[24] The most recent example is Andersen and Jordan (1968). The FRB-MIT model promises a much more sophisticated and detailed treatment of the problem. See *Federal Reserve Bulletin*, June 1969, de Leeuw and Gramlich (1969).

determination for the inter-war years. More than 50 per cent is explained by the quantity of money—but all the individual coefficients are 'insignificant at the 95 per cent level'. The poor performance of the simple quantity-of-money model in

TABLE II. I

Income and the Money Supply

Coefficient relating income and money supply

Period	$\Delta \log m(t)$	$\Delta \log m(t-1)$	$\Delta \log m(t-2)$	$\bar{R}^2$
(1) Pre-World War I 1880–1913	0·431 (0·245)	0·455 (0·275)	−0·132 (0·224)	0·287
(2) 1922–38	0·789 (0·413)	0·587 (0·453)	−0·388 (0·311)	0·518
(3) 1948–62	0·537 (0·543)	0·046 (0·544)	—	0·156

Source of period (1) and (2), Walters (1966a). Source for period (3), calculated by author from Sheppard's statistics.

the post-World War II years would not be inconsistent with the Radcliffe view that the quantity of money was not in itself an important determinant of activity.

It is interesting, however, to attempt to distinguish the monetary effect on prices from that on real output. Further analysis of the *inter-war years* shows that the primary effect of money was on the *price level* and not on real income.[25] Recent work on more satisfactory money and income series by Sheppard (1969) has shown that there is no measurable effect ($R^2 = 0$) of real money on real gross domestic private expenditure. In complete contrast the *post-war years* exhibit a marked real money–real income multiplier and a perverse price effect.[26] One example of this perversity is the famous

[25] See Walters (1966a) equation on p. 274 where the R^2 for the change in price as dependent variable is 0·607.

[26] For the 'real multiplier' see Sheppard (1969). In a draft manuscript on 'Real balances and the demand for money', Douglas Fisher has shown that there are real 'wealth effects' on consumer spending when the quantity of money is increased exogenously, although they are rather small compared with those in the United States. This is not strictly analogous to the real monetary multiplier discussed in this section, although the two concepts are closely related.

Butler downturn of 1955. The stock of money was cut back absolutely, the industrial production index followed some nine months later; but prices kept on rising at something like their previous rate of growth for about three years. The explanation of the very different paths of real income and price effects in the inter-war and post-war years is not a simple matter and, fortunately, is not the subject of this survey.[27] But historians may note that Keynes was essentially correct in his assessment of the effects of monetary expansion on *real* output and employment in the 1920s and 1930s. In real terms the U.K. was insensitive to monetary measures in the inter-war years. Oddly enough it was an old fashioned quantity theory that was then at work with T fixed and P as the variable. During the post-war years, however, attempts to control the increase in the price level by monetary means have apparently had their impact on real income and not on prices. The paradox is complete. It is small wonder that such perverse effects have been the butt of much perplexity and criticism.

A major problem in the use of monetary policy is the length of the lag in the monetary multiplier. From the correlation matrix for annual data it has been estimated that the lag is of the order of six months.[28] But such a figure must be regarded as only of a broad 'order of magnitude' since the basic data are coarsely time-defined. More recently research has suggested that the lag may well be shorter than this—perhaps as little as one quarter in the late 'fifties and 'sixties. There are, however, many methodological problems in assessing lags. For example, it is well known that some of the actions of the monetary authority are anticipated by the market—perhaps by the skill of operators, perhaps deliberately encouraged by the Bank's 'nod and wink' method. Consequently, the observed statistics would tend to bias the results towards

[27] Sir Roy Harrod, in a letter to *The Economist*, 18 July 1969, claims that the reason for increasing prices during the squeeze periods is that many industries and firms are operating with declining cost curves under conditions of imperfect competition. But the model has not been developed explicitly so it is little premature to comment at this stage.

[28] See Barrett and Walters (1966) and Sheppard (1969).

shorter lags than those which actually operate in response to the 'complete surprise' monetary change.[29] Nevertheless, it is unlikely that the lag is longer than a year or shorter than three months.

So far only monetary multipliers have been reported here. But much research is concerned with the effect of private credit, bank advances, 'encashable assets', and so on. Each of these independent variables might be thought to capture some essential expenditure stimulus which does not appear in the quantity of money. Yet the general results of these models do not seem to differ very much from those of the monetary model.[30] Furthermore, it has been shown that even the very broad definitions of money (to include the shares of building societies) do not greatly affect the general tenor of the results. Even the numerical values of the coefficients are not very different.

In search for empirical correlates of the elusive Radcliffe 'liquidity' concept, research has even widened the concept to embrace what Sheppard has called 'encashable assets'.[31] Indeed, for the *real* multiplier during the post-war period 1947–62 when the Radcliffe Committee was conducting its enquiry, encashable assets were rather *less* efficient than money as a predictor.[32] In retrospect therefore, although it is difficult to find an empirical correlate for liquidity, those close approximations that have been explored perform very much like money. There seems little to be gained and much to be

[29] Note however that one may argue that what is needed is a lag that incorporates the average foreknowledge of the market; this seems a difficult concept to formulate.

[30] I owe this conclusion to some unpublished work by Richard Barrett on 'advances multipliers' and to Sheppard (1969). See also Gibson (1967).

[31] These include money stock; deposits and shares of building societies, P.O.S.B., Trustee Savings banks, life funds, National Savings Certificates, Premium bonds, all other holdings of government securities as recorded on the Post Office Register.

[32] The coefficients of the rates of change of money and encashable assets were 0·953 and 0·824 with t ratios 4·1 and 3·2 respectively, and R^2 of 0·54 and 0·41. Note, however, that the rates of change in average consol rate and trend were also included as independent variables, so that comparison with the above multipliers is not straightforward.

lost by concentrating on the supply of 'liquidity' as the lynch-pin of monetary policy.

The second main question posed above was whether a monetary model predicts income (or consumer expenditure) better than the autonomous expenditure of the Keynesian model. As one might expect, the critical issue is the definition of what is autonomous. In Barrett and Walters (1966) the definition was investment *plus* government expenditure *plus* exports minus imports. With this definition money seems to have played the dominant role up to World War I. Yet over the whole period before the outbreak of World War II, and *including the years 1914–20*, one finds that the monetary model performs noticeably better than the Keynesian model.[33] But much of the explanatory power of the money variable from 1914 on is contributed by the war years and their immediate aftermath 1914–20. The inter-war years 1921–38 were, how-ever, Keynesian.[34] The post-World War II years were not explained by either money or autonomous expenditure; but again it must be observed that these results are for *nominal* not real values.[35] More recent work by Sheppard (1969) has redefined autonomous expenditure to exclude imports. The results for the non-war years suggest that a greater role may be attributed to autonomous expenditures than to money— but these results are for contemporaneous mid-period money and they may be much affected by the choice of the lag. These results also emphasize how critical is the definition of what is autonomous in the model.[36] As Friedman and Meisel-man have pointed out there are many definitions of auto-nomous expenditure that are apparently 'acceptable'.

[33] $\Delta \log c(t) = \text{constant} + 0.836 \Delta \log m(t-1) + 0.087 \Delta \log a(t),$
  $\qquad\qquad\qquad\qquad (0.116) \qquad\qquad\qquad (0.041)$
$\bar{R}^2 = 0.541 \qquad partial\ r - \text{money} = 0.484 \qquad partial\ r - \text{aut. exp.} = 0.076.$
[34] $\Delta \log c(t) = \text{constant} + 0.250 \Delta \log m(t-1) + 0.194 \Delta \log a(t),$
  $\qquad\qquad\qquad\qquad (0.133) \qquad\qquad\qquad (0.038)$
$\bar{R}^2 = 0.678 \qquad partial\ r - \text{money} = 0.202 \qquad partial\ r - \text{aut. exp.} = 0.650.$
[35] I conjecture that discriminating between nominal and real multipliers would pay handsome research dividends.
[36] It will be observed that all these definitions differ from the Friedman–Meiselman definitions which deducted tax receipts from autonomous expenditure.

Recently work by Andersen and Jordan (1968) has concentrated on measures of autonomous expenditure that do not reflect oscillations in income—the so-called 'full employment' expenditures. No similar analysis can easily be carried out on the data for the United Kingdom. But Artis and Nobay (1969) have constructed certain measures analogous to those of Andersen and Jordan and have tried the fiscal *versus* monetary quarterly model for the period 1958 to 1967 III. The results are quite dissimilar to those of Andersen and Jordan—giving much more emphasis to tax measures than to the money supply. They also show the economy reacts quicker to tax changes than to changes in the money supply. These results, as far as the weak money-income relationship is concerned, are similar to the quarterly results of Walters (1966a) for the period 1955 to 1962.[37] On the fiscal variables, however, it will be observed that government expenditures play an even less important role than money and advances in the Artis-Nobay equations; public expenditure does not even make the first equation. Artis and Nobay have important misgivings about both their data and the single-equation approach, and they clearly indicate their preference for a structural model.[38] The much more important role played by the government sector and the external trade account in the U.K. relative to the United States may explain part of the difference in these findings. The public sector 'borrowing requirement' has tended to dominate the money supply since the Bank felt it unwise to try to unload any substantial stock on an 'unwilling' market. The deficit in the balance of payments is reflected (*ceteris paribus*) in a reduction in the money supply; these oscillations, though not so large as the government deficit, are, of course, less 'controllable' (see Pepper [1969] and the D.C.E. development). It must also be reported that calculations such as those made by Andersen and Jordan appear to be suscep-

[37] The lag estimated by Artis and Nobay is approximately nine months.
[38] Artis and Nobay unfortunately did not discriminate between real output and prices in discussing income effects, so we cannot use their model to pursue the hypothesis that the main effects of monetary or fiscal management appear in real output and not in prices.

tible to the period chosen for analysis.[39] The issue is still quite open.

May one attempt an interim overall judgement of the results at this stage? Clearly, *any* statement will be a godsend to what the Americans call 'nit-pickers', but it is worth a try. I do believe that the results show that money, and the money stock in particular, is more important than those of us brought up in the climate of the 1940s and 1950s would have imagined. Money cannot be ignored.[40] Whether money works its wonders through the interest rate or by other portfolio adjustments on investment or consumption remains unknown—partly because of the difficulties of measuring the appropriate real interest rate and partly because of the rationing effects on credit. The precise way in which the mechanism works is not tested in any of these models.[41] One would expect that portfolio adjustment models would reveal at least some of the important channels of the effects of monetary policy. And it is to these that we turn in the final section (IV) of this survey.

IV

The empirical exploration of portfolio adjustment and the discussion of the detailed interaction of money markets, the money markets' effect on real variables and the interrelationships between government finance, money, and exchange rates, are all very new fields in the United Kingdom. Very little work has appeared in print and I am grateful to the authors who have sent me their draft manuscripts, but I cannot claim to be comprehensive.

[39] An application to the data for Canada shows almost a *volte-face* if one excludes two terminal years.

[40] The most interesting commentary on the role of money and monetary policy in economic discussion is illustrated by the N.I.E.S.R.'s *British Economy in 1975* (W. Beckerman and others, 1965). The words money and monetary policy did not even appear in the index! But things have changed; see *Britain's Economic Prospects*, Richard Caves and others (Brookings, 1968).

[41] For some information on the FRB-MIT model, see de Leeuw and Gramlich (1969).

We begin with the first published model of the U.K.'s monetary sector by Crouch (1967). This was restricted to the aggregate monetary sector and not concerned with monetary-real interactions;[42] furthermore, it did not consider different subsectors of the monetary system. The Crouch model was mainly an extension of the aggregate demand for money (divided between demand deposits, time deposits, and currency) and the aggregate supply functions; the closure of the model is achieved by a quantity theory multiplier, using lagged deposits on income. The results of Crouch's study are broadly consistent with those that have been obtained by separate inquiry into the individual functions. Marcus Miller (1968a) has however calculated the final form and latent roots of the Crouch model. The roots all lay within the unit circle so the model was not explosive, but two were complex so there were damped oscillations. The reserves-income and special-deposit income multipliers were of the order of 12 to 13. In such a model the dynamic path of adjustment is quite critical. To explore these properties of the monetary system other more complicated models with explicit concentrations on the lag structure and its effects are at present being studied by Wymer (1968).

Among the most important tasks that such models should perform is first that there should be a clear relationship between the monetary and real sectors (particularly the balance of payments for the U.K.). The effect of money on investment in different sectors and on consumer spending needs to be examined in a formal model. The Radcliffe Committee distilled many conclusions about the effects on inventory investment, overseas investment, etc., from the evidence offered. These need to be tested against the facts. A second task is to link the monetary model with the financing decisions of public authorities, the so-called 'borrowing requirements'. A direct relationship of the monetary model with the public finance model would illuminate many of the dilemmas of the authorities and sharpen the gilt-edged-money-stock issues.

[42] This also appears to be the simplification in the first stages of the 'Southampton Model', see Rowan (1969).

The analysis of a model of behaviour relationships in national portfolios and of the principles of debt management has been started by Miller (1968b). Subject to balance sheet identities, estimates have been made of the reaction of the private sector and banks in terms of their holdings of cash, deposits, bills, and securities to the (exogenous) rates on advances and Treasury bills and other instruments of monetary control.

Miller's model is a static equilibrium Tobin-style model designed to simulate the effects of policy measures throughout the financial system. Some of the results are surprising and deserve much more discussion than we can give here. The first one—a perverse result in any normal financial circles— is that if the long rate is pegged, then a rise in the short rate (via Bank rate) will increase deposits, advances, and loans and so *reduce* the cost of capital. In short, a rise in Bank rate is expansionary in its domestic impact. If, however, the long rate were not pegged, then there would be some muted increase in the cost of capital. Secondly, Miller measures trade-offs between debt service costs and credit control restrictions. One can see the great temptation of the authorities to reduce interest rates to secure cheaper debt service costs, and to take the steam out of demand by direct restrictions on credit and hire purchase. The cost of such regulation in terms of its policing and inefficiency of allocation does not appear as identified in any particular account. It is just a general loss. Many more questions can be asked of Miller's model which offers great scope for adaptation to include wealth effects.

Models of portfolio behaviour of certain types of monetary institutions are also very recent developments in the United Kingdom, see Parkin (1969) and Parkin, Gray, and Barrett (1969). These models have specified a utility function that incorporates both the mean and the variance of profits. This variation arises because the institutions cannot forecast exactly what the yields or rates are going to be; consequently, there is an error term. The sole restraint is that of portfolio balance. (Note that the restriction is not on the size of the portfolio; borrowing is the normal activity of such institutions.) These models are close relatives of those of Tobin (1966) and Bierwag and Grove (1967) and are subject to similar limitations. One of the most serious is the absence of any learning process about yields. The assumption is that over the period of observation, whatever the length (?), the errors cancel out. Observed yields do not convey any information about a change in expected yields (or about future errors). Parkin did experiment, however, with other expectation equations with little success. There does not seem to be a satisfactory way of revising expected rates, see Buse (1968). With this as one among many strong assumptions, Parkin has produced an ingenious computable model and has estimated the coefficients. His main result is to find that there are marked cross elasticities between Treasury bills, commercial bills, short bonds, call loans, and discounts and advances and that own-rate coefficients conform to expectation. The call loan rate has a very marked effect.

The discount market is part of the mystique of the City and was thought by many to be incapable of being explained in terms of a relatively simple portfolio model. Parkin has shown that a great deal can in fact be explained and that the management of the discount house performs much like other managements in switching between profitable opportunities according to their expected yield and cost. The volatility of expectations does not seem to be sufficient to upset the results.

Parkin, Gray, and Barrett (1969) have used the same model to explain the portfolio behaviour of the commercial banks. Many of the findings are very important and directly discredit the views of the Radcliffe Committee. For example, it is shown that the response of the banks to a change in the bond rate is not perverse. Furthermore, the study shows clearly what has been suggested by Crouch, Gibson, and others; Special Deposits are a nebulous instrument for controlling deposits since Special Deposits are more than offset by sales of bonds and purchases of bills by banks. On the other hand, as one might expect, a limitation on advances does create a demand for government debt and so presumably damps down and distorts domestic demand.

Somewhat similar models have been recently used on U.K. data by Rowan and O'Brien (1969) to examine the term structure of interest rates—or to be strict the difference between bills and consol yields. The authors' preliminary findings suggest that expected rates are formulated from a long series of past rates, and not only from very recent experience, and that 'errors' tend to be reversible—that is to say, the expected rate reverts to its 'normal' level. And, as in studies in the U.S.A., there appears to be no explanatory power attributable to the maturity structure of outstanding debt. Nevertheless, the various versions of the expectations hypothesis have been shown to be difficult to test[43] and since there exists an excellent survey by Telser (1967) of these problems, we may leave this subject to the specialists.

These studies have been largely concerned with the instruments of control and the supply of money and credit. Much of the discussion of the Radcliffe Committee was concerned with the methods of controlling deposits and the supply of money.[44] The Committee embraced the 'new orthodoxy'— the level of deposits was controlled by the supply of liquid assets through the 28 or 30 per cent liquidity ratio. The Committee was persuaded by the argument of Professor Sayers that the control over deposits could be exercised by reducing or increasing the supply of Treasury bills. Most of the arguments about the 'new orthodoxy' have been concerned with the *ceteris paribus* of the statements, and the 'could do' or 'would do' alternatives. But Crouch (1964) was the first to challenge the hypothesis directly by testing it against the data. He found that the 'new orthodoxy' was convincingly discredited partly because of the purchase of bills outside the discount market. A careful analysis by Goodhart (1968) has supported the hypothesis that banks could offset any reduction in Treasury bills by an increase in private sector liquid assets (such as commercial bills).

The control over the reserve base is conventionally thought

---

[43] See Buse (1968), Fisher (1968a).
[44] But oddly enough the Committee did not consider Special Deposits—nor did it discuss the implications of the emerging Euro-currency markets.

to be the main way in which the authorities influence the supply of money and credit. Yet it has been clear to many observers that there was in fact no control exercised over the reserve base; private sector claims have been determined by the level of demand at the interest rate determined by the authorities in conjunction with any increased or decreased stringency due to the need to ration credit, Goodhart (1968, appendix to Section 6). The banks have the power to adjust cash to the 0·08 ratio by switching out of Treasury bills into cash since the Bank will always supply cash to the discount houses at a rate no greater than Bank rate.[45]

One interesting aspect of the supply of money has been the alleged central role of Bank rate. The authorities and Radcliffe believed that for a given level of Bank rate they could raise the money rate of the discount houses by making them borrow at Bank rate and so force up the rate on Treasury bills. But a quantitative analysis of the period 1960–2 by Alford (1968) has suggested that borrowings at Bank rate were too small to affect greatly the money and bill rates.[46] Driving up money rates, however, is just one of the functions of Bank rate. It is hoped that an increase in Bank rate will be associated with a tightening of credit and the supply of money. Yet, with a structure of interest rates tied conventionally to Bank rate, the immediate effect is to raise the cost of holding idle balances, and so one might expect an *expansion* of credit as a consequence. This effect of changes in Bank rate has been recently observed by Marcus Miller (1968b). It thus seems possible that movements in Bank rate have a perverse effect.[47]

In this survey I do not propose to discuss any further the detailed technology of the control of the money supply. But there is one subject—the behaviour of the non-bank financial institutions—which is closely related to the control of money and credit. The argument is clearly that the N.B.F.I.s will

[45] Goodhart shows that some £200 million reductions in bank lending can be attributed to Bank 'requests'.

[46] It might be argued *per contra* that the actual amount of borrowing at Bank rate is not relevant since the marginal funds will always pay the penal rate.

[47] Bank rate movements were primarily determined by the state of the foreign reserves and unemployment, see Goodhart (1968).

frustrate policy because a reduction in the supply of money may be offset by an expansion in the credit of N.B.F.I.s or by extensions of trade credit.

There is no doubt that, secularly, credit and the deposit liabilities of N.B.F.I.s have expanded far more rapidly than the quantity of money.[48] This is simply a manifestation of improvements in the techniques of using a given amount of money; the same amount of real money goes further. For cyclical changes there is little doubt that N.B.F.I.s do tend to reduce their liabilities rather less than the banks during a downturn. But according to a study by Gibson (1967), the counter effect of the N.B.F.I. has been much exaggerated by the Radcliffe Committee and others.

A particularly interesting study of the empirical behaviour of trade credit by Brechling and Lipsey (1963) showed that trade credit was a 'strong potential frustrator of monetary policy'. But subsequent work by White (1964) and a further review of the evidence by Brechling and Lipsey (1966) (with mimeographed addenda by White and Brechling and Lipsey) seem to me to confirm that the evidence is consistent with at most only a weak frustrator of monetary policy.[49] This provisional result of the Brechling–Lipsey–White exchange discredits one of the central theses of Radcliffe—the trade credit offset. More detailed work at present proceeding on company finance should enable the detailed effects of trade credit to be charted more accurately, but I suspect that the main result will not be upset.

V

Ten years ago monetary studies were primarily the preserve of the institutionalist on the one hand and the pure theorist on the other. Statistical studies of monetary effects had only reached their infancy and had virtually no effect on the

[48] For the longest series see Sheppard (1969). See also the earlier study by Clayton (1962).

[49] The first Brechling and Lipsey conclusion was derived from *stocks* of excess credit outstanding; but all authors accepted that the relevant criteria should be the relationship between *changes* in the transfers of credit.

theorists, institutionalists, and City men who gave evidence at the Radcliffe hearings. Intuition, experience, and judgement have now been subjected to ten years' statistical and econometric analysis. What is left?

The central conclusion that liquidity was the centrepiece of the monetary system and that the quantity of money was not important, except as a determinant of the levels of interest rates, has not stood the test. The quantity of money does seem to have some effect on the level of demand. One may doubt whether as much can be done with monetary control as many people imagine; it has yet to be demonstrated that money can be used for fine tuning. (And it is at least clear to me that no selling of gilt-edged can mop up a huge government deficit such as that of 1967–8.) The danger is now that the quantity of money has been rediscovered as a not insignificant magnitude, the monetary mechanism will be asked to do too much too quickly, and too precisely. (My immediate fears are concerned with the horrifying letter of intent and the D.C.E. statistic.)[50]

One of the other main conclusions of Radcliffe was the frustration of monetary policy due to the high substitutability of credit—especially by the stretching of the monetary base by the N.B.F.I.s and by trade credit. The empirical studies show that this fear was much exaggerated. The N.B.F.I.s seem, in retrospect, to have been caricatured as the villains of the monetary play both in Britain and the United States. The evidence suggests that their role has been a minor one.

The reliance of Radcliffe on interest rates, and particularly the long-term rate, as the mechanism of control or as the instrumental variable of the system, has not been adequately tested. Monetary multipliers have used the money stock as the independent variable rather than an interest rate.[51] Furthermore, the interest rate that is useful for multipliers is one that

---

[50] See Artis and Nobay (1969) for a low-key account of the rule.

[51] The reasons for absence of results are not hard to guess. High money interest rates are usually associated with high income and so the signs are superficially perverse; see Sheppard (1969). High velocity is associated with high income and high interest rates.

is couched in real terms, and it is difficult to get convincing measures of price expectations.

As for the supply of money, the Radcliffe Committee accepted the 'new orthodoxy' that the volume of bank deposits was determined by the quantity of 'liquid assets' (Radcliffe, para. 376). The liquid assets theory has been discredited by the analysis of the data. The mechanism of Special Deposits, which strangely enough was hardly mentioned by Radcliffe, has been shown to be nebulous if not positively expansionary. On the other hand, there is some evidence that the direct ceiling on advances does limit deposit expansion.

On debt management the Radcliffe, Treasury, and Bank view was that the demand for long-term government debt was perverse—a higher interest rate would lower demand. Evidence from the portfolio models goes some considerable way towards discrediting this view. But many more models of other sectors need to be explored before such a normal demand curve is generally accepted.

Should one be surprised that so little of Radcliffe has survived the calculations of the last ten years? Perhaps not. For one of the great and lasting contributions of Radcliffe was to call forth much of the data which provided evidence for the refutation of its hypotheses. Monetary economics must at some time or other come to terms with the facts of life as they are, rather than as reported by reputable opinion. The Radcliffe Committee greatly speeded this process, in part by its provocative report. Although analytically and empirically the Radcliffe Report must be judged mediocre, the fall-out has been impressive.

REFERENCES

ARTIS, M. J. and NOBAY, A. R. (1969). 'Two Aspects of the Monetary Debate', *Nat. Inst. Ec. Review*, No. 49, August, pp. 33–51.

ALFORD, R. F. G. (1968). 'Bank Rate, Money Rates and the Treasury Bill Rate', in C. R. Whittlesey and J. S. G. Wilson (ed.), *Essays in Money and Banking in Honour of R. S. Sayers*, Oxford.

BAIN, A. D. (1968). 'Monetary Policy', in A. R. Prest (ed.), *Public Sector Economics*, Manchester University Press.

BALL, R. J. (1965). 'Some Econometric Analysis of the Long Term Rate of Interest in the U.K. 1921–61', *Manchester School of Economic and Social Studies*, XXXIII, January.

BARRETT, C. R. and WALTERS, A. A. (1966). 'The Stability of Keynesian and Monetary Multipliers in the United Kingdom', *Review of Economics and Statistics*, November.

BELL, G. and BERMAN, L. S. (1966). 'Changes in the Money Supply in the United Kingdom, 1954 to 1964', *Economica*, N.S., XXXIII(130), May.

BIERWAG, G. O. and GROVE, M. A. (1967). 'A Model of the Term Structure of Interest Rates', *Review of Economics and Statistics*, 50–62.

BRECHLING, F. P. R. and LIPSEY, R. G. (1963). 'Trade Credit and Monetary Policy', *Ec. Journal*, December.

——, —— (1966). 'Trade Credit and Monetary Policy—a Rejoinder', *Ec. Journal*, March.

BRUNNER, KARL and ROBERT CROUCH (1968). 'Money Supply Theory and British Monetary Experience', in Rudolf Henn (ed.), *Operations Research Verfahren*, Hain, Meisenheim.

BUSE, A. (1968). 'Studies in the Term Structure of Interest Rates', Ph.D. Thesis, Birmingham.

CLAYTON, G. (1962). 'British Financial Intermediaries in Theory and Practice', *Ec. Journal*, December.

COPPOCK, D. J. and GIBSON, N. J. (1963). 'The Volume of Deposits and the Cash and Liquid Asset Ratios', *Manchester School*, September.

CRAMP, A. B. (1967). 'The Control of Bank Credit', *Lloyds Bank Review*, October.

CROUCH, R. L. (1963). 'A Re-examination of Open Market Operations', *Oxford Econ. Papers*, July.

—— (1964). 'The Inadequacy of New Orthodox Methods of Monetary Control', *Ec. Journal*, December.

—— (1965). 'The Genesis of Bank Deposits—New English Version', *Bulletin Oxford Univ. Inst. of Econ. & Stats.*, 27(3).

—— (1967). 'A Model of the U.K.'s Monetary Sector', *Econometrica*, 35(3–4), July/October.

—— (1968). 'Money Supply Theory and the United Kingdom Monetary Contraction 1954–6', *Bulletin Oxford Univ. Inst. of Econ. & Stats.*, 30(2).

—— (1969). '"Special Deposits" and the British Monetary Mechanism', *Journal of Economic Studies*.

FISHER, DOUGLAS (1968a). 'The Demand for Money in Britain, Quarterly Results 1951 to 1967', *Manchester School*, December.

—— (1968b). 'The Objectives of British Monetary Policy', *Journal of Finance*, December.

—— (1969). 'Real Balances and the Demand for Money' (manuscript mimeo).

DE LEEUW, F. and GRAMLICH, E. M. (1969). 'The Channels of Monetary Policy—a further report on the Federal Reserve—M.I.T. Econometric Model', *Federal Reserve Bulletin*, June.

Dow, J. R. C. (1964). *The Management of the British Economy 1945–60*, Cambridge.

GIBSON, N. J. (1964). 'Special Deposits as an Instrument of Monetary Policy', *Manchester School*, September.

—— (1967). *Financial Intermediaries and Monetary Policy*, Hobart Paper No. 39, Institute of Economic Affairs, London.

GOODHART, CHARLES (1968). 'British Monetary Policy 1957–67' (mimeo), to appear in *Monetary Policy in the Atlantic Community*, ed. Karel Holbrik.

HETHERINGTON, P. R. (1969). 'Walters on Money', *Bankers Magazine*, July, pp. 11–17.

HUGHES, A. G. (1969). 'Leads and Lags in Monetary Economics: A New Look at the Statistical Data' (mimeo), Dept. of Economics, University of Nottingham.

KAVANAGH, N. J. and WALTERS, A. A. (1966). 'The Demand for Money in the United Kingdom 1877–1961. Some Preliminary Findings', *Bulletin Oxford Univ. Inst. of Econ. & Stats.*, 28(2), 93–116.

LAIDLER, D. and PARKIN, M. J. (1969). 'The Demand for Money Fluctuation in the United Kingdom 1953–67: Preliminary Results' (mimeo).

MELTZER, ALLAN H. (1969). 'A Survey of Monetary Demand', *Journal of Economic Literature*, I(1).

MILLER, MARCUS (1968a). 'Notes on Crouch's Model' (private memorandum, L.S.E.).

—— (1968b). 'An Empirical Analysis of the Determination of Interest Rates and the National Balance Sheet for the U.K.' (mimeo), L.S.E.

PARKIN, M. J. (1967). 'Comment on "Genesis of Bank Deposits"', *Bulletin Oxford Univ. Inst. of Econ. & Stats.*, February.

—— (1969). 'Discount House Portfolio and Debt Selection', *Univ. of Essex Discussion Paper*, No. 3, May.

——, GRAY, M. R., and BARRETT, R. J. (1969). 'The Portfolio of Behaviour of Commercial Banks', *Univ. of Essex Discussion Paper*, No. 8, June.

PEPPER, GORDON (1969). 'The Money Supply, Economic Management and the Gilt Edged Market', lecture to Institute of Actuaries.

REVELL, J. R. S. (1968). 'Changes in British Banking', *Hill, Samuel, Occasional Paper*, No. 3.

ROWAN, D. C. and O'BRIEN, R. J. (1969). 'The Monetary Sector of the Southampton Model' (mimeo), Conference on Econometric Models of the U.K., 14–17 April.

SHEPPARD, D. K. (1965a). 'Financial Statistics U.K. Banks 1880–1962', *Birmingham Univ. Discussion Paper*, A63.

—— (1965b). 'A Provincial Money Liquid Asset and Credit Series for the U.K. 1880–1962', *Birmingham Univ. Discussion Paper*, A65.

SHEPPARD, D. K. (1968a). 'U.K. Financial Institutions Balance Sheet Statistics, Bank Clearings, Interest Rates, National Savings, Money Stock, and the Stock of Institutional Credits granted to the Private Sector, 1880–1962' (mimeo).

—— (1968b). 'Changes in the Money Supply in the United Kingdom, 1954 to 1964, A Comment', *Economica*, N.S. XXXV, August.

—— (1969). Thesis submitted to Harvard University.

TELSER, LESTER G. (1967). 'A Critique of Some Recent Empirical Research on the Explanation of the Term Structure of Interest Rates', *J.P.E.*, 75, 546–61.

TOBIN, J. (1966). 'Commercial Banks as Creators of Money', *Cowles Foundation, Monograph*, 21.

WALTERS, A. A. (1966a). 'Monetary Multipliers in the U.K.', *Oxford Econ. Papers*, November.

—— (1966b). 'Bank Rate', *The Bankers Magazine*, July.

—— (1968). 'The Demand for Money Expectations Short and Long Rates', in J. N. Wolfe (ed.), *Value, Capital, and Growth*, Edinburgh.

WHITE, W. H. (1966). 'Trade Credit and Monetary Policy: A Reconciliation', *Ec. Journal*, March, pp. 165–7.

WYMER, C. R. (1968). 'Stochastic Differential Equation Model of United Kingdom Financial Markets', paper presented at Econometric Society Europlan Meeting, Brussels, September.

Discussion Papers

(a) L. DICKS-MIREAUX
(*Economic Adviser, Bank of England*)

THE great merit of any paper presented to a conference is that it should provoke discussion. In this respect Professor Walters has served us well, for his paper is undoubtedly provocative; indeed so much so that those who do not know him or his writings well might unwittingly suspect that he has written this paper with his tongue somewhat in his cheek.

The dominant theme of Professor Walters' paper is that economic hypotheses should be subject to rigorous empirical testing, especially those which underlie policy decisions. This proposition, sound enough, is perhaps well worth repeating at the outset. None the less, in this connection a note of protest should be raised at the unwarranted complaint about the Radcliffe Committee's lack of quantitative evidence. At the time, the data which the Committee had available to it was indeed sparse; and the very fact that the Committee was primarily responsible for instigating the considerable statistical improvements that have taken place in recent years must surely be taken as evidence that it did not reject a quantitative approach out of choice.

I want therefore to concentrate on the proposition that 'money does matter'. The testing of this proposition is the concern of much of Professor Walters' paper. From a policy point of view, it is obviously highly important to know whether or not money does, in fact, matter. But this is not the only proposition with which the authorities need to concern themselves when making policy decisions. If, indeed, one were to conclude that money was important—and I shall want to say more about this later—it does not necessarily follow that money should become the prime target of policy. To follow a money supply policy must imply forgoing other potential policy objectives and it may well be that the advantages of tighter control over the money supply are offset—or more than offset—by disadvantages associated with the looser control over the level and structure of interest rates, the stability of financial markets, etc. I do not claim that such disadvantages *would* necessarily follow, but merely indicate their possibility as something which should also be subjected to rigorous testing.

The first problem which presents itself with regard to the question 'does money matter?' is a statistical one. How can this particular hypothesis be tested? Professor Walters contends that it is correct to draw conclusions from direct estimation of a money multiplier equation with Y (income) as the dependent variable and M (supply of money) as the independent variable. To me this raises two further questions. First, what are the implications of M being assumed to be determined, not exogenously, but by some policy reaction function and secondly, in such an equation system, what kind of economic rationale can be given for the chosen form of the money multiplier equation?

As far as the endogeneity of the supply of money is concerned, Professor Walters admits to the possibility that the authorities, in order to meet the 'needs of trade', may increase the money supply as real income increases. Assuming no lags in both the money multiplier and the reaction functions, the two equations are econometrically identical. Professor Walters holds that this problem can be easily overcome. If, in the money multiplier equation, money is assumed to affect income with a lag, then the two equations are no longer identical and so become identifiable. Strictly speaking, he is assuming away the possibility that the reaction function also contains a lag identical with the lag in the money multiplier equation. However, since this situation would require the money stock to be adjusted in perfect anticipation of subsequent income movements, I would not quibble with his assumption. But even though the equations in a system may be considered to be identified, this still leaves us with the possibility of biased estimates in the individual equations of the system. If we take the money multiplier equation

$$y_t = \alpha + \beta m_{t-1} + u_t$$

in its stochastic form, we must next ask whether the money supply term and the error term can be truly considered to be independent of each other. The error term represents all other factors affecting the economy; and to treat it as independent of the money supply would seem a sweeping assumption worthy of a closer examination of the facts. As far as the coefficients are concerned, any positive correlation between these two terms would lead to an upward bias in the estimates of both the money multiplier and the correlation coefficient.

I shall try to illustrate this by concocting an argument which is perhaps not too implausible. Let us begin with the Chief Cashier and suppose that he is less *simpliste* than most models assume. In any case, I should not wish to take his name in vain, since he is after all not present at this Conference. He therefore controls neither interest rates nor the money supply but instead follows a policy which might be described as a trade-off between an interest rate goal and a gilt-edged sales goal. To this end, I assume he tends to sell gilt-edged when their prices are rising and to buy them when prices are falling; in neither case does he peg prices. It follows from this assumed behaviour that the money supply will clearly move in the same direction as interest-rate movements. To bring in the real world, we may assume that interest rates tend to lead movements in real variables—a commonly held hypothesis but one which in principle should also be testable. In these circumstances, it would not be difficult to obtain a relationship which, according to Professor Walters, would give support to the thesis that money matters. But does it really? As I said at the outset, I am not proposing here *the* explanation of any such positive results but merely illustrating the dangers of easy interpretation of these results.

This last point enables me to deal with the question of institutional knowledge, in this case the way in which the authorities tend to treat the gilt-edged market. I believe that such knowledge cannot be so easily dismissed as much of the empirical work would seem to do. Indeed, I would suggest that Professor Walters might have profitably and specifically mentioned at the beginning of his paper the desirability of consulting the institutionalists about the working of certain markets and policies instead of justifiably, but nevertheless solely, drawing our attention to the dangers of never testing what institutionalists say about the nature of economic relationships. Such a warning about the necessity to specify relationships in the light of what experience exists would seem, moreover, not entirely unwarranted. To take only one example from the list of research works in Professor Walters' paper, it is surely unfortunate that R. L. Crouch's econometric model of the U.K. financial sector assumes throughout cash-base control of the banking system's deposits. Some may argue that this is how control ought to be applied, but as the Bank of England have frequently said, it is, quite simply, not the way it is done in practice.

The second important question prompted by Professor Walters' paper concerns the nature of the money multiplier equation. What economic rationale underlies it? I know that there is a strand of opinion within the school of positive economics which maintains that if a relationship is found to hold in past data, this should be taken as sufficient grounds for policy-makers to act on it. I would not wish to dissociate myself entirely from this school. But it is possible to carry 'black box economics' too far and I find it unsatisfactory both from a theoretical and from a practical standpoint that this view should be held regardless of the plausibility of the transmission mechanism. It implies somehow that there is no particular merit in understanding relationships. Moreover, it requires an act of faith, even greater than that normally implicit in most policy decisions, about a relationship determined from the past continuing to hold in the future, notwithstanding the subsequent impact of policy upon it. Given the complexity of the processes connecting changes in the money supply and national income, final recourse to such simplifications may be forced upon us; but surely further work on the transmission mechanism is imperative.

At this stage, I must make it clear that I am not denying the usefulness of econometric research as such, nor indeed research which uses the simple equations of the type described by Professor Walters. On the contrary, the Bank of England have carried out several research projects in this area and have found, using regression analysis with quarterly data from 1955 to 1968, that there is some indication that various money series lead certain national income series by a short interval. Virtually the same results have been derived from cross-spectral analysis using monthly data. There is, however, considerable uncertainty about how these tentative results should be interpreted and work in this area is continuing.

So much for general considerations. I now want to deal with the more detailed results which Professor Walters quotes—particularly in Table I—concerning the money multiplier equation. For the period 1888–1913, a regression of changes in income on simultaneous and lagged changes in the money stock produces an $\bar{R}^2$ of 0·287. For the inter-war period, the $\bar{R}^2$ is as high as 0·518. However, in both periods none of the individual coefficients is significantly different from zero at the 5 per cent level, and in both cases the most significant variable is the *simultaneous* change in the money stock, leaving the direction of causation problem wide open. For the post-war period, the $\bar{R}^2$ of the relationship is only 0·156 and the coefficient on lagged changes in money is totally insignificant, a result which Professor Walters acknowledges as being consistent with Radcliffe's view that the quantity of money is not a particularly important determinant of economic activity. This is not the only evidence that is consistent with Radcliffe's conclusions. Barrett and Walters found no evidence that money was a more important determinant of expenditure than autonomous expenditures for the post-war years; and they found the inter-war years—when the influence of money was, according to the equations just discussed, at its strongest—to be highly Keynesian. Artis and Nobay found changes in the stock of money had a much weaker impact on income than fiscal policy had for the post-war period. While it is true that their results, as Professor Walters points out, could be due to the non-exogeneity of M, this objection applies equally to the results he presents in support of the monetarist case.

Nobody who has kept abreast of the American literature would be prepared to say that money did not matter at all. But it is hard to accept that empirical evidence so far for the United Kingdom compels the elevation of money to the focal point of economic policy. By most statistical tests, the evidence quoted by Professor Walters in the pages preceding his conclusion that, effectively, money matters in the United Kingdom could, I would argue, be adduced in support of the opposite conclusion.

Discussion Papers

(b) M. PARKIN
(University of Essex)

LET me begin by saying that I share the general philosophical position taken by Walters in his survey, namely that the way in which we are likely to discover things about the working of the monetary system is to specify and test hypotheses and estimate the parameters in econometric models. This approach contrasts sharply with that employed by the Radcliffe Committee of asking people for their opinions on how the monetary system works.

Walters has done an impressive job in surveying what is becoming quite a large field of work. He has, however, in my opinion, put rather too much emphasis on what we might call the Friedman/Meiselman approach and rather too little emphasis on the more disaggregated search for stable structural equations. Also, even within the Friedman/Meiselman framework, it seems to me that Walters has done less than justice to a summarization and critique of that literature.

One problem with the Friedman/Meiselman approach is that it is not obvious from a specification of reduced form equations of consumption on the money stock what is being estimated. Certainly we can have no faith in the parameter estimates on the money stock as monetary multipliers if we have not taken care to show that the equation specified is a genuine reduced form equation of the system. This requires that we correctly identify all the exogenous variables in the system and regress consumption (or some other endogenous variable) on *all* the exogenous variables that generate the endogenous variable. Only having done this can we be reasonably confident that the coefficient on the money stock is indeed the money multiplier. We can further only be reasonably happy that the reduced form equation fitted is correct if it can be deduced from a structural system, which system has itself been tested. Typically, the way in which the reduced form money multipliers model is presented is to start with a money demand function of the form

$$\frac{M^d}{p} = kY + l(r),$$

where M^d/p = money demand (real); Y = real income; r = rate of interest and then to suppress $l(r)$ and invert the function to become

$$pY = \frac{1}{k} M,$$

where M is the exogenously determined stock of money. Money income (pY) or consumption is then regressed on M, often with lags and inferences made about the money multiplier from the estimated coefficients.

What should be done, of course, is the specification of the system of *structural* equations and the derivation of a reduced form from those equations.

A further worry which one has about the Friedman/ Meiselman approach is that money is treated as an exogenous variable, or, if not exogenous, so directly controllable by a few other exogenous variables that, to assume the money stock to be exogenous, is reasonable. Central banks and central governments have the power to fix things like last resort interest rates, the net liabilities of the central bank, the stocks of, or the rates of interest on, various categories of government debt, terms on which various types of loans may be taken out, and so on. The stock of money is as endogenous a variable as consumption itself. Thus it would seem to be necessary to specify models which directly show the links between the *instrument* variables which the authorities can themselves directly determine and any intermediate variable or final target variables which are the object of monetary control.

The work which is currently being done by Marcus Miller at London School of Economics, and has been done by William Norton at the University of Manchester and myself at the University of Essex, attempts to fill some part of this gap. That is, it is work mainly directed towards dealing with questions involving the relationships between primary instrument variables and intermediate financial variables and ultimate target variables.

Walters perhaps should have put more emphasis on this work and should have shown how it is related to and represents a finer specification of the same kinds of problems which are handled in a less satisfactory manner by the Friedman/ Meiselman treatment.

To summarize, it is my judgement that the Friedman/ Meiselman approach has been no more than a set of initial explorations of the role of money in determining the level of economic activity and that important empirical contributions to an analysis of the role of money lie in the work of a more disaggregated general equilibrium nature, currently being undertaken.

SUMMARY OF THE GENERAL DISCUSSION

THE major topic of the discussion was a debate about the methodology of studies into monetary relationships. Many discussants criticized the use of reduced-form equations which attempted to link the gross aggregates of money and income in relations like demand for money equations or 'money multipliers'. This had led to the neglect of research into the structural relationships of financial markets through which monetary policy instruments influenced economic targets. This neglect led to serious problems in interpreting and using the results of empirical studies of the financial system. In some cases, it was suggested, econometricians had used reduced form equations which did not make economic sense.

The difficulty which received most attention was the problem of deciding on the correct definition of the money stock. Several speakers who had been engaged in testing aggregate money-income models claimed that it made little difference in the relationships which definition of money was used. Other speakers pointed out that for policy purposes, and for those in the market trying to predict the direction of controls, a knowledge of the exact constituents of the money stock variable was vital.

This led to a second difficulty which was concealed by working with the aggregates. It was agreed that any empirical study made assumptions about the behaviour of the authorities, the nature of market processes, etc. While it was claimed that many of these assumptions might themselves be tested, a change in assumptions must disturb the money-income relationship, and unless the structural equations describing the channels through which monetary forces operate are described, it is difficult to predict the extent of this disturbance.

The difficulty of using complicated structural research models was illustrated by the problem of explaining to operators in financial markets the particular type of data they would have to supply if such research was to be meaningful. In the discussion it became clear that the language of the academic research worker differed from that used by the economists of the institutions under study. This was seen in the different attitudes towards the concept of liquidity, which econometricians thought to be unimportant because it added little new information to any observed financial relationship but which was important to bankers because they were very aware of its balance-sheet significance.

This led to a discussion of whether anything meaningful could be said about 'liquidity' as an independent variable. The positive relation between firms' subjective judgements about their liquidity position, and the objective concept of velocity was noted; and it was claimed that because interest rates, both the 'implied' rate on demand deposits and the time-deposit rate, were flexible, market movements kept the money-liquidity ratio fairly constant so that changes in the money stock might be a good index of changes in liquidity.

Another body of comment concentrated on the choice of what interest rate should be used in econometric studies of money. This was linked with the important problem of building expectations into the model, because the relevant interest rate would partially reflect expected price changes. No satisfactory work had been done in this area and simple hypotheses such as using the difference between bond rates and equity rates had many disadvantages. The influence of price change expectations on consumer decisions might be different at different rates of price change.

Other discussants asked for more research into the links between monetary variables and the consumption patterns of different economic sectors. Research should concentrate on the impact of variables which the authorities could control. Professor Walters's reference to the ambiguous relation between monetary policy, prices, and income in the 1950s might suggest the need for more work on the cost effects of credit restraint. Other possible research areas were the links between public-sector financing and the money supply, the relation of external financing flows and the domestic financial system, and the behaviour of the gilt-edged market.

III

RECENT DEVELOPMENTS IN MONETARY THEORY—A COMMENTARY

Harry G. Johnson

Discussion Papers

(*a*) David Laidler
(*b*) R. T. Armstrong

III

RECENT DEVELOPMENTS IN MONETARY THEORY—A COMMENTARY

HARRY G. JOHNSON

(*Professor of Economics, The London School of Economics and Political Science and the University of Chicago*)

I. INTRODUCTION

THE Radcliffe Committee initiated its investigations into the working of the British monetary system at a time when the intellectual environment could be characterized as the high tide of Keynesian scepticism about the importance of monetary policy and the relevance of monetary theory. By the time its Report was published, however, that tide had begun markedly to ebb, a fact which accounts for the unexpectedly harsh reception the Report received even from what might have been expected to be intellectually sympathetic quarters. In the ensuing ten years, the tide has set markedly in the opposite direction, towards emphasis on the importance of monetary policy and concern with the theory of money (as distinct from the theory of income and employment), to the point where contemporary controversy centres on the so-called 'rise of monetarism'.

The purpose of the present paper is to survey developments in monetary theory since the Radcliffe Report, with particular emphasis on developments subsequent to two previous surveys of mine, written in 1961–2 and 1963.[1] The first of those sur-

[1] Harry G. Johnson, 'Monetary Theory and Policy', *The American Economic Review*, Vol. LII, No. 3 (June 1962), pp. 335–84, and 'Recent Developments

veys, designed to provide a comprehensive overview of the field for graduate students and non-specialist professional economists, organized the material presented within the broad analytical framework of demand for and supply of money. The second, an essay in personal interpretation unrestricted by the obligation of representation by population, took as its organizational focus six problems originating in Keynes's *General Theory*, and emphasized the two themes of the application of capital theory to monetary theory and the trend towards dynamic analysis.

For the purposes of this conference, the type of approach of the second survey referred to seems the more suitable. Accordingly, the paper discusses recent developments under a series of topical headings chosen to represent themes considered to be of general interest to monetary economists. However, in comparison with the 1963 survey, emphasis is placed rather less on unifying strands of thought and rather more on current controversy. Also, certain themes are treated in exceptional detail, in view of their presumed interest to the members of this conference—particularly the first two, the revival of monetarism and the rehabilitation of Keynes. The remaining topics are the fundamentals of monetary theory, the problems associated with financial intermediation, money in growth models, and the theory of inflation and economic policy.

II. THE REVIVAL OF THE QUANTITY THEORY AND THE RISE OF 'MONETARISM'

As already remarked, the dominant feature of the post-Radcliffe era, in the American if not quite yet the British literature, has been the revival of the quantity theory of money and the rise of the associated 'monetarist' approach to economic policy—an approach which stresses the explanatory and controlling power of changes in the quantity of money, in

in Monetary Theory', *The Indian Economic Review*, Vol. VI, No. 4 (August 1963), pp. 1–28; reprinted as chapters I and II in H. G. Johnson, *Essays in Monetary Economics* (London: Allen & Unwin, 1969).

contrast to the Keynesian emphasis on fiscal policy, and as regards monetary policy on credit and interest-rate policies. It may be useful, though it risks the accusation of putting an unwarranted motivational construction on a process of scientific development, to trace the stages in the intellectual revival of the quantity theory, which has been almost exclusively the work of Milton Friedman.

The Keynesian Revolution left the quantity theory thoroughly discredited, on the grounds either that it was a mere tautology (the quantity equation), or that it 'assumed full employment' and that the velocity factor it emphasized was in fact highly unstable. The revival of a quantity theory that could claim to rival the Keynesian theory required a restatement of it that would free it from these objections and give it an empirical content. Such a restatement was provided by Milton Friedman's classic article,[2] which redefined the quantity theory as a theory of the demand for money (or velocity) and not a theory of prices or output, and made the essence of the theory the existence of a stable functional relation between the quantity of real balances demanded and a limited number of independent variables, a relation deduced from capital theory. This version of the quantity theory, Friedman asserted, had been handed down through the 'oral tradition' of the University of Chicago. In fact, as Don Patinkin has recently shown conclusively,[3] it is to be found neither in the written tradition of Chicago—which on the contrary stressed the quantity equation and the cumulative instability of velocity—nor in the oral tradition of Chicago as Patinkin himself experienced it: 'What Friedman has actually presented is an elegant exposition of the modern portfolio approach to the demand for money which ... can only be seen as a continuation of the Keynesian theory of liquidity

---

[2] Milton Friedman, 'The Quantity Theory of Money: A Restatement', in Milton Friedman (ed.), *Studies in the Quantity Theory of Money* (Chicago: The University of Chicago Press, 1956), reprinted in Milton Friedman, *The Optimum Quantity of Money* (Chicago: Aldine Publishing Company, 1969).

[3] Don Patinkin, 'The Chicago Tradition, the Quantity Theory, and Friedman', *Journal of Money, Credit and Banking*, Vol. I, No. 1 (February 1969), pp. 46–70.

preference' (p. 47). In recent writings, Friedman has ceased to refer to the Chicago oral tradition, and has admitted that his reformulation of the quantity theory was 'much influenced by the Keynesian liquidity analysis'.[4]

Redefinition of the quantity theory as hypothesizing a stable demand function for money not only gave it an empirical content subject to testing,[5] but facilitated the interpretation by researchers of good statistical results as evidence in favour of the quantity theory and against the rival 'income-expenditure' theory (the Chicago term for the prevalent version of Keynesian economics). The next stage was to devise a set of tests of the rival theories against one another; this was the subject of the Friedman–Meiselman study for the Commission on Money and Credit of 'The Relative Stability of Monetary Velocity and the Investment Multiplier in the United States, 1898–1958'.[6]

The tests in question rested on some fundamental—and debatable—methodological principles; and the failure of the critics to understand these principles, as well as to appreciate the depth of the intellectual effort put into the tests, made their criticisms and attempted refutations less powerful and persuasive than they might have been. The crucial principle is that the test of good theory is its ability to predict something large from something small, by means of a simple and stable theoretical relationship; hence the essence of the quantity theory was specified to be the velocity function relating income to money, and the essence of the income-expenditure theory was specified to be the multiplier relationship relating income

---

[4] M. Friedman, *The Optimum Quantity of Money*, p. 73. (My personal hypothesis is that, as a result of his studies of the Marshallian demand curve and his year as a visitor in Cambridge, Friedman became enamoured of the 'Cambridge oral tradition' as a concept permitting the attribution to an institution of a wisdom exceeding that displayed in its published work, and unconsciously stole a leaf from Cambridge's book for the benefit of his own institution.)

[5] For a review of the relevant empirical studies, see David Laidler, *The Demand for Money* (London: The International Textbook Co., 1969); and Laurence Harris, 'Regularities and Irregularities in Monetary Economics', Chapter 5, pp. 85–112 in C. R. Whittlesey and J. S. G. Wilson (eds.), *Essays in Money and Banking in Honour of R. S. Sayers* (Oxford: The Clarendon Press, 1968).

[6] 'Commission on Money and Credit', *Stabilization Policies* (New Jersey: Prentice-Hall, 1963), pp. 165–268.

to autonomous expenditure (for the purposes of the tests, these relationships were redefined in terms of consumption rather than income, to avoid pseudo-correlation). This principle is in sharp contrast to the more common view that the purpose of theory in this context is to lay out the full structure of a general equilibrium model in the detail necessary to produce an adequately good statistical 'fit'. A second principle is that behavioral relationships should be invariant to institutional and historical change; hence the Friedman–Meiselman emphasis on a long run of data. A third principle, whose practical application has given rise to legitimate criticism, is that since Keynesian theory does not specify exactly what is to be treated as 'autonomous' and what as 'induced' in an economy with governmental and foreign trade sectors, the classification must be effected by statistical tests of independence and interdependence.

According to the Friedman–Meiselman tests, the quantity theory consistently out-performed the Keynesian theory, with the exception of the 1930s sub-period. A conscientious, or nonchalant, Keynesian might well have interpreted these results as confirming the master's insight, insofar as the tests could be considered relevant at all. Instead, a number were provoked into attempting to disprove the findings; and, as mentioned, their efforts were generally vitiated in their impact by violation of one or another of the rules of the game as laid down by Friedman and Meiselman.[7]

As restated by Friedman, the quantity theory still laboured under the handicap of two potentially powerful criticisms. The first was the long-standing traditional criticism of the quantity

---

[7] Donald D. Hester, 'Keynes and the Quantity Theory: A comment on the Friedman–Meiselman CMC Paper', and M. Friedman and D. Meiselman, 'Reply to Donald Hester', *Review of Economics and Statistics*, Vol. 46, No. 4 (November 1964), pp. 364–8 and 369–76; Albert Ando and Franco Modigliani, 'Velocity and the Investment Multiplier', Michael de Prano and Thomas Mayer, 'Autonomous Expenditure and Money', Milton Friedman and David Meiselman 'Reply', and 'Rejoinders', *The American Economic Review*, Vol. LV, No. 4 (September 1965), pp. 693–728, 729–52, 753–85, 786–90, 791–2. For a commentary on the issues, see Stephanie K. Edge, 'The Relative Stability of Monetary Velocity and the Investment Multiplier', *Australian Economic Papers*, Vol. 6, No. 9 (December 1967), pp. 192–207.

theory, that the theory is irrelevant because the quantity of money supplied responds passively to the demand for it—the 'Banking School' position which remains strong in popular thinking on monetary policy. This criticism was quelled by the publication of the long-awaited, monumental volume by Friedman and Schwartz on the monetary history of the United States,[8] and the companion volume by Cagan on the supply of money in the United States.[9] These works demonstrated both the independent determination of the supply of money, and the significant influence of monetary changes on U.S. economic history. The second criticism stemmed from the strongly-held belief that the great depression of 1929 and after was the consequence of the collapse of the willingness to invest and proved conclusively the inability of monetary policy to remedy mass unemployment. The Friedman–Schwartz volume demonstrated as conclusively as possible the causal role played by rapid and substantial monetary contraction in the depression of the 1930s, and thus paved the way for a dismissal of the Keynesian analysis as based on a misinterpretation of the facts of experience.[10] There remains, however, acute controversy over the interpretation of the emergence of large holdings of excess reserves by the American banking system in the latter part of the 1930s.

While, as already mentioned, Friedman's restatement of the quantity theory of money should probably be interpreted as an appropriation of portfolio-balance analysis on Keynesian lines for use against those Keynesians who have neglected the monetary side of Keynes's theory in favour of the income-expenditure side, there is one important difference between the Friedman (quantity theory) approach and the Keynesian approach to that analysis which is of considerable importance

[8] Milton Friedman and Anna J. Schwartz, *A Monetary History of the United States, 1867–1960* (Princeton, N.J.: Princeton University Press for the National Bureau of Economic Research, 1963).

[9] Phillip C. Cagan, *Determinants and Effects of Changes in the Stock of Money, 1867–1960* (New York: Columbia University Press for the National Bureau of Economic Research, 1965).

[10] See Milton Friedman, 'The Monetary Theory and Policy of Henry Simons', *The Journal of Law and Economics*, Vol. 10 (October 1967), pp. 1–13; reprinted in M. Friedman, *The Optimum Quantity of Money*, chapter 4, pp. 81–93.

both theoretically and practically. This difference is that the restated quantity theory introduces explicitly, and emphasizes, expected changes in the price level as an element in the cost of holding money and other assets fixed as to both capital value and yield in money terms, whereas Keynesian portfolio-balance theory almost invariably starts from the assumption of an actual or expected stable price level (though this assumption may subsequently be modified).[11] The assumption in question has the great theoretical advantage of endowing money with an absolutely certain yield of zero per cent, and hence making it a fixed point of reference for portfolio choices; but this advantage is bought at the cost of giving money in the portfolio attributes of safety which in general it does not possess. Moreover, from the standpoint of application of monetary theory to the interpretation of actual events and policies, the assumption is likely to be consistently misleading, because it encourages practitioners of the approach to interpret changes in market interest rates on monetary assets as indicators of changes in monetary ease or tightness, without proper allowance for the effects on the relation between money and real rates of interest of changes in expected rates of inflation or deflation.

This difference is in an important sense the essence of the differentiation between the 'monetarist' and the alternative 'Keynesian' approach to problems of economic policy. The monetarist approach stresses the unreliability of money interest rate changes as economic indicators, owing to the influence on them of price expectations, and concentrates instead on changes in the money supply as a variable over which the monetary authority has control and whose meaning is theoretically clear. In addition, and more fundamentally, the monetarist approach rests on the assumption that velocity rather than the multiplier is the key relationship in the understanding of macro-economic developments in the economy. This was the point of the Friedman–Meiselman test already discussed. Subsequently, the focus of the controversy

[11] See for example James Tobin, 'Money and Economic Growth', *Econometrica*, Vol. 33, No. 4 (October 1965), pp. 671–84.

has shifted from autonomous expenditure *versus* money supply to fiscal policy *versus* monetary policy as the subject of empirical testing. In this connection, tests performed at the Federal Reserve Bank of St. Louis under the inspiration of Karl Brunner have been advanced in support of the monetarist as against the Keynesian approach; but these tests too have been the subject of considerable criticism.[12]

As mentioned above, Friedman's restatement of the quantity theory obtained the immediate tactical advantage of freeing it from the Keynesian criticism of assuming an automatic tendency towards full employment in the economy, by making it a theory of the demand for money without commitment to the analysis of prices and employment. This advantage, however, has proved something of an embarrassment subsequently, given the success of the quantity theory counter-attack on Keynesianism and the rise of the monetarist approach to economic policy, since it apparently leaves the quantity theorist with nothing to say about the relative impact of short-run variations in the money supply, and hence in aggregate demand, on money prices on the one hand and physical output on the other. (It may be noted that a similar problem arises for the Keynesian theory, under conditions of near full employment, which the Phillips curve analysis seeks to resolve but which it resolves rather unsatisfactorily—see below.) The obvious answer to this problem, in neo-quantity-terms, lies in an application of expectations theory to the determination of the division of an increase in monetary demand between changes in money wages and prices and changes in employment and output; but thus far no satisfactory theory along these lines has been produced.[13]

In concluding this section, a brief reference should be made

[12] Leonall C. Andersen and Jerry L. Jordan, 'Monetary and Fiscal Actions: A Test of Their Relative Importance in Economic Stabilization', *Federal Reserve Bank of St. Louis Review*, Vol. 50, No. 11 (November 1968), pp. 11–23; further discussion may be found in the April 1969 and August 1969 issues of the *Review*.

[13] The issue is discussed in detail in Chapter 2 ('The General Theoretical Framework') of Friedman and Schwartz's forthcoming *The Monetary Statistics of the U.S.*; this chapter is scheduled for separate publication in *The Journal of Political Economy*, under the title 'A Theoretical Framework for Monetary Analysis'.

to recent extensions of the monetarist approach to problems of balance-of-payments analysis and policy. As regards individual countries, prevailing theory emphasizes the balance of aggregate demand and aggregate supply capacity on the one hand, and the relation between domestic and foreign price levels on the other, as the key determinants of the balance of payments. A monetarist approach, on the other hand, as reflected in the new I.M.F.—inspired emphasis of British economic policy on 'Domestic Credit Expansion', emphasizes the relation between the growth of domestic demand for money and the growth of supply intended by the monetary authority as the key determinant of international reserve gains or losses. As regards the international monetary system as a whole, the monetarist approach emphasizes the relation between the growth of total desired reserves and the growth of overall reserve supplies as determining the need for some countries to have deficits, and the relation between national growth of desired money balances and national expansion of domestic credit as determining which countries will have the necessary deficits.[14]

III. THE REHABILITATION OF KEYNES

The quantity-theory counter-revolution discussed in the preceding section has been directed against the so-called 'income-expenditure' school, by which is meant those economists in the Keynesian tradition who have concentrated their analysis and policy prescriptions on the income-expenditure side of the Keynesian general equilibrium apparatus. (This focus has been the dominant impact of the Keynesian Revolution on governmental and other practical thinking on economic forecasting and policy-making.) There is, it should be remarked, nothing to prevent the absorption of the empirical evidence of a stable demand function for money into the corpus of the Keynesian general equilibrium model—a stable

[14] For an example of the monetary approach to balance-of-payments theory, see R. A. Mundell, 'Real Gold, Dollars and Paper Gold', *American Economic Review, Papers and Proceedings*, Vol. 59, No. 2 (May 1969), pp. 324–31.

demand function for money is in fact implicit in the liquidity-preference component of the standard Hicksian IS–LM diagram—other than the conditioned Keynesian reflex against the 'quantity theory' label and the conditioned Keynesian belief that 'money does not matter' (or, at least, 'does not matter much').

'Keynesian economics' came very rapidly to be epitomized by the IS–LM diagram of the textbooks, in terms of which Keynesian under-employment equilibrium depends either on the rigidity of money wages or on the special case of the 'liquidity trap' (a perfectly interest-elastic liquidity preference function) keeping the rate of interest above that consistent with full-employment equilibrium between saving and investment; and this special case was disposed of by the critics through the introduction of the 'Pigou effect' of a falling price level on the real value of money balances and hence on real wealth and consumption. As a result, Keynes has become 'the greatest economist of modern times' (an obituary remark indicating that his contribution was so indisputable as to require no explanation) and the *General Theory* has been shelved as a 'classic' (meaning an acknowledged great book that no one reads, for fear of discovering that the author was himself not clear about the message his disciples derived from his work). Put differently, Keynes has been assigned to the shadow regions, as one who had a tremendous influence on popular (i.e., undergraduate-level) economic theory and on the thinking of the makers of public policy, but whose theoretical contribution considered at the highest scientific level was shamefully amateurish, if not downright clownish, and is best passed over with a curt but fulsome general acknowledgement.

The position thus assigned to Keynes in contemporary economic folk lore has been challenged in a recently-published monumentally scholarly work of exegesis and interpretation of the *General Theory* by Axel Leijonhufvud.[15] Leijonhufvud dis-

---

[15] Axel Leijonhufvud, *On Keynesian Economics and the Economics of Keynes* (London: Oxford University Press, 1968); see also ibid., *Keynes and the Classics* (London: The Institute of Economic Affairs, Occasional Paper 30, 1969).

tinguishes sharply between 'Keynesian economics'—essentially the IS–LM analysis summarized above—and 'the economics of Keynes', as represented by the *General Theory* and the *Treatise on Money*, on which the *General Theory* built to a greater extent than Keynes's followers have appreciated; and he seeks to show that the latter economics is both quite different from, and far more subtle and profound than the former. In this endeavour he draws heavily on some very recent work unfamiliar to most monetary economists, notably R. W. Clower's attack on the extension of the Walrasian general equilibrium apparatus to a monetary economy by Patinkin and others (to be discussed subsequently), and the work of Alchian and others on the economic theory of market information and search; and the structure of his argument rests importantly on one proposition that readers who think they have understood Keynes may have difficulty in accepting as essentially to Keynes's thought, namely the assertion of a 'second psychological law of consumption', according to which a fall in the rate of interest increases consumption by increasing the 'perceived wealth' of the community (described as Keynes's 'windfall effect').

Leijonhufvud's re-interpretation of Keynes's economics, and differentiation of it from 'Keynesian economics', can be briefly but crudely summarized in the following propositions. First, what Keynes was challenging, and what he found most difficult to escape from, was the concentration of received economic theory on a dynamic adjustment process in which prices moved instantaneously to equilibrate markets. His dynamic adjustment process focused on quantity adjustments; and quantity adjustments by producers give rise to destabilizing feedback processes, epitomized in the multiplier analysis. If Walras's Law held in reality, any excess supply of one commodity (or labour or money) would imply an excess demand for others, and produce an adjustment process consistent with full employment. But in a monetary economy, Walras's Law refers to potential and not to 'effective' demands, because goods and labour are exchanged proximately for money and only ultimately for labour and goods; there is an 'income-constrained process' by which an excess supply of labour ('involuntary unemployment') appears not as an excess demand for goods signalling to producers the need to increase output and demand for labour, but as an equilibrium position in which the excess demands of the unemployed either proximately for money or ultimately for goods are not 'effective' and hence do not work to restore full employment equilibrium.

Second, the core of Keynes's analysis is 'liquidity preference', the unwillingness of asset holders to allow an equilibrating fall in the rate of interest, motivated by inelastic expectations about future rates of interest based on past experience. The cause of underemployment equilibrium is neither interest-inelasticity of investment demand—because Keynes aggregated bonds and real assets, and a fall in the rate of interest means a rise in the demand price for real capital— nor interest-inelasticity of saving—because while Keynes discounted the pure intertemporal substitution effect of interest-rate changes, he attached (or so Leijonhufvud asserts) considerable importance to the 'windfall effect' described above—but the prevention by liquidity preference of the equilibrating fall in interest rates necessary to counteract a decline in the inducement to invest. For economic policy it follows that, for an economy in the neighbourhood of full employment equilibrium, stabilization policy should rely primarily on monetary policy, to keep market rates of interest in line with the 'natural rate'. But for an economy in deep depression, interest rates may well be low enough for consistancy with full employment equilibrium, and the problem may instead be depression of entrepreneurial expectations requiring fiscal policy of a pump-priming nature to restore a full-employment level of activity. For a near-full-employment economy, however, Leijonhufvud reasons that the logic of the 'income-constrained process' implies that fiscal policy will not be a powerful tool, because, short of a general liquidity crisis, the public will be able to maintain its normal consumption levels by drawing on its financial assets.[16] Leijonhufvud,

[16] Leijonhufvud, *Keynes and the Classics*, pp. 40–5.

incidentally, argues that Keynes in fact recognized the real balance effect of a reduction in wages and prices, but attached predominant importance to the interest-rate effect precisely because he believed that both investment and saving were highly sensitive to the influence of lower interest rates in raising the values of real assets.

Leijonhufvud's rehabilitation of Keynes is virtually certain to be widely acclaimed by economists of most persuasions, not merely on the scientific account of its scholarly grasp and range, but also for the broadly political reason that it writes 'Keynesian economics' as it has been developed by mathematical economists, primarily in America, out of the 'true' Keynesian tradition, and that it does so by the application of concepts and approaches either developed by or congenial to contemporary quantity theorists—especially, the application of the 'human capital' approach to labour and wage-determination and of expectations theory to the determination of wages and interest rates. Hence it provides common ground of an intellectually appealing kind on which both 'old-line' Keynesian revolutionaries (such as Joan Robinson) and neo-quantity-theory counter-revolutionaries (such as Milton Friedman) can unite in condemnation of their common enemy, the dominant school of orthodox macro-economic theory based on the IS–LM model. From the point of view of scientific progress in the understanding of macro-economics and monetary theory, Leijonhufvud's work provides an extremely useful assemblage and conspectus of emerging concepts and approaches on which further theoretical work is required, and also clears the air of a number of prevailing myths about the true nature of the Keynesian Revolution. In a very broad sense, his work carries forward the process of transformation of monetary theory by the application of capital theory concepts and the analysis of dynamic processes discussed in my 1963 survey.

IV. FUNDAMENTAL ISSUES IN MONETARY THEORY

As recorded in my 1962 survey, one of the major contributions to the development of monetary theory consequent on

the Keynesian Revolution was Patinkin's integration of monetary and value theory within the framework of Hicksian
general equilibrium analysis.[17] That integration rested on the
conception of money as 'outside money'—an asset of the
community matched by no corresponding debt of the community to a monetary institution—and the mechanics of the
analysis depended heavily on the real balance (real wealth)
effect of a change in the money price level. Subsequently,
Gurley and Shaw developed an alternative 'inside money'
model, in which the mechanics of the analysis rested instead
on the substitution effect of a change in the ratio of privately-
held money to privately-held assets of other kinds. The
'neutrality of money' issue on which the Patinkin–Gurley
and Shaw controversy focused need not detain us here, since
the essential rules of the game are clear enough in retrospect.
What is more relevant from the contemporary perspective is
the distinction introduced by the debate between 'inside' and
'outside' money, and the ensuing proclivity of monetary
theorists to distinguish between models built on the two
alternative assumptions about the institutional nature of
money, one involving both a wealth and a substitution effect
and the other involving only a substitution effect.

The validity of the distinction between 'inside' and 'outside' money has been successfully challenged in a recent book
by Boris Pesek and Thomas Saving,[18] distinguished on the
one hand by its insight into relevant questions and on the
other by analytical confusions into which it stumbles. Put very
briefly, Pesek and Saving have shown that, for purposes of
model-building, the relevant distinction is not between
'inside' and 'outside' money, but between money bearing a
zero rate of interest (or more generally money bearing a rate
of interest fixed in nominal terms, of which zero interest is a
special case), and money bearing an interest rate competitive with rates of return on other available assets. In the
former case the services of money, being 'monopolized' in a

[17] H. G. Johnson, *Essays in Monetary Economics*, pp. 17–21.
[18] Boris P. Pesek and Thomas R. Saving, *Money, Wealth, and Economic Theory*
(New York: Macmillan, 1967).

sense, have a scarcity value for the community and hence a wealth value for the community as a whole; in the latter case the services of money become a free good and hence have no wealth value, though the fact that they are a free good maximizes community welfare. Unfortunately Pesek and Saving fail to understand the distinction between a zero alternative opportunity cost of money services to money holders, and a zero purchasing power of money itself in terms of goods and services: the former involves the payment of competitive interest on real balances, the latter will result from the absence of any restriction on the freedom of the banking system to expand its issue of (assumedly costless) paper credit.[19] Hence the initial insight, which has important implications for the efficiency of monetary arrangements and for various monetary-theoretic problems such as optimal monetary growth (see below), is vitiated by illogical analysis and absurd conclusions.

The main purpose of the Pesek and Saving analysis, however, was to establish an *a priori* theoretical definition of what should and what should not be counted in practice as part of the money stock for purposes of monetary analysis, and in particular to establish the medium-of-exchange function as decisive (i.e., to validate the conventional definition of money as currency in circulation plus deposits subject to cheque). A parallel attempt has been made by Newlyn,[20] and subsequently by Yeager,[21] to arrive at an *a priori* definition of money in terms of 'neutrality', by which is meant that the use of the monetary item can affect aggregate expenditure on goods and services without affecting the market for loans, rather than in terms of non-interest-bearingness. Friedman

[19] On these issues see Harry G. Johnson, 'Inside Money, Outside Money, Income, Wealth, and Welfare in Monetary Theory', *Journal of Money, Credit and Banking*, Vol. I, No. 1 (February 1969), pp. 30–45; also 'Comment', ibid., No. 3 (August 1969), pp. 535–7.

[20] W. T. Newlyn, 'Definitions and Classifications', *Theory of Money* (Oxford: The Clarendon Press, 1962), Chapter 1, pp. 1–11.

[21] Leland B. Yeager, 'Essential Properties of the Medium of Exchange', *Kyklos*, Vol. XXI (1968), Fasc. 1, pp. 45–69.

and Schwartz[22] have recently shown that both efforts rest on special sets of assumptions—about the banking system in the former case and about the nature of relevant monetary transactions in the latter—and that properly interpreted both lead back to the identification of money with the cash base provided by the central bank. The definition of money for purposes of empirical application of monetary theory therefore remains an empirical question.

Patinkin's integration of monetary and value theory rested on a particular way of incorporating money into the general equilibrium framework, namely through the attribution of 'utility' to the services provided by real money balances. As has long been recognized, money can be incorporated into a general equilibrium system in an alternative way, as part of the budget restraint that conditions the maximization of utility from the consumption of real goods and services. This alternative approach is represented by the inventory-theoretic analysis of transactions demand for cash developed by Baumol and Tobin. It has significant implications for the national income accounting aspects of monetary theory,[23] important in some theoretical contexts (see below on money in growth models). Though the concept of money as a producers' good (as well as a consumers' good), which incorporates the essence of the inventory approach, has long been a part of the neo-quantity-theory conceptual approach to monetary theory,[24] the lines of battle between contemporary quantity theorists and Keynesians have gradually been drawing up on the issue of the 'utility approach' versus the 'transactions-cost approach' to monetary theory.[25] This line of division is

[22] Milton Friedman and Anna J. Schwartz, 'The Definition of Money: Net Wealth and Neutrality as Criteria', Journal of Money, Credit and Banking, Vol. I, No. 1 (February 1969), pp. 1–14.

[23] See Don Patinkin, Money, Interest, and Prices: An Integration of Monetary and Value Theory, 2nd edn. (New York: Harper and Row, 1965), Chapter VII.

[24] Milton Friedman, 'The Quantity Theory of Money: A Restatement', and 'The Optimum Quantity of Money', chapters 2 and 1 in The Optimum Quantity of Money.

[25] See for example James Tobin, 'Notes on Optimal Monetary Growth', The Journal of Political Economy, Vol. 76, No. 4, Part II (July/August 1968), pp. 833–59.

unlikely to prove fruitful in the advancement of knowledge in the field. On the one hand, the utility approach is to be interpreted as an 'as if' or 'revealed preference' means of introducing the notion that the demand for money is subject to the ordinary analytics of choice among rival assets; it is thus unspecific enough to absorb any more specific theory based on the precise circumstances of choice. On the other hand, insofar as there is an empirically resolvable conflict between the two approaches, it must imply either a prediction as to which of alternative empirical variables will produce the better econometric results (e.g., measured current income as a proxy for transactions *versus* 'permanent' income as a proxy for wealth), or a prediction of the empirical magnitude of a statistical elasticity coefficient (e.g., the transactions approach predicts interest and scale elasticities of the demand for real balances significantly below unity); and the empirical studies of demand for money available so far provide little clear support for the transactions-cost approach.[26] In addition, the inventory approach is open to the general theoretical objection that it takes the patterns of payments and receipts as given, whereas these patterns can be construed instead as an optimizing response to the social usefulness of money as a medium of exchange and store of value.

The integration of monetary and value theory that has ensued on the Keynesian Revolution, the work of Lange, Patinkin, and many others, has built on the Hicksian formulation of general equilibrium theory. As applied by these writers, the approach treats money as parallel to any other good that is the object of utility-maximizing choice. In my 1962 survey, I called attention to certain difficulties that arise in treating money—as a capital good with a service flow—on a par with current flows of perishable consumption goods in a utility-maximization process subject to a budget constraint involving both current income and inherited money capital.[27] More recently, Robert Clower has attacked this type of for-

[26] See for example David W. Laidler, *The Demand for Money*, *passim*.
[27] Ibid., p. 20, text and footnote 1.

mulation of the economic theory of a monetary economy, as making money just like any other good and therefore omitting from the analysis the essence of the difference between a monetary and a barter economy, which is precisely that in a barter economy goods exchange for other goods without differentiation of the goods, whereas in a monetary economy money plays a unique role distinct from that of goods, because goods have to be exchanged for money and money for goods. In consequence of this difference, economic actors have to be considered as constrained in their choices, not by the potential worth of their initial endowments of goods and money, but as purchasers by their initial cash balances (the 'expenditure constraint') and as sellers by the value of desired intra-period receipts of money income (the 'income constraint').[28] The outcome is a drastic reformulation of the general equilibrium theory of a monetary economy, some of the implications of which have been discussed above in connection with Leijonhufvud's rehabilitation of Keynes. It may be remarked that in its own way Hicks's recent re-examination of the transactions demand for money,[29] intended indirectly to support the Radcliffe Report position, has attempted to cope with the same problem, though Hicks has been justly criticized for failing to realize that the transactions demand for money is conditional on and inseparable from its characteristic as a store of value, and that the pattern of use of money for transactions is, in anything longer than the very short run, the resultant of acts of choice and therefore not 'involuntary'.[30] Similar questions can be raised about Clower's sharp distinction between purchasers and sellers and between the budget constraints to which they are subject.

[28] R. W. Clower, 'A Reconsideration of the Microfoundations of Monetary Theory', *Western Economic Journal*, Vol. VI, No. 1 (December 1967), pp. 1–8.
[29] Sir John Hicks, *Critical Essays in Monetary Theory* (Oxford: The Clarendon Press, 1967), Chapter 1.
[30] N. J. Gibson, 'Foundations of Monetary Theory: A Review Article', *The Manchester School of Economic and Social Studies*, Vol. XXXVII, No. 1 (March 1969), pp. 59–75; and Laurence Harris, 'Professor Hicks and the Foundations of Monetary Economics', *Economica*, Vol. 36, No. 142 (May 1969), pp. 196–208.

V. FINANCIAL INTERMEDIARIES AND THE 'NEW VIEW' OF MONETARY THEORY AND POLICY[31]

As mentioned in the Introduction, the Radcliffe Committee's emphasis on 'the liquidity of the economy' as the key variable for monetary analysis and policy represented the high tide of Keynesian disbelief in the practical relevance and theoretical importance of money as formulated in traditional monetary theory, and as such met a harsh critical reception from the spokesmen of resurgent monetarism. In my 1962 survey I remarked that one important group working in the Keynesian liquidity preference tradition had yet to be heard from: those pursuing the Markowitz 'portfolio-balance' approach to monetary analysis under the leadership of James Tobin at Yale University.[32] The collective works of this group have recently been published in three Cowles Commission monographs,[33] which constitute something of a delayed Yale counter-blast against the Chicago School's famous *Studies in the Quantity Theory of Money*.[34] These monographs, and especially Monograph 21, *Financial Markets and Economic Activity*,[35] may be interpreted as providing belatedly the intellectual foundations of the Radcliffe Committee's position on monetary theory and policy—what has come to be described in the American literature, following a phrase in Tobin's important essay on

[31] For an extended treatment of the subject matter of this and the following section, see Allan H. Meltzer, 'Money, Intermediation, and Growth', *Journal of Economic Literature*, Vol. VII, no. 1 (March 1969), pp. 27–56.

[32] H. G. Johnson, *Essays in Monetary Economics*, p. 30.

[33] Donald D. Hester and James Tobin (eds.), *Risk Aversion and Portfolio Choice*, Cowles Foundation Monograph 19; *Studies of Portfolio Behavior*, Cowles Foundation Monograph 20; *Financial Markets and Economic Activity*, Cowles Foundation Monograph 21: (New York: John Wiley and Sons, 1967). For a textbook presentation of the Yale approach, see Basil J. Moore, *An Introduction to the Theory of Finance: Assetholder Behavior Under Uncertainty* (London: Collier-Macmillan, 1968).

[34] M. Friedman (ed.), *Studies in the Quantity Theory of Money* (Chicago: University of Chicago Press, 1956).

[35] Monographs 19 and 20 are concerned with the applications of the portfolio-balance approach to the micro-economics of investor and of institutional behaviour, and hence fall outside the field of interest of this paper.

'Commercial Banks as Creators of "Money"',[36] as the 'new view' of money.

In the general approach of the Yale School, 'monetary theory broadly conceived is simply the theory of portfolio management by economic units: households, businesses, financial institutions, and governments. It takes as its subject matter stocks of assets and debts (including money proper) and their values and yields; its accounting framework is the balance sheet. It can be distinguished from branches of economic theory which take the income statement as their accounting framework and flows of income, saving, expenditure, and production as their subject matter.' This distinction is admitted to be artificial, but useful because 'the processes which determine why one balance sheet or portfolio is chosen in preference to another are just beginning to be studied and understood'.[37] One of the major implications of this approach is the necessity 'to regard the structure of interest rates, asset yields, and credit availabilities rather than the quantity of money as the linkage between monetary and financial institutions on the one hand and the real economy on the other'[38]—hence the relevance to Radcliffe.

The crucial distinction for the Yale School, then (as for the Radcliffe Committee), is between the financial sector and the real sector (or between stock and flow analysis) rather than between the banking system and the rest of the economy (as various versions of the contemporary quantity theory would have it) or between liquid and illiquid assets (which Leijonhufvud interprets to be the essential distinction drawn in Keynes's own theory). Their central contribution is an elaborate analysis of the competition between banks and non-bank financial intermediaries—acknowledged to stem from the earlier work of Gurley and Shaw[39]—from which emerges

---

[36] Deane Carson (ed.), *Banking and Monetary Studies* (Homewood, Illinois: Richard D. Irwin, 1963), pp. 408–19; Chapter 1, pp. 1–11 in Monograph 21.

[37] Quotations from 'Foreword' (to the series), Monograph 21, pp. v–vi.

[38] J. Tobin, 'Commercial Banks as Creators of "Money"', Monograph 21, p. 3.

[39] In connection with the discussion of the work of Gurley and Shaw in my 1962 survey (*Essays in Monetary Economics*, pp. 36–7), it may be remarked that the

the conclusions that 'the quantity of money as conventionally defined is not an autonomous variable controlled by governmental authority but an endogenous or 'inside' quantity reflecting the economic behaviour of banks and other private economic units'; that 'commercial banks differ . . . from other financial units less basically in the nature of their liabilities than in the controls over reserves and interest rates to which they are legally subject';[40] and that controls over non-bank financial intermediaries may increase the effectiveness of monetary policy in influencing the real sector.[41]

As its authors acknowledge, this last proposition is not particularly impressive or useful, since there is no obvious economic gain discernible in enabling the monetary authority to operate on the economy by smaller rather than larger monetary policy operations. The main argument for controls on financial intermediaries is in fact the rather disreputable one of shielding the interest-cost of the public debt from the impact of general economic policy, and so forcing the burden of adjustment to changes in general economic policy onto the private sector; and the practice of such controls raises the question of the effects on the efficiency of the economic system as a whole. It is the first two propositions that raise fundamental issues in monetary theory.

Both of these propositions are rendered difficult to deal with by the strict separation of the monetary and the real sectors assumed by the basic approach, and particularly by the assumption of prices of real goods and services fixed autonomously in terms of money, on which the analysis rests, and which precludes consideration of many of the aspects of the problem that would naturally occur to a quantity theorist.

empirical volume that was to have validated their theoretical work on financial intermediation has not yet appeared.

[40] Quotations from 'Foreword', Monograph 21, p. viii; these two propositions are developed in Tobin, op. cit.

[41] James Tobin and William C. Brainard, 'Financial Intermediaries and The Effectiveness of Monetary Controls', *The American Economic Review*, Vol. LII, No. 2 (May 1963), pp. 383–400, reprinted as Chapter 3, pp. 55–93, of Monograph 21; see also William C. Brainard, 'Financial Intermediaries and a Theory of Monetary Control', *Yale Economic Essays*, Vol. 4, No. 1 (Fall 1964), pp. 431–82, reprinted as Chapter 4, pp. 94–141, of Monograph 21.

The second proposition on its positive side is essentially that controls on banks place the latter in the position of making a 'monopoly' profit on marginal business, so that an increase in reserves will automatically induce them to expand the scale of their operations, whereas other institutions are marginally in equilibrium so that their response to changes effected by monetary policy or otherwise will involve a general equilibrium adjustment in asset values and yields. This is certainly a possibility. But it fits easily into the general framework of analysis of the efficiency effects of controls mentioned in the previous paragraph (and also into the Pesek–Saving analysis of the wealth effect of an expansion of 'inside' money discussed in Section IV); and its does not suffice to equate banks in the really relevant respects with non-bank financial intermediaries, the negative side of the proposition. Further, what it implies is only that on impact an increase in bank reserves will have a wealth effect on the economy; when all the repercussions of an increase in the cash base are taken into account (including the repercussions on prices) there should be no change in the relative size of the banking sector, in spite of the marginal excess profitability of banking.

The crux of the matter is the first proposition, that the quantity of money as conventionally defined is an endogenous variable. This proposition derives its force by contrast with a straw man, the 'text-book' old view that the quantity of bank deposits is determined by a mechanical multiplier process operating on bank reserves, in which the preferences of the public play no part. Even in theoretical analyses of the determination of the money supply long pre-dating the Keynesian Revolution, the preferences of the public, in the form of the desired ratio of currency to deposits, played an essential part in the determination of the volume of bank deposits erectable on a given cash base provided by the monetary authority.[42] The contemporary theory of money supply, which has

---

[42] See for example J. E. Meade, 'The Amount of Money and the Banking System', *Economic Journal*, Vol. 44 (1934), pp. 77–83, reprinted as Chapter 5, pp. 54–62 in American Economic Association, *Readings in Monetary Theory* (Homewood, Illinois: Richard D. Irwin, 1951).

developed very rapidly since my 1962 survey, has incorporated all the relevant influences of the choices of the public among competing monetary and near-monetary liabilities and of the financial institutions (both bank and non-bank) among reserves and other assets in the theory of the relation of the conventionally-measured money supply to the cash base provided by the central bank.[43] The crucial issue is whether the interrelationships (deduced from rational maximizing behaviour on the part of all economic actors) in the financial sector are stable enough to permit changes in the monetary base (or, more proximately, changes in the conventionally-measured quantity of money) to be used to analyse and predict changes in the real sector (including both output and price level changes), or whether detailed understanding of the financial sector and the effects of monetary changes on the 'structure of interest rates, asset yields, and credit availabilities' is a necessary prerequisite of this endeavour. In this connection, the 'new view' is long on elegant analysis of theoretical possibilities, but remarkably short on testable or tested theoretical propositions about the way the economy works, and specifically how it responds to monetary impulses, when the interaction of the monetary and the real sectors is taken into account.

VI. MONEY IN GROWTH MODELS AND MONETARY EFFICIENCY

In concluding my 1962 survey, I remarked that 'almost nothing has yet been done to break monetary theory loose from the mould of short-run equilibrium analysis . . . and to integrate it with the rapidly developing literature on economic growth'.[44] The period since has seen a rapid development of theorizing in this direction, to the point where a whole issue of the new *Journal of Money, Credit and Banking* has been

---

[43] For discussion see Allan H. Meltzer, 'Money, Intermediation, and Growth', op. cit., and Karl Brunner, 'Yale and Money' (mimeographed).

[44] H. G. Johnson, *Essays in Monetary Economics*, p. 66.

devoted to publication of the proceedings of a conference held of this precise subject.[45] This literature has raised in a fresh form many of the fundamental problems of monetary theory, notably those of the role and functions of money in the economy; as yet, however, it has barely approached the question of quantification of the influence of money and monetary policy on economic growth. It does, however, overlap with an emerging body of analysis dealing with the requirements of efficiency in the organization of the monetary and financial sector, of considerably more relevance to practical economic policy.

The starting point of the latter body of analysis is the proposition that money, as an instrument of exchange and an item of wealth, is socially virtually costless to create (though not necessarily socially costless to use) and hence that the stock of it should be maintained at the satiety level for society. In the context of the problem of monetary efficiency, this proposition implies that taxes on the use of money, such as are involved in the imposition of required reserves in the form of non-interest-bearing currency and deposits at the central bank and other restrictions on commercial banking, as well as restrictions on the freedom of competition among financial intermediaries, restrict the use of money and money substitutes to sub-optimal levels and hence reduce the efficiency of the economy. (If restrictions are applied to commercial banks only, there may be an extra-optimal resort to non-bank intermediary services.[46]) This proposition refers to optimization of the holding of real balances; if banks are left free to compete without restriction in providing nominal money, the gains from using costless paper as a medium of exchange and store of value will be dissipated through inflation. The proposition also abstracts from the practical point that the payment of interest on currency holdings is

---

[45] *Journal of Money, Credit and Banking*, Vol. I, No. 2 (May 1969).

[46] Recognition of these points motivated, at least in part, the *Report on Bank Charges* of the National Board for Prices and Incomes, which argued against traditional methods of monetary control in the United Kingdom and in favour of more competition in banking.

infeasible.[47] If this last point is taken as being of predominat-
ing importance, monetary efficiency requires the establishment of a zero money rate of interest on other financial claims
to parallel the assumedly inherently institutionally necessary
zero money rate of return on currency. To analyse the condition for accomplishing this, the analysis must move from a
static to a dynamic framework, and appeal to the Fisherian
distinction between the real and the money rate of interest, as
separated by the expected rate of inflation or deflation. The
conclusion then emerges that monetary efficiency and the
optimization of social welfare require management of the
growth of the money supply so as to cause the price level to
fall at a rate equal to the real rate of return on capital.[48]

Recent work on the problem of introducing money and
monetary policy into models of economic growth, however,
has started from a quite different analytical framework,
namely the artificial conventions of 'real' growth models.
These models postulate a constant ratio of savings to income
(real output), and proceed to determine (i) the conditions
under which the model will converge on a steady-state growth
path, the rate of growth being determined by the exogenously-
given rates of growth of the population and of technological
efficiency, and (ii) that savings ratio which will maximize
consumption per head along the steady-state growth path.
The problem of introducing money into such a model

[47] On these issues see my 'Problems of Efficiency in Monetary Management',
The Journal of Political Economy, Vol. 76, No. 5 (September/October 1968),
pp. 971–90.

[48] For a recent analysis leading to this conclusion, couched in quantity theory
terms and rich in the application of relevant capital theory, see M. Friedman,
The Optimum Quantity of Money. Besides being misleadingly titled, since the analysis
refers to a growing and not a static economy, this essay is rather distracting in its
pursuit of theoretical side-issues suggested by past controversies and its intrusive
concern for a quantification of potential welfare gains which is provided only
fragmentarily and inconclusively; the need for the rather embarrassing 'final
schizophrenic note' could have been avoided by presenting the argument more
frankly as a logical exercise. It may be recalled that the pre-Keynesian quantity
theorists recognized the problem of the optimal trend of the price level, but
tended to interpret it as a problem of social justice in the division of the gains
from technical progress between the active and the retired population, because
they failed to understand the link between the money and the real rate of
interest provided by the expected rate of inflation.

presents itself as the problem of incorporating money and monetary growth into the concept of 'income' to which the assumed fixed savings ratio is to be applied, and deducing the influence of variation in the rate of monetary expansion (or proximately the trend rate of change of prices) on the proportion of physical output available for investment in additions to the physical capital stock. It has been recognized that this problem has a close affinity to Metzler's classic article on the neutrality of money in a short-run Keynesian system.[49] A subsidiary problem has been the interpretation of the welfare implications of the consumption-maximizing savings ratio, epitomized in 'the golden rule of accumulation'.[50] So long as the actual savings ratio is above the consumption-maximizing ratio, no problem results, because by reducing the savings ratio society can increase its consumption level at all points of time, present, and future, which must be accounted an indisputable welfare gain; but if the actual ratio falls short of the consumption-maximizing ratio, the welfare implications of a movement towards the latter are ambiguous, because the move involves a sacrifice of present consumption for the sake of future consumption, and the model contains no specification of the terms on which such an intertemporal substitution between present and future consumption can be analysed.

Subtleties of welfare analysis apart, the problem is how to introduce money and monetary growth into the 'real' model of accumulation described above. For this purpose, 'money' has been generally defined as an asset bearing interest at a rate fixed in monetary terms—usually taken as zero by convention—so that its real rate of return is determined by the (assumed to be fully expected) rate of inflation or deflation determined by monetary policy. The original analysis of the problem by Tobin[51] treated money as an asset pure and simple, contributing nothing to real income and welfare;

[49] L. A. Metzler, 'Wealth, Saving and the Rate of Interest', *The Journal of Political Economy*, Vol. 59, No. 2 (April 1951), pp. 93–116.

[50] E. S. Phelps, 'The Golden Rule of Accumulation: A Fable for Growthmen', *The American Economic Review*, Vol. 51, No. 4 (September 1961), pp. 638–48.

[51] James Tobin, 'Money and Economic Growth', *Econometrica*, Vol. 33, No. 4 (October 1965), pp. 671–84.

hence monetary growth entered the model purely as a capital gain additional to current production, which added to perceived income but subtracted from the saving available for real investment, and hence reduced real output per head. Thus inflation appeared to be 'a good thing', if the savings ratio fell short of the consumption-maximizing ratio and the intertemporal choice problem was ignored.

My own analysis of the problem[52] stressed the necessity of allowing money a function in a monetary economy, and therefore of attributing to the presence of money an increase in economic welfare and so in the base to which the assumed constant savings ratio was applied, thus introducing two conflicting terms in the effect of the presence of money and the exercise of monetary policy—the Tobin capital-gains effect of real monetary growth reducing the real savings ratio and the Johnson consumption-of-cash-balance-services effect raising it—with an ambiguous result for the specification of optimal monetary policy. My contribution violated some of the canons of sound national income accounting in attempting to capture intra-marginal consumers' surplus in the representation of the income-augmenting effect of cash-balance services. Levhari and Patinkin[53] have subsequently explored the implications of a more conventional valuation of the services of cash balances (at their marginal value) for income and consumption accounting, with the predictable consequence of making their conclusions depend on the elasticity or inelasticity of demand for cash-balance services.

Other writers, especially the late Miguel Sidrauski,[54] have departed from the confining influence of the Metzler assumption that saving is inversely related to wealth, and placed their analytical emphasis on time preference, that is,

[52] Harry G. Johnson, 'Money in a Neo-Classical One-Sector Growth Model', Chapter IV, pp. 143–78, in *Essays in Monetary Economics*. See also H. G. Johnson, 'Inside Money, Outside Money . . .', *Journal of Money, Credit and Banking*.

[53] D. Levhari and D. Patinkin, 'The Role of Money in a Simple Growth Model', *The American Economic Review*, Vol. 58, No. 4 (September 1968), pp. 713–53.

[54] Miguel Sidrauski, 'Inflation and Economic Growth', *The Journal of Political Economy*, Vol. 75, No. 6 (December 1967), pp. 796–810.

on some minimum acceptable rate of interest as the ultimate determinant of the accumulation of material capital per head. In such a theoretical framework, or in one in which the savings ratio is regarded as amenable to influence by fiscal policy, the analysis must return to regarding the optimization of the quantity of money at any point of time as a separable problem from that of maximizing consumption of real goods and services per head, in which case its solution (again assuming the infeasibility of paying explicit interest on currency) must be management of the money supply so as to produce a rate of price decline equal to the real rate of interest—as pointed out above in connection with the static problem of monetary efficiency. In this connection, it should be noted, the same conclusions follow whether money is regarded as 'productive', and/or yielding utility, or whether it is treated on transactions-demand theory lines as the cheapest means of reconciling different temporal patterns of receipts and payments—in which latter case money balance holdings affect economic welfare via the observable flow of goods and services rather than via the 'utility' yielded by money services.

VII. THE THEORY OF INFLATION AND OF ECONOMIC POLICY

The objectives of macro-economic policy for the government of a contemporary 'mixed-capitalist' country have come to be formulated as the maintenance of high employment without inflation, consistently with the achievement of an adequate rate of economic growth and the preservation of balance-of-payments equilibrium. In this context a major contribution to the theory of economic policy—in my judgement the only significant contribution to emerge from post-Keynesian theorizing—has been the 'Phillips curve'.[55] The Phillips

[55] A. W. Phillips, 'The Relation Between Unemployment and the Rate of Change of Money Wages in the United Kingdom, 1862–1957', *Economica*, Vol. 25, No. 100 (December 1958), pp. 283–99.

curve is an empirical relationship between the rate of unemployment (taken as an index of demand conditions in the labour market) and other variables on the one hand, and the rate of increase of money wages on the other. From it can be deduced, through the assumption that the trend of prices is determined by the trend of wages via the deduction of the rate of increase of productivity, a 'trade-off function' between the rate of inflation and the rate of unemployment; and the policy-makers can either be assumed to choose a point on this function according to their or the community's preferences, or advised to choose a point on it that maximizes social welfare (minimizes social loss).[56]

Much work has been done on the econometric refinement and testing of the Phillips curve. Recently there has been a recurrence of the initial doubts about the concept, namely about whether the assumed rounded-L shape of the curve does not represent an arbitrary and illegitimate linkage of the behaviour of the labour market under conditions of approximately full employment and of mass unemployment.[57] More fundamentally, the concept of the curve has been attacked as being logically inconsistent in ignoring the influence on the wage-fixing process of expectations about the rate of wage and price inflation, which expectations themselves are derived by a learning process from past experience of the rate of inflation chosen by the policy-makers. On the assumption that inflation eventually becomes fully expected and translated into wage and price-fixing behaviour, the trade-off for the policy-makers is not between a 'permanent' rate of unemployment and a 'permanent' rate of inflation, but between the gains from less unemployment now and the losses

[56] See, for example, G. L. Reuber, 'The Objectives of Canadian Monetary Policy, 1949–61: Empirical "Trade-offs" and the Reaction Function of the Authorities', *The Journal of Political Economy*, Vol. 72, No. 2 (April 1964), pp. 109–32.

[57] See for example Bernard Corry and David Laidler, 'The Phillips Relation: A Theoretical Explanation', *Economica*, Vol. XXXIV, No. 134 (May 1967), pp. 189–97; also A. G. Hines, 'Unemployment and the Rate of Change of Money Wages in the United Kingdom 1862–1963: A Reappraisal', *Review of Economics and Statistics*, Vol. L, No. 1 (February 1968), pp. 60–7.

from more inflation later.[58] The most elegant statement of this position is to be found in Milton Friedman's Presidential Address to the 1967 Meetings of the American Economic Association,[59] which argues forcefully that in the long run monetary policy cannot control real variables—notably the real rate of interest and the level of unemployment—but can only control nominal money variables—the behaviour of the price level and of the money rate of interest.

The Friedman argument from the quantity theory of money raises the empirical question of the effects of introducing the expected rate of inflation into the estimation of the Phillips curve. If the coefficient of the expected rate of inflation is unity, the Phillips curve vanishes, and only one rate of unemployment—'the natural rate of unemployment', in Friedman's terminology—is consistent with a constant rate of inflation (which may—and may as well—be zero) in the long run. While various recent writers have attempted to investigate this empirical question, the most thorough examination of it is to be found in a rather obscure source, a symposium held at New York University on 31 January 1968.[60] Empirical evidence produced by Robert M. Solow strongly supports, and evidence produced by Phillip Cagan (on a somewhat different methodological approach) does not effectively refute, a coefficient for expected inflation significantly below unity (in the neighbourhood of one half). The outcome is a 'sophisticated' Phillips curve, based on a dynamic version of 'money illusion', which still offers a trade-off to the policy-makers, though its slope is steeper than that implied by the 'naive' Phillips curve.

Recognition of the Phillips curve relationship has prompted

[58] E. S. Phelps, 'Phillips Curves, Expectations of Inflation and Optimal Unemployment Over Time', *Economica*, Vol. XXXIV, No. 135 (August 1967), pp. 254–81.

[59] Milton Friedman, 'The Role of Monetary Policy', *The American Economic Review*, Vol. 58, No. 1 (March 1968), pp. 1–17; reprinted as Chapter 5, pp. 95–110, in M. Friedman, *The Optimum Quantity of Money*.

[60] Stephen W. Rousseas (ed.), *Proceedings of a symposium on Inflation: Its Causes, Consequences and Control* (Wilton, Connecticut: The Calvin K. Kazanjian Economics Foundation, Inc., 1969). Tobin's comment (pp. 48–54) is especially apposite.

governments, particularly in the United Kingdom, to resort to 'incomes policy' as a way to alter the Phillips curve and permit the achievement of fuller employment consistently with the maintenance of price stability. The Phillips curve approach has suggested an obvious test of the effectiveness of incomes policy as practised on past occasions, namely its effectiveness in shifting the Phillips curve to the left in the standard diagram. Such tests have almost invariably shown incomes policy to have been of negligible effectiveness in terms of the relevant policy objective.[61] Very recently, R. G. Lipsey has argued that this formulation of the problem is wrong, and that the purpose of incomes policy is to change the slope of the Phillips curve (specifically, to flatten it) rather than to change the constant term that determines its location. The empirical work on the British data by Lipsey and Parkin[62] shows that incomes policy, interpreted this way, has in fact been successful; but that because the policy-makers have reduced the level of employment simultaneously with the introduction of incomes policy, they have in fact achieved the pessimum result of increasing both the level of unemployment and the rate of inflation.

VIII. CONCLUDING COMMENTS

Since the Radcliffe Committee was appointed, and even more since it reported, there has been a tremendous surge of interest in and research into the general field of monetary economics. This paper has attempted to survey the major topics of probable interest to participants in this decennary conference. One topic important for the development of British monetary economics has been deliberately omitted as not yet lending itself to generalization: the long and frequently confused debate over the theory of the money supply process

---

[61] See for example David C. Smith, 'Incomes Policy', Chapter III, pp. 104–44 in R. E. Caves and Associates, *Britain's Economic Prospects* (Washington: The Brookings Institution, and London: George Allen & Unwin, 1968).

[62] R. G. Lipsey and J. M. Parkin, 'Incomes Policy: A Reappraisal', presented to the 1969 (Essex) meeting of the Association of University Teachers of Economics.

in the United Kingdom and the role and objectives of the Bank of England, a debate sparked by the Radcliffe Report itself and strongly influenced by the development of theory and research in the United States. Of the topics surveyed, the one probably of greatest current interest is the rise of monetarism and particularly the implications of monetarism for the theory of the balance of payments. Perhaps the greatest disservice that Keynes rendered to the development of economics in this country was to develop the theory of macro-economics and money on the assumption of a closed economy. The extension of Keynesian theory to an open economy—which has been largely the work of economists in other countries, though the classic contribution of James Meade must be recognized[63]— has been built on the manifestly unsatisfactory assumption of money illusion on the part of the wage-earners, which assumption is necessary to permit exchange rate changes to be treated as producing changes in real price relationships. Much work remains to be done in developing a monetary economics appropriate to the analytical and policy problems of the British economy.

[63] J. E. Meade, *The Theory of International Economic Policy*, Vol. I: *The Balance of Payments*; Vol. II: *Trade and Welfare* (London: Oxford University Press, 1951 and 1955).

Discussion Papers

(a) DAVID LAIDLER
(*University of Manchester*)

PROFESSOR Johnson's paper covers a very wide scope, and no discussant can hope to deal with all the topics he has touched upon. I will confine myself to dealing with three points, the first two of which are fairly general.

First I would like to say something about the very important methodological questions Professor Johnson raises in his discussion of the Friedman–Meiselman debate. I believe that these questions have far wider relevance than Professor Johnson explicitly accords them. There are two views that one may take of the role of theory in economics. They may be termed 'Walrasian' and 'Marshallian'.[1] Briefly, and hence at considerable risk of producing caricatures, we may describe these two views as follows. A 'Walrasian' regards the role of theory as being to encompass as many empirical possibilities and complications as possible. A theory is better the 'more fruitful' it is: this phrase being interpreted to mean that more facts are compatible with a theory. To the 'Marshallian', 'more fruitful' is also better, but means something quite different. A more fruitful theory is one that rules out more logically conceivable possibilities than some rival and is not confronted with empirical evidence to the effect that some fact it has ruled out has occurred. The 'Marshallian' criterion is not straightforward though, because, for a given level of fruitfulness, a simpler theory is to be preferred to a more complex one, a simpler theory being one that needs less information and fewer assumptions to yield its predictions. It is almost

---

[1] I borrow these convenient labels from R. W. Clower. The reader should beware of reading too much historical significance into them.

invariably the case that greater simplicity is bought at the price of less fruitfulness so that the choice of theories becomes a subjective matter; it must be based upon the weight one wishes to give to the two competing criteria. The weights selected will usually depend upon the problem at hand; for some problems the 'Marshallian' will select one theory and for other problems he might select another.

The Friedman–Meiselman paper is by no means the only work to be founded on a 'Marshallian' methodology. Virtually all the theoretical and empirical work that has been done on the monetarist side of the debates of the last few years has been based on this approach. The counter-currents, particularly the 'New View' to be found at Yale, are more 'Walrasian' in character. Much of the debate, summarized so thoroughly by Professor Johnson, has been futile because of the failure of the two sides to realize that there is disagreement at this fundamental level—though I think a perusal of the lierature would show the monetarists to be the less guilty of this on the whole.

Let me illustrate these points. Friedman has treated the supply of money as exogenous and velocity as independent of interest rates for some problems, while admitting elsewhere that the money supply is partly endogenous and that velocity is affected by interest rates and rates of inflation.[2] Alan Meltzer has treated the U.S. as having a single, stable, aggregate demand for money function and simultaneously treated firms as being a case apart from the household sector.[3] To a 'Marshallian' all this is the result of different

[2] Cf., respectively, Friedman, M. and Meiselman, D. 'The Relative Stability of Monetary Velocity and the Investment Multiplier in the United States, 1898–1958', in *Commission on Money and Credit: Stabilization Policies* (Englewood Cliffs, N.J.: Prentice-Hall, 1963); Friedman, M. and Schwartz, A. J., *A Monetary History of the United States 1867–1960* (Princeton, N.J.: Princeton University Press, for the National Bureau of Economic Research, 1963); Friedman, M. 'The Quantity Theory of Money, A Restatement', in Friedman (ed.) *Studies in the Quantity Theory of Money* (Chicago: University of Chicago Press, 1956).

[3] Cf., respectively, Meltzer, A. H., 'The Demand for Money: the Evidence from the Time Series', *Journal of Political Economy*, 71 (June 1963), pp. 219–46, and, Meltzer, A. H., 'The Demand for Money: A Cross Section Study of Business Firms', *Quarterly Journal of Economics*, 77 (August 1963), pp. 405–22.

problems requiring different degrees of simplicity in the theories applied to solve them. The test contained in the papers cited, and in many others not mentioned here, are to be regarded as valuable experiments designed to find out just how fruitful are theories of differing degrees of simplicity. The same work, viewed through 'Walrasian' eyes, represents theoretical and empirical casualness of the worst sort, whose lack of consistency disqualifies it from serious consideration.

To the 'Walrasian', if the money supply is in fact partly endogenous, it must be treated as such; if velocity is interest elastic this must always be allowed for; if firms behave differently to households, they should be analysed separately, and aggregation should be explicitly and correctly carried out. All this, of course, makes it difficult to produce simple models that yield testable predictions, and the 'Walrasian's' rigorous theorizing is, to the 'Marshallian', vacuous and sterile. Though I hope we can avoid methodological discussion for its own sake, I believe that it will help us considerably if we bear these differences of method in mind when we discuss the contrast between the monetarist and the Yale view of monetary economics. It might also help to be similarly cautious in discussing the Clower attack on orthodox monetary theory. He too sometimes gives the impression of being more concerned with deriving results from descriptively accurate premises than with the empirical content of those results.

Now the contrasts I have drawn in the last few paragraphs are sharp ones, perhaps even over-sharp, and no doubt my own basically 'Marshallian' prejudices are quite apparent. Before leaving the matter, then, let me stress that 'Marshallian' flexibility can sometimes lead to trouble. As Professor Johnson has noted, the 'Yale view' lays great stress on the endogeneity of the money supply, but the point they have to make here is perhaps more serious than he allows. It is often the case that monetarists analyse the world in terms of a model in which the money supply is totally exogenous and in which, on the demand side, currency and bank deposits are both treated as money. For the supply of money to be totally exogenous, given modern monetary institutions, the public's currency-demand deposit ratio would have to be constant; these two assets would have to be perfect complements. However, to treat them both as 'money' requires them to be perfect substitutes. Flexibility and willingness to deal in approximations is one thing, but inconsistency within a given model is another; if this particular inconsistency has not led monetarists into serious trouble with their predictions, and I do not believe that it has on the whole, then they should be trying harder than they have in the past to understand and explain why it has not. This, I believe, is the real burden of the Yale school's insistence on the endogeneity of the money supply.

My second point has to do with recent advances in the fields of monetary efficiency and the interaction of the real and monetary sectors in economic growth models. I think Professor Johnson could have laid greater stress on the importance of introducing time preference into the analysis of these problems. As he notes, those models that contain a function that simply makes saving a function of income do not enable us to say anything about the effects of the introduction of money on economic welfare when this introduction leads to a sacrifice of current consumption for the sake of future consumption. This is because the model does not tell us how to weight consumption at different moments in time. It is strange indeed that a model which seeks to analyse the behaviour of income and consumption over time should leave the allocation of consumption over time to be determined by a 'rule of thumb' rather than by an explicit hypothesis about utility maximizing behaviour. Models such as that of Sidrauski, which use the rate of time preference as the determinant of saving behaviour, are not open to such criticism, and do permit such welfare judgements to be made. It seems to me to be an important consequence of the introduction of money into growth theory that this problem has been highlighted. Moreover, there is another characteristic of the Sidrauski type of model that is worth bringing out explicitly. Such models can be interpreted as attempts to integrate monetary theory and value theory, and more successful attempts than that of

Patinkin; they are open neither to the criticism that they treat stocks and flows as equivalents nor to the criticism that deal with choices made over an unduly short horizon.

Finally, the fact that such models enable us to make welfare statements and to integrate value and monetary theory does (as Alvin Marty has pointed out) give us a theoretical framework in which financial innovation may be studied.[4] For example, some innovations, such as the introduction of money itself, economize on real resources and increase economic welfare; others, such as perhaps the introduction of credit card systems, use real resources to economize on cash balances and lower economic welfare. Work along these lines has hardly begun, but may well turn out to be one of the most fruitful, not to say empirically relevant, offshoots of recent developments in monetary theory.

My third and final point is more specific than the other two. I would argue that Professor Johnson is too ready to accept at face value Solow's evidence that the current rate of inflation moves less than in proportion to the anticipated rate of inflation. Professor Johnson is right to conclude that, if such a result were true, it would imply that the authorities had open to them a long run choice between inflation and unemployment, something which the Phelps–Friedman view of the role of expectations in an inflationary process would deny. However, he fails to note that, in this Phelps–Friedman approach, the expected rate of inflation affects the current rate of inflation through its influence on the money wage bargain. To maintain equilibrium at a given *real* wage the money wage must rise at the expected rate of inflation, and, associated with equilibrium in the labour market, is a given 'natural' unemployment rate to which the economy will always tend to return in the long run.

Now the function fitted by Solow is

$$p_t = b_0 + b_1 ucl_t + b_2 f_t + b_3 cu_{-1} + b_4 p^e_{-1},$$

[4] Cf., Marty, A. L., 'Notes on Money and Economic Growth', *Journal of Money, Credit and Banking*, I (May 1969), pp. 253–65.

9—M.I.B.

where p is the percentage rate of change of the price level, ucl is the percentage rate of change of unit labour costs (the rate of change of money wages adjusted for changes in the average product of labour), f is the percentage rate of change of farm prices, cu_{-1} is an index of capacity utilization lagged one quarter, and p^e_{-1} is the 'expected rate of inflation' lagged one quarter, this variable being measured as a geometrically weighted average of present and past levels of the rate of change of prices, with a variety of weighting patterns being tried.[5] As the reader will note, even if it is true that p^e_{-1} does indeed represent the expected rate of inflation in this model, money wage rate changes are also independently included in it. Thus, at best, the coefficient of p^e_{-1} would pick up only those effects of anticipated inflation on the current rate of inflation that were not being transmitted through the labour market. It would be surprising indeed if the coefficient of p^e_{-1} came out equal to 1 in these circumstances; the fact that Solow finds it to be in the region of 0·4 is in no way inconsistent with the Phelps–Friedman proposition that there is no long run trade off between inflation and unemployment. Moreover, p^e_{-1}, calculated in the way that it is, may turn out to be a significant variable in Solow's equation, not because it represents the expected rate of inflation, but because the other variables in the expression act upon the rate of change of prices with a distributed lag.

None of this is to say that the Phelps–Friedman hypothesis about the role of anticipated inflation in the wage bargaining process is correct; all I have argued is that Solow's evidence does not refute it. It is worth noting, though, that if Solow and Tobin were correct, and there did exist the type of 'dynamic money illusion' to which Professor Johnson refers, then we should expect to observe real wages, and labour's share of national income, falling during inflationary periods. This 'wages lag' hypothesis goes back at least to David Hume,

---

[5] Cf., Solow, R. M., 'Recent Controversies on the Theory of Inflation: An Eclectic View', in Bousseas, S. (ed.), *Symposium on Inflation: Its Causes, Consequences and Control* (New York, 1968), pp. 6–17. The regression results are reported on p. 15. Note that Solow also used a dummy variable for post-1966 observations.

but history, particularly recent history, does not seem to have produced much evidence in its favour. Thus I am less willing than Professor Johnson to abandon the view that the inflation-unemployment trade-off is, at best, a short run phenomenon.

Discussion Papers

(b) R. T. ARMSTRONG
(H. M. Treasury)[1]

I SHALL discuss Professor Johnson's paper as a practitioner in monetary policy. I should emphasize that what I shall say represents the view of a practitioner, not necessarily of the practitioners.

Richard Sayers has referred to the differences and shades of views he encountered in his dealings with representatives of what Radcliffe called 'the authorities'. There are five or six of us here from the Treasury and about the same number from the Bank of England. All of us contribute, with others, in one way or another to the discussion and formulation of monetary policy. For this purpose each of us must have worked out for himself, more or less explicitly, some kind of position on the way in which monetary measures work. I dare say that no two of us have the same view, and that between us we cover a pretty wide spectrum. None the less, advice has to be given, and decisions have to be taken, not necessarily at the time we would choose. Sometimes all of us might give broadly the same advice, sometimes there may be shades of differences in the advice from different advisers. In the end the Chancellor of the Exchequer takes the decisions, and his decision may correspond exactly with none of the advice given to him. It follows that you should not deduce the position of any one of us from your scrutiny of the actions or the pronouncements of the authorities.

It follows too that what I have to say is very much one man's view. I think that most of my colleagues here would

---

[1] Mr. Armstrong was secretary to the Radcliffe Committee, 1957–9.

endorse what I say, and probably put it very much better; but I must accept responsibility for it. I must also remind you that I comment not only as a practitioner but as someone trained in a different academic discipline and following a different career structure from almost all of you. If you feel that I am commenting on an altogether lower level of sophistication than most of the discussion you have heard, that is deliberate: not only am I doing what comes naturally, but it will give you some idea of the problems of communication which worry me and which, I think, should worry you.

Economists have been accused of over-hasty reading and fastening on catch phrases. How much more must this be so for the non-economist coming to discussion on this subject. Perhaps I can give you a foreshortened perspective of the development of monetary theory as it might look to someone from outside who followed it from journalistic comment.

We start from the famous quotation from the Radcliffe Report: 'Monetary measures can help, but that is all'. The Radcliffe Committee took a 'weak' view of the efficacy of monetary policy. 'Liquidity' was a vague concept, but we could apprehend what the Committee was driving at, and in any case because monetary policy was 'weak' the vagueness did not matter too much. Changes in money supply were of more interest to the academic than to the policy-maker.

Then suddenly one day we were made aware of Friedman, rather on the lines of Professor Johnson's description of Keynes, as the greatest monetarist of modern times in that his contribution was so indisputable as to require no explanation. The catch phrase is 'money matters after all'. We probably do not distinguish between Friedman and the more extreme Friedmanians—I hasten to say that I am thinking more of transatlantic than of British adherents to the Friedman school in this. There is a hazy awareness that it is not quite simple, that there are considerable lags between changes in money and their effects. But now there is some disenchantment with fiscal policy, because it now seems weaker than it did or because there has already been a pretty hefty dose of it. So there is a predisposition to look again at monetary policy as

a short-run regulator and at money supply as a more important indicator for the policy-maker.

I should not like you to think that this is a typical policy-
maker's view: developments in monetary theory achieve
different depths of penetration at different points in the soft
under-belly of the authorities. A number of my colleagues are
highly versed in these developments, and there is some
important econometric work being done within the official
machine.

I came here hoping that the discussion would make me
more informed about how monetary theory has developed and
is developing, and about the implications which these developments have for the policy-maker who has to read the book of
instructions while he is trying to run the machine. I do know
much more about how the theory is developing, thanks to
Professor Johnson's admirable paper. Professor Laidler
referred to its density: that is especially difficult for the non-
academic, but one is amply rewarded by the richness of its
content. I think that I can detect chinks of light for the
policy-maker in the discussion we have had, for instance in
some of the econometric developments which were described
by Prof. Walters. But on what I conceive to be the main
issue, summed up as 'liquidity versus money', the message I
get is that the debate is still on: the Yale people have still to
produce the empirical evidence against which to test the
'elegant theoretical possibilities' in the 'new view', but the
possibilities have at least not been shown to be false.

May I tell you the lacks which I, as a non-economist policy-
maker who has been around in this business for quite a time
now, have come to feel? You know that we have developed
an apparatus of financial forecasting which takes as its
starting point the current price versions of the national income
forecasts and derives from them sectoral flow of funds forecasts. Because a financing forecast cannot (in the present
state of the game) be done until after the constant and current
price national income forecasts have been completed, the
scope for 'feedback' from the financing forecast to the national income forecast is limited. This practical difficulty

could perhaps in due course be overcome. More serious, to my mind, is the difficulty of providing a theoretical justification for inviting the national income forecasters to modify their forecasts on account of implausibilities in the financing forecasts. Their work is based on a coherent framework of propositions and relationships, tested by a series of empirical studies; and of course this framework has been institutionalized into the official processes of policy-making. We do not have and badly need a correspondingly coherent and tested framework of propositions and relationships on the monetary side, as a basis for synthesis between national income and balance-of-payments analysis and forecasting on the one hand and monetary analysis and forecasting on the other. I was encouraged by a sentence in Professor Johnson's paper to think that this might be a possibility, one day; but the drift of the discussion leads me to think that that day may be some way off.

Incidentally I do not think that this is a job for another Radcliffe Committee. I sympathize with those who wish that there had been a chapter or appendix in the Radcliffe Report about the monetary theory on which its conclusions were based. But, if you want a major contribution to the development of monetary theory, you do not set up that sort of committee. Committees of that kind are set up to be a different kind of job. You may or may not think the job worth doing; I do think that it was, and probably would be again, though it is arguable, now that there is so much more statistical information, that monetary policy and the working of the monetary system are less appropriate subjects for the work of such a committee. But I think that criticism of the Radcliffe Committee for not doing a job on monetary theory is in some sense misconceived.

The lacks which I as a policy-maker feel, must be supplied, I think, by the work of the monetary economists. I have been impressed by the amount of econometric work that has been going on, and I sympathize very much with the proposition that an 'elegant analysis of theoretical possibilities' needs to be tested and verified by empirical studies. Much work, I am sure, remains to be done, as Professor Johnson has said, in developing 'a monetary economics appropriate to the analytic and policy problems of the British economy'; and some arbitration or reconciliation between the 'monetarists' and the 'new view' men may perhaps be achieved in the process. I also understand your desire to look for propositions and relationships that are valid independently of institutional factors, though the policy-maker has to work within the limitations set by the existence of a complex structure of financial institutions.

But I come back again to the problem of communications. Whatever the academic stature of the work that is done, unless it can be related to the work of the policy-maker it is not going to help people like me with our day to day problems. This is partly a matter of the direction given to the work, and partly a matter of communications: we need to find some means of distilling the policy implications from the results of work expressed in the complex and symbolized forms which much of your discussion uses. I have found this conference very stimulating, and I hope that it will lead to others of the same kind. But I do not think that conferences like this can solve alone the problem of communications; fascinating though they are, it is not enough for us just to overhear your discussions. Unless and until the work is done and the significance of the results can be injected into policy-making discussion, developments in monetary theory will continue to be less clearly and directly reflected than they should be in the formulation of monetary policy.

SUMMARY OF THE GENERAL DISCUSSION

THE discussion began with a claim that the survey had neglected the important theoretical and empirical research into the term structure of interest rates which had been carried out in the 1960s. It was explained that this subject had been omitted deliberately because it did not seem to have been a relevant feature in explaining the evolution of monetary policy.

A major debate arose over the claim in the survey that Friedman and Schwartz had made a major contribution in showing the extent of the responsibility of the monetary authorities for the Great Depression. It was suggested that the importance of monetary influences had been recognized before Friedman and Schwartz, but the discussion concluded that their *Monetary History of the United States* had been important in showing how the existence of the Federal Reserve had played a positive rather than a neutral role in preventing the economic system from stabilizing itself, and had helped push the economy into even deeper depression in 1931.

Several discussants cast doubts on the value of theoretical work on the question of the optimum money stock for economic growth. The small contribution to welfare which might result from following the conclusions reached by the theorists could not justify the institutional upheaval which would result even though, it was admitted, most changes suggested by economists were like this. In this connection it was also noted that there was precedent for such policies as paying interest on currency, which had been discussed by writers in this field.

Theories of the role of money in a growing economy were also challenged because they failed to make adequate provision for expectations and required the existence of steady-state conditions. Against this criticism it was claimed that expectations only provided difficulties for the theory when they were based on irrational behaviour, and there was no need to assume that such behaviour was common. In particular, the rate of interest on debt would adjust to reflect expectations about changes in the price level and provide another mechanism towards stability.

The survey's conclusion that the Phillips curve analysis of the price-employment trade-off had been the only major extension of the *General Theory* was criticized by discussants who suggested that a similar price-wage mechanism could be found in Keynes's *Treatise on Money*. Similarly, Keynes could be defended from the charge that he had only considered his system in a closed economy, by reference to the *Treatise* which contained references to the impact of external factors.

In reply, it was re-emphasized that Keynes had been writing a political document to have an influence on the particular circumstances of the 1930s. In this context it was not surprising that the analysis stopped at a closed economy and concentrated on output determination rather than the dynamics of the wage-price process. There was still a great need for more work in these areas, and this was amply illustrated in the ensuing discussion about the shape of the Phillips curve, when several speakers claimed that the evidence from the conference papers mentioned in the survey could be interpreted to suggest a vertical Phillips curve.

Finally, the discussion considered the exogeneity of the supply of money in the economy. It was noted that the currency-deposits ratio in the United Kingdom has been quite variable, but that the demand for currency has been a very stable proportion of transactions or income. This meant that the authorities, because they control the currency supply, could use this relationship as a policy instrument. However, at present they choose to disregard this weapon.

IV

THE U.K. FINANCIAL SECTOR
SINCE RADCLIFFE

1. The Evolution of Monetary and Financial Institutions
R. J. CLARK

2. Non-Clearing Banks
T. RYBCZYNSKI

3. Monetary Policy and the Clearing Banks
J. E. MAYCOCK

Discussion Papers
(*a*) P. DAVIDSON
(*b*) A. B. CRAMP
(*c*) G. CLAYTON

IV

THE U.K. FINANCIAL SECTOR
SINCE RADCLIFFE

---

1. *The Evolution of Monetary and Financial Institutions*

R. J. CLARK

(*Economic Adviser and Head of International Planning,*
National Westminster Bank Ltd.)

PREFACE

THREE points of clarification must be made at the commencement of this paper. First, it has been prepared within one of the clearing banks and almost inevitably has been written from a clearing bank point of view. This may not be a serious disadvantage because, although the relative importance of clearing banks has declined over the past decade, they remain the most prominent feature of the British monetary system.

Secondly, no attempt has been made to provide a history of institutional developments over the past decade. Rather, the purpose has been to select some of the changes that have taken place and comment on the reasons for them. Thus a comparison is made between the situation in 1958–9 and that which now exists.

Thirdly, this paper is also selective in another sense. It does not cover the whole gamut of institutions as did the Radcliffe Report, but only those engaged more or less directly in banking. Thus the insurance companies, superannuation and pension funds, investment trusts, and unit trusts are not dealt with at all; and others covered by Radcliffe are referred to only indirectly.

The following are some of the matters that seem most deserving of attention:

(a) the diversification of financial services;
(b) the decrease in specialization between different groups of financial institutions;
(c) the proliferation of overseas banks, of subsidiaries of the clearing banks and of joint ventures;
(d) the growth of the so-called parallel markets;
(e) the changed position of the clearing banks;
(f) the mergers.

This is a purely personal selection and others might well have chosen differently. Moreover, although these form the main section headings, there is unavoidably a considerable amount of overlapping. The sections dealing with changes in the clearing banks have deliberately been left to the last. The remainder, except that relating to the parallel markets, have been dealt with rather summarily and, indeed, have been included by way of reminder and for the sake of completeness.

I. INTRODUCTION

Since 1959, when the Radcliffe Report was published, the pace of change in financial institutions has quickened perceptibily. This is not to say that the Report was the signal for the start of wholesale innovation. Many recent developments were already in train before 1959 and others have arisen out of circumstances that were scarcely envisaged ten years ago and have little to do with the thinking of the Radcliffe Committee. Nevertheless, the exercises involved in preparing evidence to put before the Committee and the Report itself, like the more recent Prices and Incomes Board and Monopolies Commission reports, caused banks and other financial institutions to re-examine themselves and this re-examination hastened the processes of change. Furthermore, all three reports stimulated public discussion and helped to stimulate demand for new financial services.

The whole environment has been conducive to change. Technological developments, rising standards of living, the re-structuring of industry that has been going on, the reduced role of sterling and the controls that have resulted from the persistent weakness in the balance of payments, and even the credit squeezes that have been characteristic of this period, have all exerted pressures making for change in the financial institutions. Rising costs and staff shortages, common to all forms of enterprise, and increasing competition have also contributed.

From all these factors one may be singled out as being significantly different in the ten years after Radcliffe from what it had been in the ten preceding years. Throughout the post-war period economic controls of many kinds have been in force; but, whereas in the 'fifties both monetary and non-monetary restrictions were being eased, in the 'sixties monetary restrictions have been intensified. Thus at the present time, while most categories of control have been relaxed or abolished, monetary controls are tighter than they have ever been. This has contributed to the appearance of new financial institutions, the switching of business from one group to another, and to the progress of the parallel markets. These trends are illustrated by Table IV.I.

II. DIVERSIFICATION OF FINANCIAL SERVICES

Partly in response to public demand, partly due to demands that they themselves have created, all financial institutions have widened the range of services they offer. These include money transmission services, additional forms of credit, investment, and advisory services. None is, strictly speaking, new; they are all variants or extensions of well-established practices.

The developing services are of various kinds. One group relates in one way or another to the payments mechanism and ranges all the way from facilities for obtaining cash—cash dispensers—to substitutes for cash, such as credit cards. It includes improved machinery for the transmission of money associated with the use of computers as well as the giro systems of the banks and G.P.O.

TABLE IV.1

All Financial Institutions—Market Share of Deposits

	1958		1968	
	£ million	Per cent	£ million	Per cent
London Clearing Banks	7,199	38·8	10,736	24·2
Scottish Banks	747	4·0	1,137	2·6
Northern Ireland Banks	137	0·7	267	0·6
Accepting Houses	212	1·1	1,877	4·2
British Overseas Banks	573	3·1	2,744	6·2
Foreign Banks	171	0·9	959	2·2
American Banks	129	0·7	5,301	11·9
Other Overseas Banks			2,710	6·1
Trustee Savings Banks	1,160	6·2	2,365	5·3
Post Office Savings Banks	1,646	8·9	1,779	4·0
Other National Savings	3,643	19·6	4,399	9·8
Post Office Giro			10	—
Local Authorities	376	2·0	1,763	4·0
Hire Purchase Companies	128	0·7	614	1·4
Building Societies	2,479	13·3	7,757	17·5
Total Deposits	18,600	100·0	44,418	100·0

Of greater interest are newer forms of lending. Apart from convenience, one of the attractions of the credit card, particularly the 'community' type card, is the borrowing facility that it offers to users. So far neither the individual borrowings, nor the totals, are of great importance; but, of course, under squeeze conditions it has not been open to sponsors of credit cards to make much of this aspect. If we ever get free of restrictions on consumer credit, the amounts borrowed by way of credit cards may well increase very greatly.

The period since Radcliffe has seen, not only a great expansion of the use of hire purchase in connection with consumer goods, but also the extension of this type of facility to the purchase of industrial and agricultural machinery. Factoring has also become an established method of providing companies with working capital. In taking over their book debts for cash, a finance house not only provides clients with funds, but also relieves them of risk and a good deal of their accountancy work.

Equipment leasing, which is rapidly gaining ground, is another way of providing companies short of working capital with the means of acquiring capital goods necessary for the expansion of their business. Though often especially attractive to small, under-capitalized concerns, its appeal is by no means limited to them. The latest development is the provision by a consortium of financial institutions of leasing facilities to airlines for the purchase of aircraft, and before long the principle may be extended to ships.

One item that has grown substantially, particularly in the last two years, in the books of the banks is their cut-price lending for exports and, to a much smaller extent, for shipbuilding. This long-term lending at $5\frac{1}{2}$ per cent is guaranteed by E.C.G.D., and so is risk free as far as the banks are concerned; it is also outside the 98 per cent ceiling. But it involves a great deal of work and is, at current rates of interest, unprofitable to the lenders. Nor is it right in principle that exports should be subsidized by private institutions. If such a subsidy is deemed desirable, it should be made out of public funds.

The bulk of this type of export finance is, of course, provided by the clearing banks who, in any case, lend altogether too cheaply and on terms that often give them inadequate control of their own balance sheets. There has been a considerable widening of the spread of rates on loans and overdrafts since the days of Radcliffe, when it was normally only from $\frac{1}{2}$ to $1\frac{1}{2}$ per cent above Bank rate. Today it may go from

$\frac{1}{2}$ to 3 per cent above Bank rate, but very rarely higher than that. This is still not a realistic spread in the sense that it is not wide enough to cover the differences in risks and administrative costs of different loans. Moreover, the 'blue chip' rate at 1 per cent over Bank rate is an incentive to borrow from the banks in order to lend elsewhere. This probably does not happen to any significant extent but it is certainly true that a corporate treasurer who can borrow at this rate would see no particular reason for disturbing any liquid assets he may hold elsewhere in order to repay a bank loan.

The banks would be in a better position to control their lending in the short term if bank borrowing were by way of fixed loan rather than by way of fluctuating overdraft as the major proportion is at present. Small facilities tend to be fully used but many big borrowers have limits far in excess of their normal day-to-day needs. Such limits may be used on only a few days in the year. Indeed, the overall ratio of utilization to total limits is rarely much in excess of 60 per cent. Big limits may, however, be used quite without warning and if the bank's own liquidity is tight it may in effect be compelled itself to borrow at market rate, or sell securities at a loss, in order to lend at blue chip rate.

It is in the direction of loans rather than overdrafts that bank lending should be moving. If, in addition, a higher proportion of such loans were negotiated for repayment on an amortization basis, the banks would be able to extend very considerably their term lending. For good measure, many of us would like to see the negotiation of compensating balances a regular feature of bank lending. One welcome feature of tight and dear monetary conditions is that they are pushing us in this general direction.

The other big area of diversification is in what may be called 'related banking services'. Most of these in one form or another have been provided by the merchant banks for a long time; but they, on the whole, have been rather selective in accepting clients, whether companies or private persons, and it is the clearing banks that have begun to enter the mass market for such services as investment portfolio management.

The newcomers to the list of related services are chiefly those that can be handled by computer, e.g. the handling of repayments of house loans for building societies or of payrolls for companies with large numbers of employees.

III. DECLINE OF SPECIALIZATION

There has been an increase in the numbers of specialists in virtually all types of financial institutions. At the same time there has been a breakdown of the specialization between institutions that was once a particularly marked feature of the City. The process began long ago. For instance it is now sixty years since the clearing banks trespassed in to the territory of the accepting houses by departing from their exclusively domestic banking role and opening specialist branches for the handling of foreign business.

In the years since Radcliffe, and particularly since the early 'sixties, the movement has accelerated. It is, indeed, one aspect of diversification, which may well go further in the direction of 'one stop', 'department store' banking. Not that the days of the smaller specialist institutions are over, but they will probably have to survive by innovating, taking advantage of the fact that big banks, like all big concerns, are inevitably somewhat cumbersome.

IV. NEW FINANCIAL INSTITUTIONS

In the period under discussion, the City, and not only the City, has seen the appearance of a number of entirely new entities, the establishment of branches of old institutions and old institutions in new guises. Some of these are subsidiaries of big banks; some have been set up by groups of banks, often with both British and foreign participation; and some are branches of overseas banks. The motives behind the establishment of these new entities are mixed, the most important being the creation or exploitation of new markets for financial services, at home and abroad, the circumvention of restrictions and the defence of existing market positions.

The proliferation of these new institutions is a tribute to the continuing importance of the City as a financial centre, which is in part due, in spite of severe exchange control, to the free-trading atmosphere that still persists. As Professor Ira O. Scott wrote recently: 'The Empire may have disintegrated and the U.K. may now be a third-rate military power, but the City of London has staged a come-back which would be the envy of any child movie star reaching maturity.' The other side of the coin from the point of view of the older banks in London is that competition, particularly for deposits, has been notably intensified and this has not been without its effect on rates of interest.

The subsidiaries of the banks are engaged in three main lines of activity, hire purchase finance, e.g. Forward Trust; merchant banking, e.g. County Bank; and the taking and placing of funds in the parallel markets, e.g. Westminster Foreign Bank. Though the last two functions are mentioned separately, they clearly overlap in practice; the first customarily stands on its own.

In its report on bank charges the Prices and Incomes Board commented adversely on the establishment of subsidiaries by the clearing banks and recommended that the work done by the former should be undertaken by departments of the parent banks. There seems no very good reason for adopting this recommendation and several excellent reasons for doing otherwise.

For example, a subsidiary can bid for large deposits in the open market, paying competitive rates, without disturbing the rate paid by the parent on the great bulk of its deposits, most of which are individually small. The subsidiary operates in markets where the turnover is high, the administrative costs low and the turn on individual transactions very small indeed. Because of the far greater administrative costs involved in operating small accounts and the cash and liquidity ratios—particularly the former—that it is required to maintain, it would be quite uneconomic for the parent bank to compete for general deposits at rates applicable to very large amounts.

From the point of view of the clearing bank account-holder, as has often been stressed, there is little difference in liquidity between a current account and a deposit balance; significantly higher rates on deposits, unless accompanied by much more rigid practices than at present observed regarding transfers between accounts in the same name, would probably lead to a big movement from current to deposit account, with important consequences for the banks' net earnings. The high general level of interest rates in the past few years has produced some movement in this direction.

A subsidiary operating in a wholesale rather than a retail market is also far better placed than the parent to match deposits and placings. Since funds of this kind are highly volatile, this is a matter of great importance. It is highly doubtful whether a clearing bank itself could afford, as the specialist subsidiaries do, to make medium- and even long-term loans out of funds of this kind.

There is also the question of expertise of kinds different from those normally required in clearing banks. Hire purchase finance, for example, demands skills not normally required for the more traditional types of bank lending. The same applies even more obviously in connection with merchant banking services. Of course, expertise can be bought; but, just as there is nothing to be gained by unnecessarily upsetting an existing pattern of interest rates, so it is more convenient not to disturb salary structures. It is, moreover, easier to give autonomy to a subsidiary company than to a department.

In addition, it has been felt that activities for which subsidiaries have been set up do not fit in very well with the balance sheet of a clearing bank. It can, for instance, be argued that equity participations are inappropriate to banks, the bulk of whose resources are the property of depositors and not of their shareholders. Even though the subsidiaries are wholly-owned this argument is not entirely without substance.

The new entities, such as Midland & International Banks Ltd. and International Commercial Bank, have a different purpose. These, and others like them, are jointly owned by banks of different types based in different countries. They engage in international, medium-term lending which the individual participants might find difficult; and they secure for each a geographical and customer coverage that would be costly, perhaps impossible, for any one of them to obtain acting alone. These institutions have grown rapidly in size and have prospered. They operate in quite a different manner from commercial banks in that, instead of taking deposits which they then proceed to lend, they actively seek out lending opportunities and then find the necessary funds.

Their main weakness is their heavy dependence on the Euro-dollar market as a source of funds for their international lending. Though they no doubt have substantial stand-by borrowing facilities with all the banks that own them, they have not themselves branch networks through which to gather deposits. Thus they have to buy their money and, to a great extent, match the terms of their loans with the periods for which money is obtainable in the market. Unmatched terms make them extremely vulnerable to rising interest rates.

Under the heading of new entrants to the City, the most dramatic increase has been in the numbers of branches of foreign banks, particularly American. These have come for three main reasons. The first is that a London address is good for public relations back home. The second is defensive. With an increasing number of their company clients doing business in various ways in the U.K. an American bank without the means of servicing such customers may find itself at a disadvantage domestically. Thirdly, and most important, American banks come to London to participate in the Euro-dollar market, which they cannot do without a London office. This last reason has been given added force by the tightness of money in the U.S. and by the encouragement given to U.S. companies with overseas operations to borrow abroad.

V. PARALLEL MARKETS

The Euro-dollar market, which has been the magnet drawing U.S. banks to London, developed to fill a gap in international financial arrangements. It was stimulated by national measures to control capital flows, in particular those that give rise to interest rate differentials between countries and those that force international companies to meet their borrowing requirements outside their country of origin; and it was made possible by a certain degree of freedom for capital to move across national boundaries. So long as these conditions persist, the Euro-currency markets in some form or other will continue. The size of the market and the supply of funds in relation to the almost insatiable demand, and hence interest rates, will depend on the tightness of monetary conditions in the countries that are the main providers of Euro-currencies, notably of course the U.S.

This market was already in being before the Radcliffe Committee finished its work and it is a little surprising that its report contains no reference to it. Throughout its relatively short history London has been the predominant centre of the Euro-dollar market. This is probably due to two factors—the expertise of the City, particularly of its foreign exchange dealers, and the fact that the gap the market came to fill was that left as a result of the decline of sterling.

Though, in spite of the persistent weakness of the pound, the sterling system has been an unconscionable time adying—largely because international traders enjoy change no more than the rest of mankind—its gradual decline left a gap to be filled. Meanwhile the short-term liabilities of the U.S. in the form of dollar balances in the hands of non-residents of the U.S. had grown enormously and their employment in the U.S. become relatively unprofitable. Thus increasing demands for finance developed alongside excess dollar balances lacking employment. Merchant banks and other institutions in the City saw the opportunity for profit in this situation and soon built up a substantial business.

Initially the business done by banks in London was mainly in the nature of brokerage. They progressed before long from broking to banking, to the making of medium-term loans in Euro-dollars and to the issue of Euro-bonds.

This market is frowned on by some national monetary

authorities because it is outside their control and its existence may frustrate domestic monetary restrictions. Also it has been seen as the medium by which high levels of interest rates are transmitted from one country to another. While the first has validity, the second has not. If money is tight and expensive in the leading financial centres, interest rates will be high elsewhere, whether there is a Euro-currency market as we know it or not. The world hunger for capital is in itself sufficient to ensure this.

From the commercial point of view there seem to be two dangers. First, a bank placing funds in this market has no control over their ultimate use and may have no knowledge of the final user. Secondly, there is no lender of last resort, as Lord Cromer has recently observed. Thus there is the possibility that the failure of a large taker of funds in this market could result in further failures and this could spread almost indefinitely. Both these dangers may be exaggerated. The contrast between the practices in this market and those of commercial bankers in their ordinary lending is not as great as has been suggested. Even the commercial banks do not always know the quality of the customers with whom their borrowers are doing business. They simply set a limit to what they will lend to any particular borrower, which is really what banks that employ funds in the Euro-dollar market do. Furthermore, though it is true that there is no formal lender of last resort, there is in every chain of lenders and borrowers at least one institution of sufficient strength to prevent a chain reaction resulting from a failure.

VI. LOCAL AUTHORITY MARKET

U.S. government action was one of the factors stimulating the rise of the Euro-dollar market but it was action by our own government that caused local authorities to be among the main takers of funds in another new market. Towards the end of 1955 the Chancellor of the Exchequer instructed local authorities to meet their needs as far as possible in the market before turning to the Public Works Loan Board. The government's economic policy at that time included restrictions on stock issue by local authorities and, in any case, long-term interest rates were at levels that it was then believed would not last long, which made temporary borrowing appear to be in the interests of rate-payers as well as a sheer necessity.

Accordingly the local authorities began to take short-term funds, mainly in the form of deposits, and these grew before long to very big figures. In the first quarter of 1969, short-term borrowing by local authorities totalled over £2,000 million, of which almost three-quarters was repayable within seven days. This money came and, though the local authorities now have easier access to the P.W.L.B., still comes from a variety of sources—private persons, industrial companies, and banks—and not a little from overseas.

Thus the local authorities are operating in a highly competitive market, in which their own demands have at times noticeably added to the competitive pressures. Moreover, in so far as they take funds originating abroad, they are in a market subject to sudden sharp contractions of supply, particularly when confidence in sterling is shaken for any reason. In such circumstances, for example at the end of 1964, the local authorities' lenders of last resort are the commercial banks, who have at times had to increase their local authority lending in conditions most unfavourable for the banks.

At least one bank chairman was moved to comment in his annual statement on the difficulties these arrangements created for the banks. The local authorities are not themselves entirely to blame; they are placed in an anomalous position by the central government, which compels them, in gathering a large part of their funds, to behave as if they were in the private sector, though they are wholly in the public sector with regard to their expenditure.

Incidentally, the Radcliffe Committee was critical of the arrangements for local authority finance; but it did not apparently foresee that the local authorities would be driven to the large-scale taking of deposits that we have since observed.

In the market for funds the local authorities have been in direct competition with the hire purchase finance houses.

This is a group whose deposit-taking activities, in both large and relatively small sums, have increased enormously in the past decade. With expanding business and a very profitable return on their lending, they have been almost indifferent to the price of deposits. Even more than the local authorities, they must have the money, which is one reason for the intensity of demand that has frequently occurred in this market. Tables IV.2 and IV.3 illustrate some aspects of the development of hire purchase and other instalment credit facilities.

TABLE IV.2

Hire Purchase and Other Instalment Credit (£ million)

End of period	Total outstanding	Owing directly to		
		Durable goods shops and department stores	Finance houses	Other instalment credit retailers*
1958	559	227	332	—
1959	849	327	522	—
1960	935	325	610	—
1961	934	316	618	—
1962	887	318	569	—
1963	959	345	614	—
1964	1,280	361	754	165
1965	1,386	360	836	190
1966	1,261	307	756	198
1967	1,226	276	742	208
1968	1,269	281	766	222

* Comprising general stores (other than department stores), general mail order houses and co-operative non-durable goods departments.

VII. INTER-BANK MARKET

Related to, but separate from, both the Euro-dollar market and the local authority/finance house market is the inter-bank market. Banks are active in both the first two but they are not the sole participants: deposits come from sources other than banks and banks are not the only users of funds.

TABLE IV.3

Commodity Analysis of Hire-Purchase and Other Credit Instalments Outstanding at Year End (£ million)

	1958	1959	1960	1961	1962	1963	1965*	1966*	1967*	1968*
Private and Commercial motor vehicles and caravans	256	394	454	461	416	451	617	534	536	548
Farm and industrial equipment	26	37	52	68	66	73	112	118	116	111
Household goods	261	396	394	366	372	397	50	36	22	18
Other goods	13	22	35	32	33	33	58	68	67	89
Total	556	849	935	927	887	954	837	756	742	766

* Finance Houses only.
Source: Board of Trade Journal; Credit.

The inter-bank market, on the other hand, is one in which banks, other than the clearing banks, borrow exclusively from, and lend exclusively to, banks.

In a country like Britain, in which the commercial banks do not borrow directly even from the central bank, such a market seems very strange. But there are good reasons for its existence. The banks operating in the inter-bank market are engaged in business that is very different in character from that traditionally undertaken by the clearing banks or, until recently, by other financial institutions in the City. Moreover, a number of the newcomers are American banks who, back in the United States, have been accustomed to dealing in the Federal Funds market, which in principle is quite similar to the inter-bank market.

The banks in this market, probably numbering over 150, the majority of which are, of course, also active in the Euro-currency market, are wholesalers. Thus their business tends to be lumpy, which is one reason why they find the inter-bank market attractive, if not essential. Each bank knows that it can place excess funds or borrow to meet deficiencies at the going rate and therefore need not be inhibited from accepting deposits for which it has no immediate borrowers nor, within limits, from undertaking lending business for which it has no immediate funds.

VIII. CLEARING BANKS

The clearing banks have changed considerably over the past decade. They have overhauled their management structure, their recruiting and their staff training, refined their money transmission services with the aid of computers, embarked on a wide range of financial services on the periphery of deposit banking and greatly extended their international interest. The biggest outward change, however, has been that resulting from mergers and takeovers.

At the time of the Radcliffe Report there were eleven clearing banks—the Big Five, Martins, District, Glyns, Coutts, Williams Deacons, and National, with much of its business in Ireland. Shortly there will be only six. Four of these—Barclays with Martins, National Westminster with Coutts, a wholly-owned subsidiary, Midland and Lloyds— now hold 97 per cent of clearing bank deposits, the remaining 3 per cent being in the hands of William Deacons, Glyn Mills, and the non-Irish part of the much reduced National (now being merged to form Williams and Glyn Mills Ltd.).

The Monopolies Commission was not much impressed by some of the reasons given for the proposed Barclays–Lloyds– Martins merger. Nevertheless, there is a clear need for a rationalization of the expensive branch network; there are economies of scale in the use of computers; and there is a need for bigness in the international field. Alongside these structural changes, and of greater importance, has been the relative decline of the clearing banks in relation to the monetary system as a whole which is illustrated in Table IV.I (above, p. 134). In the table the term 'deposits' is interpreted pretty broadly and there is a good deal of double counting. Moreover, the 1968 figures are swollen by those for the American banks, a large proportion of whose deposits are not domestic but are monies taken in the Euro-dollar market and lent by the London branches to their American head offices. Nevertheless, the table shows the proportions of the total market held by various groups of institutions in 1958 and 1968 and indicates that between these two dates the proportions in the hands of the London Clearing Banks declined significantly. Every other major group gained ground. The Building Societies in particularly enlarged their proportion from 13·3 per cent in 1958 to 17·5 per cent in 1968, which means that more small savings than formerly are being channelled to the Building Societies for investment in housing. Whether in current circumstances this represents the best possible allocation of scarce resources is a question that perhaps lies outside the scope of this paper.

Any discussion of the clearing banks must obviously include reference to the vexed subject of bidding for deposits and the related question, already touched upon, of the rates charged for loans, even though much of what can be said on the former has already been said.

The banks might present a better public image if they were to abandon their cartel agreement in deposit rates; but if they were to do so it is inconceivable that in practice the rates offered would ever differ from bank to bank to any significant extent. The most that could be expected would be that, at very considerable administrative cost, they would dress up their advertising to make their terms look different. This surely would benefit no one. The fact is that the banks pay for the deposits they get primarily in terms of service and the public are prepared to leave money with them for the sake of convenience. What the public places on deposit, as opposed to current account, is attracted as much by the 'moneyness' of a clearing bank deposit as by the rate offered.

In any case, whatever the merits or demerits of free rate competition between the banks for deposits, the authorities have the last word. This was clearly given as recently as 25 July 1969 by the Chancellor of the Exchequer in the House of Commons in a written reply to Mr. Sheldon:

The Government has reviewed the arrangements under which the London clearing banks and the Scottish banks respectively agree among themselves as to the rates which they pay upon deposits and charge upon certain types of lending, in the light of the views expressed by the National Board for Prices and Incomes in its report on bank charges and by the Monopolies Commission in its report on the proposals for a merger between Barclays, Lloyds and Martins Banks.

It can be argued that the abolition of these arrangements would in the long run be in the public interest as conducive to greater competitiveness in the banking system. So long, however, as the banks are being asked to operate under a system of tight credit control which narrowly restricts their ability to compete in their lending they would not in practice be able to make any significant use of the opportunities for greater competition that abolition of the cartel would in theory provide.

The Government has, therefore, concluded that the public interest would not be served, at any rate *at the present time*, by urging the banks to abandon their agreement upon deposit and lending rates. The representatives of the banks concerned have been informed of this conclusion.[1]

Competition between the banks and other financial institutions is perhaps a separate question. Apart from leakages, which may not be very important, it seems fairly clear that though the ownership of deposits may change—they

[1] Official Report, 25 July 1969, Written Answers, Col. 604.

may pass from a non-financial company or private individual to a merchant bank or building society—they are not in general lost to the clearing bank system unless they go to an institution in the public sector. When the ownership changes in this way, the position of the deposit holder is only marginally different—his asset is now in slightly less liquid form—bank deposits are in total unchanged but the other financial institution now has resources to lend that it did not previously have. In other words, competition by the clearing banks with other financial institutions would be aimed at depriving the latter of resources for lending rather than at directly gaining deposits. Unless the clearing banks were then able to increase their own lending the consequences for the economy would be deflationary.

If one had to make a forecast, however, it would be that the share of the financial markets held by the clearing banks themselves will continue to decline, but that this relative decline will be more than made up by the further acquisition or establishment of subsidiaries by the clearing banks. Through these they will increase their share of the market by providing a wider and wider range of financial services; some of these are already available through one channel or another, and others will be introduced to meet new requirements. Possibly the side of their activities most open to expansion, again largely through subsidiaries, is the international. Here they will encounter severe competition; but the opportunities are enormous.

Much has been omitted from this survey. Nothing has been said of the probable impact of the Post Office Giro, of the progress of credit cards or of developments resulting from the increasing use of computers and all that goes with them. Nor has it been necessary to discuss the question of disclosure, since this has already been voluntarily agreed by the banks in advance—if only just in advance—of compulsion to do so. Enough has, however, been said to indicate how the main financial changes of the last ten years look from inside a clearing bank and, perhaps, to suggest the lines on which further changes are to be expected.

2. Non-Clearing Banks

T. RYBCZYNSKI

(Lazard Bros. and Chairman of the Business Economists Group)

I. INTRODUCTION

THE non-clearing bank financial intermediaries which the Radcliffe Committee included in its review comprised in addition to the Scottish banks and discount houses two different types of institutions, those undertaking banking business, that is accepting deposits and providing payment and transfer facilities, and those collecting savings but not engaged in banking. The former group included accepting houses, overseas and foreign banks, and hire purchase and finance houses; the latter comprised insurance companies, superannuation funds, investment and unit trusts, and building societies. This paper is concerned mainly with the non-clearing bank financial intermediaries carrying on banking business and above all accepting houses and overseas and foreign banks. It does not deal with the hire purchase houses, simply because their deposit taking activities have been and continue to be confined predominantly to obtaining funds from other financial institutions (nowadays mainly by using the parallel markets) and do not involve the acceptance of deposits from the public to any significant degree. It also excludes the non-bank types of financial institutions.

The evolution of the non-clearing banks since Radcliffe can be seen best by first presenting a bird's eye view of the role they played in the financial system of the U.K. in the late 'fifties, then discussing briefly the changes in their position which have occurred since and finally trying to see the factors which have been responsible for and contributed to the developments in this area during the last ten years or so and what influence and bearing monetary and other policies have had on them.

II. THE POSITION OF NON-CLEARING BANKS
AT THE TIME OF RADCLIFFE

Examining the role played by the accepting houses and overseas and foreign banks, the Radcliffe Committee came to the conclusion that their domestic banking business in relative and absolute terms was fairly small, that it was incidental to their other business, but that these institutions were important in the acceptance market, being responsible for a very large proportion of the total bills outstanding.

The accepting houses which in 1958 numbered eighteen and which were described in the Report as 'merchant bankers who have made the acceptance of bills of exchange an important part of their business' were in the Committee's opinion 'domestic bankers on only a minimal scale' such business being 'in the main ancillary or incidental to their acceptance or issuing business' but their acceptances—which 'added to the total of liquid assets' . . . 'accounted for between 20 and 25 per cent of all bills outstanding and for rather under half the bank bills (i.e. bills eligible for discount or advance by the Bank of England)'. The overseas and foreign banks, the Report said, were relatively unimportant in the domestic financial scene and 'accept the domestic business only incidentally to their main business'. Their total acceptances, however, as reported to the Committee, were half as great as those of the accepting houses.

The relative unimportance of the non-clearing banks in the purely domestic setting in the late 'fifties and their significance in the acceptance market, can be attributed to the nature of their business and above all to their direct and intimate involvement in foreign trade and other external transactions. This is reflected in the statistics submitted by these institutions to the Committee. These suggest that the accepting houses' domestic sterling deposits in 1959, of £220 million, accounted for about 1·3 per cent of the total domestic sterling deposits and those of the overseas and foreign banks, of £215 million, were responsible for only 2·5 per cent of the total. At the same time sterling advances made by the accepting houses to U.K. residents, which amounted to £40 million, were equivalent to slightly less than 2 per cent of the total, while those of the overseas and foreign banks, of £140 million, were responsible for about 7 per cent of the total. However, in the field of acceptances (including acceptances both for domestic and foreign clients) altogether in 1959 these banks accounted for more than two-thirds of the total.

While in domestic banking, in terms of resident sterling deposits and advances, accepting houses and overseas banks played a very modest role, they were very significant as far as non-resident sterling deposits and advances were concerned. This can be seen from their share of non-resident sterling deposits. In 1958 the accepting houses' non-resident sterling deposits, of £112 million, can be estimated to have accounted for some 12 per cent of the total, including those held by the Bank of England, and those of the overseas and foreign banks at that date (of £707 million) for approximately three-fifths of the total.

These three main features of the non-clearers' business—a small share in the domestic banking business, the important role played by them in the sterling acceptance business, and their very significant role in non-resident sterling business—were the direct result of these banks being concerned principally with foreign transactions. In fact from their beginnings in the late eighteenth century, the accepting houses have been outward looking. The acceptance facilities they developed to finance British exports and imports were later on extended to finance trading between third countries and were supplemented by sterling banking facilities for non-residents which were developed because of the international position of sterling and the key currency role it has occupied. It is on this basis that the accepting houses also built up other services, catering chiefly for all types of foreign transactions, such as foreign issues, foreign exchange, and other business.

The key currency position of sterling was also the basis of the business of the overseas and foreign banks, whose principal activities, as described by the Report, were in the late 'fifties 'to act as exchange dealers, to finance foreign trade and to employ in London funds arising from their general business'.

Another important factor which was responsible for the position of the accepting houses and overseas and foreign banks in the late 'fifties in the U.K. financial system was limited competition for the type of business they undertook. Specialization along different functional lines, established during the inter-war years and before with clearing banks showing very limited interest in this area and based on the supremacy of sterling, was strengthened even more after World War II before the introduction of external convertibility of sterling and other currencies.

In these years various groups of banks continued to rebuild their business, which had contracted during the War, along the lines developed before the War. Monetary and other policies affected the banking business carried on by the accepting houses and overseas and foreign banks by influencing the course of U.K. foreign trade, by making it easier or more difficult for other countries to finance their trade in London, and finally by making the holding and the use of sterling by non-residents more or less attractive.

III. CHANGES SINCE RADCLIFFE

In the ten years which have elapsed since the publication of the Radcliffe Report, the position of accepting houses and overseas and foreign banks has changed significantly in many respects.

First, the number of overseas and especially foreign banks, but not the number of accepting houses, has increased by leaps and bounds. While at the time of Radcliffe the membership of the Association of Foreign Banks and Affiliates was only 19 and the number of American banks only 7, the total now stands at no less than 135. This increase in numbers, which is still continuing, has meant increasing competitive pressures.

Secondly, these banks have increased greatly their share of the U.K. domestic sterling business. Excluding sterling deposits of other U.K. banks and sterling certificates of deposit, the accepting houses and overseas and foreign banks now hold no less than £2,060 million of domestic deposits, a figure which can be estimated to account for some 15 per cent of the total as compared with 3·5 per cent ten years ago.

The great expansion both in relative and absolute terms has been shared by all the six groups of banks making up the category of non-clearing banks but has been particularly striking in the case of the accepting houses and American banks, whose deposits during that period increased by some 500 per cent. This trend has also been accompanied by a rapid increase in these banks' sterling loans and advances to U.K. residents (excluding banks) which in late 1969 (in gross terms) amounted to £1,185 million, and accounted for more than 15 per cent of the total.

Thirdly, there has been little expansion in the sterling deposits held by and advances made to non-residents by these banks. At the end of June 1969 non-resident sterling deposits held by them amounted to £1,069 million as compared with some £820 million in 1958. It is interesting to note that all the increase of some £250 million has accrued to non-clearing banks other than accepting houses, the non-resident sterling deposits held by the latter having remained almost unchanged. Sterling lending to non-residents, other than by way of acceptances, has likewise remained at the level at which it was ten years ago. Between December 1958 and June 1969 sterling loans and advances extended by these banks to non-residents rose from £165 to £205 million, an increase of only £40 million, of which an appreciable part is due to the inclusion of new banks in the statistical net rather than to a genuine rise in lending.

Fourthly, the non-clearing banks have experienced a large rise in their acceptances business. Their total acceptances, for U.K. and overseas residents, amounted in mid-1969 to £755 million, an increase of £567 million, or 300 per cent, on £188 million in December 1968. The bulk of this rise occurred in acceptances for U.K. residents, which expanded during that period from £94 to £493 million, or 440 per cent, while those on foreign account increased from £77 to £261 million, or by 240 per cent.

The fifth important change in the non-clearing banks' sterling business has been the large growth in sterling deposits from other U.K. banks and the appearance of the sterling certificate of deposit as a medium for attracting funds. The former (sterling deposits from other banks) stood at nearly £1,200 million in September 1969, accounting for nearly a quarter of these banks' gross sterling deposits. The latter (sterling certificates of deposit), which were introduced in 1968, amounted a year later to £280 million, representing about 6 per cent of the gross sterling funds at their disposal.

Finally, the most significant and important change in the position of non-clearers as compared with 1958 is their very large involvement in the currency business. While non-sterling business was not unknown during the 'fifties, its relative importance was very limited, and it is only during the last ten years that this activity has come to occupy a very important place. The gross currency deposits held by non-clearing banks, including subsidiaries of the clearing banks, amounted in June 1969 to nearly £14,500 million. These deposits are denominated predominantly in Euro-dollars but include also other Euro-currencies, such as Euro-deutsche-marks, Euro-Swiss francs, etc. Of the total £14,500 million, about a quarter represented funds deposited by other U.K. banks, nearly two-thirds covered deposits from overseas residents including banks, 7 per cent were obtained by way of dollar certificates of deposit and the remaining 3 per cent, currencies owned by U.K. residents.

IV. FACTORS RESPONSIBLE FOR AND CONTRIBUTING TO THE CHANGE IN THE POSITION OF NON-CLEARERS

What are the factors which have been responsible for the changes which have occurred in the functions and the relative position of the non-clearing banks during the last ten years and what part have monetary and other policies played in this transformation?

Of the six important changes mentioned in the last section, the relative fall in the non-clearing banks non-resident sterling business, i.e. deposits and advances (but not acceptances which are discussed separately), can be attributed principally to the changed position of sterling in the world economy and in part to direct government measures.

The total increase of U.K. sterling liabilities by more than £2,000 million over the last ten years, has been principally confined to the holding of non-interest-bearing notes and Treasury bills by overseas monetary authorities, including the I.M.F., and has reflected, in the main, increased indebtedness on the part of the government. Non-resident holdings of current and deposit accounts during that period remained virtually unchanged. This development can be said to have been associated with and closely related to the difficulties experienced by the U.K. economy and the increasing use of the U.S. dollar as an international transaction currency. It should be stressed that the U.K. authorities have not imposed any restriction on the use of non-resident owned sterling since the introduction of external convertibility in 1958. What they have done as part and parcel of their policy, and what has affected the non-clearing banks' business of this type, has been to restrict from time to time U.K. sterling lending to non-residents (as well as restricting non-resident access to sterling acceptances and re-finance facilities in London as discussed later on), thus reducing the attraction and the actual use of sterling as an international currency.

Monetary policy has played a relatively minor part in this process. However, inasmuch as the interest rates resulting from the authorities' policies were higher in London after taking account of the forward cover than those obtainable in other centres, and above all New York, London was in a position to attract funds from overseas in accordance with the classic gold standard mechanism.

Interest-rate arbitrage has worked to attract foreign capital on a number of occasions, but becomes ineffective when the forward premium increases very substantially, something which has happened frequently since the authorities have decided not to support forward rates. Some element of stability, in the sense of making it less attractive for non-residents to withdraw sterling funds from London, has been introduced by the Basle Agreement, under which sterling balances held by Sterling Area countries enjoy a *de facto* exchange guarantee. This arrangement, however, has provided a cushion against withdrawals of sterling rather than a positive incentive to add to sterling balances.

The lack of growth in non-resident sterling business—a factor which has influenced the strategy of non-clearing banks—has also been accompanied by much stronger competitive pressures. These have appeared as one result of the entry of a number of new banks and also because of a change in the attitudes of the clearing and other banks which have decided to compete for such deposits at full market terms, either directly or through their subsidiaries.

The large expansion in the domestic sterling business of the non-clearing banks, including the rapid growth of both sterling deposits from other banks and sterling certificates of deposit, has been due to a number of complex but not entirely unconnected factors. Among these the following three can be singled out as having been especially significant: the large rise in the demand for highly specific but relatively cheap short-term bank (and other) finance; the increased sophistication and complexity of the financial system in satisfying different requirements while making the best use of financial resources; and the absence of restrictions on interest rate paid by these banks, together with increasing competition among them.

The last few years have been a period during which requirements for specialized types of finance have been growing very rapidly. This demand has come from final borrowers such as local authorities and the corporate and personal sectors and various financial institutions catering for their needs. Unhampered by the restrictions on interest rate, non-clearing banks (and the subsidiaries of clearing banks) have tried to satisfy these requirements by attracting the deposits needed for this purpose and, in so doing they have developed the wholesale market in which interest rates have tended to be much more flexible. In retrospect, as pointed out by writers such as Revell,[1] the trend toward the segmentation of the financial market and greater specialization of the various financial institutions, which makes it possible to increase the velocity of circulation, is a secular development characterizing mature economies. The relatively more important role now played by the non-clearing banks in domestic banking can be regarded, to a large extent, as a reflection of this development which is likely to be affected only indirectly by the monetary policy. This trend can be expected to continue in the future.

Although in many ways the growth of the acceptance business of the non-clearers can be looked upon in the same light, there is little doubt that direct restrictions on lending, which did not in the first instance embrace non-clearing banks but did do so later on, have been an important contributory factor in this process. However, inasmuch as the acceptance facilities provided by the non-clearers had been used to finance British exports they were included in the privileged category, and the growth in this business has been the direct result of government policy.

The large involvement of the non-clearing banks in currency business, particularly in Euro-currency banking, can fairly be attributed to developments in international monetary and financial conditions and to the measures taken by various national governments. The development of the Euro-currency markets has made it possible for the U.K. to finance some of its overseas transactions in currencies other than sterling, thus reducing the balance of payments pressure arising from the banking function associated with the international position of sterling.

Access to this market by U.K. firms is of course governed by exchange control regulations; but it has also been influenced by developments such as the invoicing of U.K. exports in currencies other than sterling and the consequent transfer to other currencies of the burden of financing U.K. foreign trade.

---

[1] See Revell, J. R. S., 'Changes in British Banking', *Hill, Samuel Occasional Paper*, No. 3, 1968.

V. CONCLUSION

This brief and primarily descriptive survey of the non-clearing banks appears to suggest that the changes in the business and position of non-clearing banks have been largely the result of the long-term secular trends and that the influence of monetary and other policies has been limited. This is not to deny that specific measures have had a direct bearing on the behaviour of these banks. Their precise impact, however, is something which has as yet to be evaluated.

3. Monetary Policy and the Clearing Banks

J. E. MAYCOCK

(*Economic Adviser, Midland Bank*)

I. INTRODUCTION

THE appropriate starting point for this paper is the examination in Chapter VI of the Radcliffe Report of 'The influence of monetary measures'. In this part of the Report, although some consideration is given to ratio controls and the effects of interest rate changes, attention is mainly and repeatedly directed to direct control of clearing bank advances in times of emergency. Otherwise, 'in any ordinary situation we cannot find that there would be sufficient advantage to justify discriminatory action against the banks' (para. 508).

The key passage is to be found in paragraph 395. This accepts that the banks hold a special position in the liquidity structure, since for most borrowers and for most short-term purposes they are much the most convenient institutional source of funds, and often the only source. But it is emphasized that any special concern, in times of emergency, with the lending operations of the banks, and any extreme measures

... are to be aimed at the banks as key lenders in the system, and not at the banks as 'creators of money'. It is the level of bank advances rather than the level of bank deposits that is the object of this special interest; the behaviour of the bank deposits is of interest only because it has some bearing, along with other influences, on the behaviour of other lenders.

This view is reaffirmed a little later: '... a monetary authority in a tight corner may well decide to strike directly at the banks. It is however at bank advances that they should strike' (para. 397h).

Ever since 1959, as was the previous practice, control of bank lending on the lines prescribed in Radcliffe has invariably been included in the 'package' of official measures of restraint whenever the authorities have felt restrictive action to be necessary. Selective controls over bank lending have been operating for more than one-half of the last ten years and, save for a few months in 1967, quantitative restraints on lending have been continuously in force from the end of 1964 up to the present day. Meanwhile the clearing banks have been required to observe a minimum ratio of liquid assets to deposits, a requirement first made specific in 1955. This has been supplemented by special deposits, a new instrument of control. The arrangements for calling for special deposits from the banks had been worked out before the Report was published, but were brought into operation for the first time in 1960; since April 1965 the system has been in continuous use. Bank rate has been actively used by the authorities in reinforcement of other action, having been changed twenty-four times since 1959. These movements have been immediately reflected in clearing bank deposit and lending rates since the links with Bank rate have been maintained.

II. QUALITATIVE AND QUANTITATIVE CONTROLS

Apart from minor measures in 1960—the first call for Special Deposits and the raising of Bank rate—there have been three main periods of credit restraint since Radcliffe: from July 1961 to October 1962, from November 1964 to April 1967, and from November 1967 to the present day. In each of these periods the authorities indicated selective criteria that were to be applied to bank lending, on the one hand the categories of borrower to be accorded priority and on the other those to be discouraged. The guidance given has followed a common pattern, with advances related to consumption at home, notably personal and professional borrowing, hire-purchase finance companies, speculative building and property development, and other speculative transactions of all kinds marked out for special restraint; and finance to assist exports or to save imports given priority.

Within this general pattern, changes of emphasis have occurred from time to time. In November 1967, for example, finance for exports, always given the highest priority, was extended to cover invisible exports. The priority to be given to regional development, productive investment, and agriculture, has also varied. In July 1965, the banks were for the first time categorically asked to restrain the growth of finance for imports and to examine requests for credit for this purpose even more carefully than before, particular reference being made to imports of manufactured goods for home consumption and imports for stockbuilding.

In recent years the selective controls, which involve some measure of restraint on total lending, have been reinforced to a much greater degree than previously by expressly indicated quantitative controls, described by Radcliffe as 'the most drastic form of control of bank advances' (para. 527). These have taken the form of an indicated ceiling for bank lending within which the total was to be contained. Radcliffe had suggested (para. 527), though not very forcefully, that when quantitative restraint was required each bank should have its own ceiling expressed as a proportion of its deposits, as an alternative to a collective overall ceiling. It was argued that this more refined method of control would involve somewhat less restriction of competition between the banks, since any one of them would be able to increase its business if it could attract deposits away from the others, which would correspondingly come under greater pressure. It was not felt, however, that the difference between a proportional and absolute ceiling would be great in the short run; what was important was that action should be directed at the banks' advances.

In the event the absolute ceiling method has continued to be pursued, and more rigorously than before. In July 1961, the banks were asked in general terms to cut the rate of increase in lending considerably by the end of the year. In the next period of restraint the initial request—in December 1964— was similar, namely that the rate of growth should be reduced; but five months later the requirement was made more specific, the banks being told that the increase in lending during the twelve months to March 1966 should not exceed an annual rate of about 5 per cent. For the first time the ceiling applied only to lending to the private sector, and also for the first time to their acceptances and purchases of commercial bills. This widening of the ceiling requirement to cover all lending —advances and bills—has been maintained since, and so too have the exclusion from its application of finance for the public sector.

Early in 1966 the ceiling set for the following March was continued 'until further notice', but in the event was removed just over a year later, its removal being accompanied by the indication that only a modest increase in the total would be permitted, and also that henceforth greater reliance would be placed on a more flexible use of Special Deposits to influence bank lending. This respite for the banks was short-lived. In the new situation created by devaluation, the accompanying package of measures included the imposition of a limit on lending to the private sector, excluding finance directly related to exports, to the November 1967 level until further notice. The limit was fixed in amount, with allowance made for seasonal factors but not for movements in the price level or other indicators.

The ceiling requirement has remained in force ever since, though the formula for determining it has been changed, first by raising the nominal ceiling but bringing within it export finance, and then by reducing it to 98 per cent of the November 1967 level but excluding from it medium- and long-term finance for exports and shipbuilding against official guarantees. The new, and more restricted target, was to be achieved by March 1969, but by contrast with earlier periods the clearing banks have experienced considerable difficulty in meeting the requirements of the authorities. In August 1969, for example, they were collectively as much as $4\frac{1}{2}$ per cent above the 98 per cent ceiling.

III. RATIO REQUIREMENTS

The clearing banks have remained subject to cash and liquidity ratio requirements, but as in the years up to 1959 the authorities have not operated on the banking position by limiting the supply of cash. As recorded by Radcliffe (para. 376) the Bank of England has since the war accepted the desirability of 'reasonable stability' in the Treasury bill rate; it has preferred to furnish cash far more readily than before the war so that in practice it has become virtually interchangeable with Treasury bills. However, the fixity of the cash ratio, which has been maintained at 8 per cent of gross deposits, contributes to the control of the authorities over short-term rates.

Thus the effective base of bank credit had by the late 'fifties become the liquid assets holdings of the banks, and the ratio an accepted instrument of monetary regulation. This was the position at the time of Radcliffe and so it has remained. As the Bank of England confirmed in the December 1968 issue of its *Quarterly Bulletin*, 'one of the assumptions which is now implicit in official policy is that it is the total liquid assets of the principal deposit banks and not their cash alone, which influences their ability to lend to the private sector'.

Like the cash ratio, the liquidity ratio is required to be maintained, but because of seasonal swings is a minimum or floor rather than a fixed point. The ratio requirement itself has altered.[1] In 1951 the Governor of the Bank of England indicated that a figure of between 28 and 32 per cent would be expected, although exceptionally a minimum of 25 per cent might be permissible. By 1955, 30 per cent was regarded as the

---

[1] So too has the definition of liquid assets; see Wadsworth, J. E., 'Banking Ratios Past and Present', in *Essays in Money and Banking in Honour of R. S. Sayers*, ed. C. R. Whittlesey and J. S. G. Wilson (Oxford: The Clarendon Press, 1968). As currently defined, liquid assets comprise cash (balances with the Bank of England plus cash in tills and vaults), money at call and short notice (advances to the London discount market, plus loans of under one month to other members of the money market, jobbers and stockbrokers, bullion dealers, and other U.K. non-clearing banks), some foreign currency balances, the banks' own holdings of tax reserve certificates, U.K. Treasury bills discounted, other bills discounted (mainly bank and trade bills, foreign government treasury bills, local authority bills, foreign currency bills, and bills or promissory notes drawn under the short-term export credit scheme with a tenor of six months or less), refinanceable credits (principally advances relating to medium-term export credits guaranteed by the E.C.G.D. and falling due for repayment within eighteen months) and some fixed-term shipbuilding credits.

appropriate minimum level and in 1957 the Governor of the Bank of England told the Radcliffe Committee that he had 'left the banks in no doubt ... that they should not allow their liquidity ratios to fall significantly below 30 per cent'.

This remained the figure until 1963. The banks were then experiencing considerable pressure on liquidity, and at the same time the Government was anxious to avoid a restriction in bank credit. In the spring the Bank of England indicated that it would take a less rigid view of the newly-established minimum level of 30 per cent, and in the autumn the banks were advised that they could 'aim to achieve a liquidity ratio of not less than 28 per cent between now and the make-up date in April 1964'. In practice, 28 per cent has continued to be accepted as a suitable minimum, and when individual banks have on occasion failed to achieve it, they have been reminded by the central bank of their obligation to do so.

IV. SPECIAL DEPOSITS

The Radcliffe Committee (para. 508) considered a variety of methods for restraining lending by the banks to the private sector through raising reserve requirements or similar devices, among them the Special Deposit arrangements drawn up by the Bank of England and the clearing banks in 1958. It found little to choose between a straightforward power to vary the liquidity ratio requirement and some such system as Special Deposits. However, the latter has been brought into use in succeeding years to reinforce other ways of restricting credit.[2]

Under the system, the clearing and the Scottish banks—but not other banks—are required to place with the Bank of England a deposit equivalent to a stated percentage of their gross deposits, to be held there until released. Such calls are made by the Bank with the approval of the Chancellor of the Exchequer, and the amounts earmarked are provided by the banks out of liquid assets, but can no longer be treated as such.

[2] For reasons for the choice of Special Deposits rather than a variable liquidity ratio, see 'Bank liquidity in the United Kingdom', *Bank of England Bulletin*, December 1962.

Hence the banks' liquidity ratio is correspondingly reduced along with their ability to increase their lending. The Special Deposits system is therefore akin to a variable liquidity ratio.

In 1960 the first call for special deposits was made, and by 1961 they were at their highest levels yet recorded—3 per cent

TABLE IV.4

Special Deposits—London Clearing Banks

Date of Announce-ment	Date of Transfer	Call or release		Cumulative total		Liquidity ratio*
		Percent of gross deposits	£m†	Percent of gross deposits	£m.†	Percent of gross deposits
Calls						
1960						
April 28	by June 15	1	70	1	70	31·4
June 23	by July 20	½	35	1½	105	31·2
	by Aug. 17	½	38	2	143	31·4
1961						
July 25	by Aug. 16	½	38	2½	185	32·9
	by Sept. 20	½	36	3	221	34·3
Releases						
1962						
May 31	on June 12	½	36	2½	185 ⎫	
	on June 18	½	36	2	149 ⎭	33·4
Sept. 27	on Oct. 8	½	38	1½	113 ⎫	
	on Oct. 15	½	38	1	75 ⎭	33·5
Nov. 29	on Dec. 10	½	39	½	38	34·0
	on Dec. 17	½	38	Nil	Nil	35·9
Calls						
1965						
April 29	by May 19	½	44	½	44	29·8
	by June 16	½	43	1	87	30·1
1966						
July 14	by July 20	½	47	1½	140	29·9
	by Aug. 17	½	49	2	189	30·3

* Immediately after call or release.
† The amounts fluctuate in accordance with movements in gross deposits.

for the clearing banks and $1\frac{1}{2}$ per cent for the Scottish. (The rate for the Scottish banks has always been one-half that applying to the clearing banks.) The banks were free from calls for Special Deposits during the whole of 1963 and 1964, but the arrangements were brought into use again in May 1965 and have been employed ever since. The history of calls and releases for the clearing banks, and the combined liquidity ratio at the appropriate dates, are shown in Table IV.4.

Thus the system, as employed, has not been particularly flexible, nor has the original intention that it should replace 'directive' controls over advances been fulfilled. This intention was reiterated in the April 1967 Budget; the ceiling on bank advances was then removed, but the Chancellor of the Exchequer stated that 'the Special Deposits system will be used in future in a new and more flexible manner' with a view to exercising a more continuous control over lending. Whereas previously a call for deposits had been regarded as in the nature of a crisis measure, in the future it was intended to be used as a 'routine adjustment to conditions as they develop'. Before this intention could find expression in action, devaluation of sterling had become necessary, and the level of Special Deposits has now remained unchanged at 2 per cent for over three years.[3]

V. THE INTEREST RATE AGREEMENTS

Radcliffe came to the conclusion (para. 507) that moderate use of the interest-rate brake was of little effect on the expansion of advances, but that some restraint could be effected by imposing losses on the banks on sales of securities before maturity. The authorities have continued to use variations in interest rates, along with other measures, and have used them more particularly with reference to the external situation. In times of crisis Bank rate has been raised sharply, and once—in February 1969—it was specifically indicated that the intention

---

[3] Chart 1 illustrates some of the features dealt with in this and the preceding two sections.

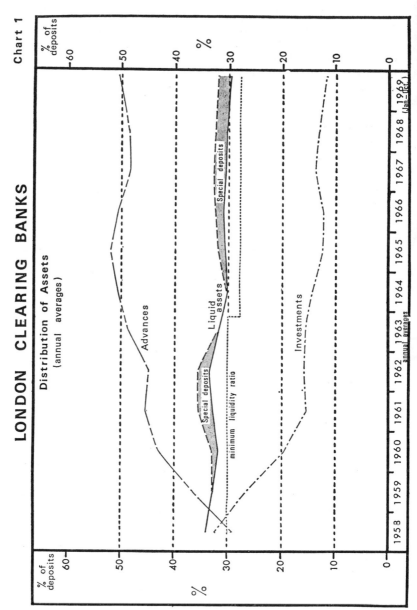

LONDON CLEARING BANKS

Chart 1

Distribution of Assets
(annual averages)

of the increase was to help to curb demand for bank finance. Meanwhile the general rate structure observed by the clearing banks has remained unaltered. They have by agreement kept the rate of interest allowed on deposits at seven days' notice firmly linked to Bank rate, at 2 per cent below, and rates charged on advances are still mostly arranged on the traditional formula—a stated margin above Bank rate subject to a minimum. The banks have, however, been attempting to push up the minimum; to widen the margin; and to impose 'commitment' charges where facilities have been agreed for a specific purpose well in advance of the need to borrow and in other special circumstances.

More recently—in September 1969—the clearing banks announced that, with the approval of the Bank of England, all lending rates, except for the concessionary rates applying to export and ship-building finance, were to be increased by ½ per cent as from the beginning of October. The purpose was to narrow the gap between bank lending rates and other market rates and so to reduce the pressure on bank lending. This move still left rates charged linked to Bank rate, but the 'blue chip' rate—the finest rate to the highest class of commercial borrower—now moved from the long-standing ½ over Bank rate to 1 per cent over, with a minimum of 5 per cent per annum.

The Radcliffe report had little to say about the inter-bank rate agreements, but in subsequent years they have come under considerable criticism from official quarters as well as academic and other commentators. Paradoxically, in view of later indications of official attitudes, the first public criticism came from the then Governor of the Bank of England, Lord Cromer, in April 1963 when he asked: 'Is the considerable rigidity in interest rates which has grown up in the banking world in the last twenty years or so an encouragement to the growth of bank deposits?'[4] In the following year he stated, however, that it was lack of flexibility rather than uniformity of rates which he was questioning, for he accepted

[4] The Earl of Cromer, *Speeches 1959-66* (Bank of England, 1967; published privately).

the argument that the degree of competition in banking was such that it was unlikely that widely differing rates would be maintained for any length of time. Following his earlier comments, it became widely known that some limited proposals for rate competition were drawn up by the banks, but were rejected by the authorities, on the grounds that they would increase interest rates generally, including lending rates.

The agreements subsequently came under more detailed scrutiny in two official inquiries. The National Board for Prices and Incomes, in its report on bank charges published in May 1967,[5] implicitly accepted that no interest should be paid on current accounts, but specifically recommended the abandonment of the agreements on rates on deposit account and those relating to lending, with the exception of advances for exports and shipbuilding. It said: 'Historically, a case can be made out for an agreement between the banks on the rate of interest to be paid on time deposits so long as the banks remained the predominant financial intermediaries. . . . We would question, however, whether such a justification any longer holds good.' This followed from its view that other financial intermediaries were taking deposits from the banks. The Board also considered that 'insufficiently attractive deposit rates are likely to inhibit the banks from experimenting with more diversified lending. We view the abandonment of the banks' present cartel agreement on deposit rates as a necessary step towards the creation of a system in which the banks could play a greater role than they do at present by developing a more diversified pattern of lending.'

Besides recommending the abandonment of the agreement on the rate offered on time deposits, the Board also suggested that the banks should 'feel free to offer a range of time deposits of varying maturity dates carrying different rates of interest'. If the deposit rate agreement were ended, 'it follows that there should also be a dissolution of the collective agreements maintained by the banks on lending rates'. The Board noted that 'within the framework provided by these agree-

[5] Cmnd. 3292.

ments the banks compete for advances business agressively. . . . Nevertheless, the framework of agreements inhibits rate competition. . . . We think that these agreements should be dissolved, on the grounds that they are liable to operate against the most effective allocation of funds.' It was thought that 'these suggestions would have greater implications for the relative lending rates of different intermediaries than for the general level of lending rates. . . . We would . . . expect some diversion of borrowers from higher cost sources to the banks, so that even if a rise in bank lending rates occurred, the overall average of lending rates could remain unaffected.'

Just over a year later the Monopolies Commission, in its report on the proposed Barclays–Lloyds–Martins merger,[6] took a similar line. It stated: 'Many times it emerged clearly from the evidence we received that competition between clearing banks is severely limited by the agreements on maximum rates payable on deposits and minimum rates chargeable on certain types of advances.' It noted that 'the banks all hold the view that, without the agreements, they would end up paying more for the deposits they already receive and would therefore be unable to finance industry and commerce so cheaply'. It also noted the preference of the banks for competing through subsidiaries, and the hindrance of the imposed liquidity ratio.

Official views on the interest rate agreements were in contrast to those expressed five years previously. Before the Monopolies Commission, the Governor of the Bank of England accepted the arguments put forward by the banks in support of their present practices, while 'the Treasury representatives went further and said that they would wish the present arrangements to survive because they believed that they enabled the major part of the credit requirements of the country's industry and commerce to be satisfied at lower rates than would otherwise be the case'. Following publication of the report, the President of the Board of Trade stated that, in the light of the Commission's criticisms, 'we shall again review the arguments which have hitherto led to the conclu-

[6] House of Commons Papers, 1968; 319.

sion that these agreements are not, on balance, against the public interest'.

It would seem that the review is now completed, and the conclusion reached, as reported to the House of Commons by the Chancellor of the Exchequer,[7] is that 'at any rate for the present time' the public interest would not be served by urging the banks to abandon their agreement upon deposit and lending rates. The Chancellor said that it could be argued that the 'abolition of these arrangements would in the long run be in the public interest, as conducive to greater competitiveness in the banking system. So long, however, as the banks are being asked to operate under a system of tight credit control which narrowly restricts their ability to compete in their lending, they would not in practice be able to make any significant use of the opportunities for greater competition that abolition of the cartel would in theory provide.'

In addition to the arguments for maintenance of the agreements, as put by them to the two official inquiries, the banks have also pointed to the development of their subsidiary and associated undertakings, not subject to cash and liquidity ratio requirements, which operate outside the rate agreements and which are able to attract funds insofar as they are sensitive to interest rate levels. They have also questioned the general impression given especially by the National Board for Prices and Incomes that lending rates are agreed between themselves. The position was explained by the chairman of the Midland Bank as follows:

... apart from the rather special arrangements applying to the discount market, the only important agreement between the banks is the one which establishes a minimum figure, of ½ per cent over Bank rate, to be charged to 'blue chip' borrowers. Moreover, although this minimum rate is agreed between us, each bank decides to which of its borrowing customers the minimum shall apply—there is no uniform definition. For the rest, where uniform rates are in operation this is generally at the instance of the authorities.[8]

Chart 2 illustrates changes in short-term interest rates since 1958.

[7]. Official Report, 25 July 1969, Written Answers, Col. 604. The Chancellor's reply is given in full on p. 148.
[8] Statement to the shareholders, January 1969.

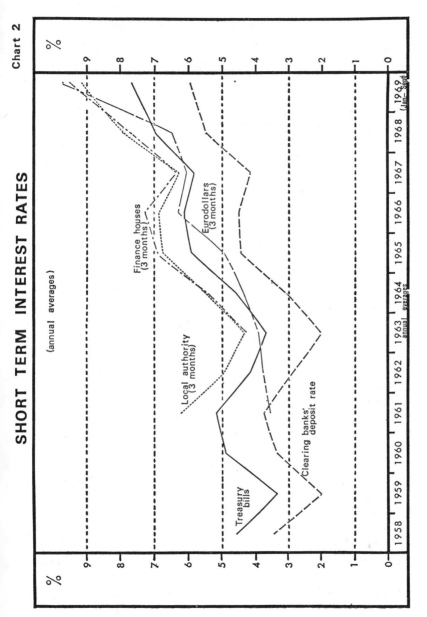

Chart 2

SHORT TERM INTEREST RATES
(annual averages)

VI. MOVEMENTS IN DEPOSITS

Until relatively recently, movements in the level of bank deposits, as an important constituent of the money supply, have attracted little official attention. Radcliffe found that for the purpose of monetary policy, bank deposits were important but they were not the main aspect of bank activity to be brought under investigation; 'the amount of money, in the sense of the amount of notes and bank deposits, is of considerable significance' (para. 392), but it is 'only part of the wider structure of liquidity in the economy. It is the whole liquidity position that is relevant to spending decisions, and our interest in the supply of money is due to its significance in the whole liquidity picture. . .' (para. 389). 'The authorities thus have to regard the structure of interest rates rather than the supply of money as the centre-piece of the monetary mechanism. This does not mean that the supply of money is unimportant, but that its control is incidental to interest rate policy' (para. 397).

As may be seen from Table IV.5, net deposits have risen consistently over the past ten years, to give an increase of over one-half over the whole period. The increase has, however, been somewhat less pronounced than that recorded for the national income; expressed as a proportion of the latter, net deposits have fallen from 33·5 per cent in 1958 to 29·2 in 1968. This was a much slower rate of decline than in earlier post-war years. Moreover, movements in the past few years have been relatively modest, and exceptionally an increase was recorded between 1967 and 1968.

Meanwhile banking turnover has continued to rise rapidly, broadly at the same rate as the rise in gross national product; indeed, the Midland Bank Index of Business Turnover has moved very closely with the annual national income figures for 'final expenditure'. In effect then, an increase in the velocity of circulation has offset a relative decline in the crude quantity of money. Nevertheless, the rise in velocity since Radcliffe—which could not 'find any reason for supposing, or any experience in monetary history indicating, that there is any limit to the velocity of circulation . . .' (para. 391)—has been less pronounced than over the previous ten years. The income velocity of circulation, as measured by relating the Midland Bank Index of Business Turnover to gross national product, rose by less than one-fifth between 1962 and 1968.

TABLE IV.5

Net Deposits of the Clearing Banks (Annual Averages)

Year	£ million	Per cent change on previous year	As per cent of national income
1958	6,230	3·1	33·5
1959	6,499	4·3	33·2
1960	6,743	3·8	32·3
1961	6,909	2·5	30·9
1962	7,084	2·5	30·3
1963	7,409	4·6	29·8
1964	7,891	6·5	29·4
1965	8,316	5·4	29·1
1966	8,675	4·3	29·0
1967	9,024	4·0	28·8
1968	9,645	6·9	29·2
1969	9,760	1·2	

The importance now being given to the money supply, or rather the concept of 'domestic credit expansion', and the implications for the banks are noted below. Here attention may be drawn to the problems of defining the money supply. The official definition goes much wider than currency in circulation with the public, balances in sterling on accounts with the joint stock banks—primarily the clearing banks and their counterparts in Scotland and Northern Ireland—and deposits with the National Giro, which together comprise the final means of payment. The widening of the definition to include all deposits by U.K. residents with other institutions making up the banking sector as a whole—the discount market, accepting houses, and overseas and other banks—as well as non-sterling deposits, can be questioned.[9]

The grounds for doing so are the primary effect of a transfer of funds from a clearing bank to another private sector intermediary is merely a re-shuffling of the ownership of clearing bank deposits, but no reduction of them. As a secondary effect, the banks may be affected adversely, but how significantly is far from clear, nor, it must be admitted, are the implications for monetary policy, except that if control of the money supply is a major objective, then it would seem that attention should be mainly directed to the course of clearing bank deposits.

The increase in deposits placed with non-clearing bank intermediaries, which has been such a notable development since Radcliffe, is attributable in part to the active use, during the period, of interest rates as an instrument of policy, bringing them to appreciably higher levels than for many years past (see Chart 2).[10] This has also had consequences for the clearing banks themselves. First, the proportion of deposits held on interest-bearing accounts has been significantly higher than previously; it rose from 37·4 to 43·9 per cent between 1959 and 1968. Secondly, the sector composition of deposits has changed, with deposits of persons rising appreciably faster than those of companies, which have become increasingly sensitive to interest rate differentials in the disposition of their 'idle' funds. In 1968, the proportions for companies and 'other' (persons and unincorporated businesses) were 18·4 and 71·3 per cent respectively, against 26·2 and 60·1 per cent in 1959.

VII. NEW TRENDS IN POLICY

To summarize the story so far, in the exercise of policy in relation to the clearing banks the authorities have employed the traditional methods of changes in interest rates, imposition

[9] See 'Money Supply and the Banks', *Midland Bank Review*, February 1969.

[10] U.K. interest rates have also risen in response to movements in overseas financial centres.

of qualitative and quantitative controls on lending, and maintenance of the liquidity ratio requirement supplemented by the relatively new system of Special Deposits. In these ways they have attempted to influence respectively the demand for credit, the willingness of the banks to supply it, and their ability to do so.

Recently, pressures of a kind not experienced for forty years have also come into play, bringing particular consequences for the banks. This new development follows from the return to prominence in official thinking of the supply of money. By the time of the devaluation of sterling, in November 1967, it was becoming apparent that the growth of the money supply in the United Kingdom was regarded as a serious weakness in the situation, both in this country and by critics and creditors overseas, and the Letter of Intent addressed to the International Monetary Fund included the following undertaking: 'Bank credit expansion will be sufficiently limited to ensure that the growth of money supply will be less in 1968 than the present estimate for 1967, both absolutely and as a proportion of g.n.p., despite the expected substantial recovery of reserves.'

The Bank of England also has been giving more attention to the money supply. Ten years ago the then Governor commented that the total level of bank deposits was no less important than the level of bank advances, but then the whole subject seemed to be dropped until October 1968, when the present Governor was more specific. He acknowledged weighty opinions which do not consider that the trend of the money supply has any reliable significance in the context of the level of internal demand. But, he went on, 'I for my part believe that we should be more concerned with it, as indeed I know many informed observers overseas feel we should be.... I do not accept that controlling the money supply is simply a question of the proper use of central banking techniques, as some appear to believe. Much more fundamental matters are involved.'[11]

At all events, increasing weight seems to have been given to

[11] *Bank of England Quarterly Bulletin*, December 1968.

movements in the money supply in the formulation of official policy, and in 1969 a specific commitment was given to the I.M.F. in respect of the wider concept of 'domestic credit expansion'. Whatever the impulse, the post-devaluation Budget and other measures brought about a sharp change in the Exchequer situation in the financial year 1968–9. This resulted in a net repayment of debt of £287 million, the first year this had been possible since 1950–1 and comparing with a net borrowing requirement of over £1,300 million in 1967–8. For the current financial year (1969–70) an even greater net repayment of debt is in prospect, the Budget estimates showing an overall surplus of £826 million. This massive turn-round in government finance is bringing increasingly severe pressures on bank liquidity.

At the same time, the banks' efforts to maintain or restore liquidity in the classic way, by realizing part of their investments, have been made difficult by another important development in official policy. This took the form of a significant change in the tactics followed by the authorities in their operations in the gilt-edged market, which implied also a new emphasis in official policy. The change in tactics first became evident late in 1968, and was acknowledged in the March 1969 issue of the *Bank of England Quarterly Bulletin*. This clearly pointed to the conclusion that the authorities had been significantly less willing to intervene in the market as buyers than they would have been in similar circumstances previously, an interpretation borne out by the movements in gilt-edged prices themselves.

This policy 'of allowing any weakness' in the market 'to be fully reflected in prices' seems to have been maintained in 1969. Thus the banks have been, in the words of Radcliffe (para. 507) 'brought sharply up against realization losses' even though the surrounding circumstances are not quite as envisaged in the Report. One circumstance that has changed since 1959 is the size of the banks' holdings of investments. Today these represent little more than 10 per cent of deposits, against three times that figure in 1958, so that the 'cushion' available for realization, even at a loss, is now far from comfortable. And with the ratio of advances to deposits having risen correspondingly, the banks have become more sensitive to the liquidity position.

VIII. THE EFFECTIVENESS OF POLICY

The effectiveness of various measures directed at the banks over the past ten years cannot easily be assessed, for one thing because they have often been associated with other action. In particular it is not easy to judge to what extent increases in Bank rate, with corresponding movements in rates charged to borrowers, have helped to curb demand for finance from the clearing banks. The Radcliffe Report noted (para. 138) that 'the banks believe that in general customers are almost indifferent to the rates', and subsequent experience does not suggest any substantial modification of this view. The unusually high rates experienced in recent years seem to have had some effect on demand from 'weaker' borrowers, although it is not possible to say whether knowledge that in any event credit was unlikely to be forthcoming has not been a more important factor. Another factor is that part of the cost of borrowing is offset by tax relief, though under the Finance Act 1969 interest on personal borrowing, with some exceptions, is no longer being allowed as a charge against tax. Except to a quite small extent at the margin, availability rather than cost of credit has probably been the dominant consideration, especially as the clearing banks have remained a relatively cheap source of finance, even after the general increase in rates that started to become effective in October 1969.

It is also difficult to measure how effective have been the qualitative controls, notwithstanding the efforts of the banks to apply the selective criteria as laid down from time to time. In the classification of advances statistics only two borrowing categories which have been consistently placed under special restraint, namely personal and hire-purchase finance, and one—agriculture—which has generally been accorded priority can be broadly identified. The course of lending to these

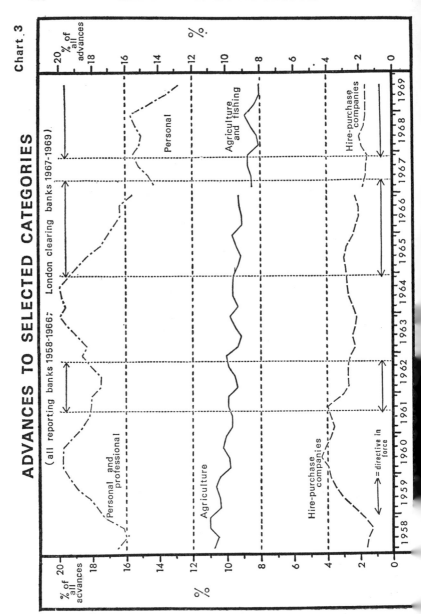

ADVANCES TO SELECTED CATEGORIES

Chart. 3

(all reporting banks 1958-1966;   London clearing banks 1967-1969).

three categories, plotted in Chart 3, suggests that the wishes of the authorities have been substantially met.

For the rest, the categories covered by the 'requests' cannot be matched in the statistics. Advances are classified according to the most important activity of the borrower, the analysis following the Standard Industrial Classification. Moreover, finance obtained from the banks will go into a company's general stock of working capital, and cannot be specifically identified as, say, finance for production for exports rather than for the home market.

During most of the 'squeezes' of the 'sixties, the qualitative 'directives' were reinforced by requests to the banks regarding the total of their lending. The influence of these on movements in advances can be assessed by reference to Table IV.6 below. After the middle of 1958, when bank lending was free of all restraint for the first time since the war, advances rose sharply—by over 30 per cent in 1959 and about 24 per cent in 1960, this upsurge being mainly financed by a running down of investment portfolios (see Chart 1). But in 1961 bank credit was brought under restrictions that, taken together, were more severe than those imposed at any other time since the war. They comprised the re-imposition of selective controls, a jump in Bank rate from 5 to 7 per cent, and a further call for Special Deposits; it was made plain that the impact of these measures was to fall on the level of bank advances, but in any event investment portfolios, the second line of reserves, had by then been sharply reduced. The outcome was a marked slowing down in the rate of increase in advances to under 8 per cent in 1961, and in the following year to under 2 per cent.

During 1962, with official policy now directed to re-expansion of the economy, lending restrictions, and special deposit requirements were gradually removed, and subsequently the minimum liquidity ratio was brought down from 30 to 28 per cent. Once more advances moved on to a pronounced rising trend.

With the return of monetary restraints late in 1964 and their tightening in the first half of 1965, the growth of advances again slowed down. Further measures were taken in mid-1966,

and for the year as a whole, advances were less than 2 per cent
higher than over the previous twelve months and in the following year no increase at all was recorded, notwithstanding
freedom from ceiling considerations and reductions in Bank
rate for a period.

TABLE IV.6

Advances of the Clearing Banks (Annual Averages)

Year	£ million	Per cent change on previous year	As per cent of national income
1958	1,923	2·9	10·3
1959	2,522	31·1	12·9
1960	3,123	23·8	15·0
1961	3,357	7·5	15·0
1962	3,408	1·5	14·6
1963	3,880	13·8	15·6
1964	4,328	11·5	16·1
1965	4,653	7·5	16·3
1966	4,732	1·7	15·8
1967	4,725	−0·1	15·1
1968	5,075	7·4	15·4
1969	5,328	5·0	

The measures taken in 1961–2 and 1964–6 therefore had a
quite discernible effect on bank lending, but the course of
events since November 1967 has been less clear. The monetary
measures that accompanied the devaluation followed a
familiar pattern, with a rigid ceiling placed on bank advances
and Bank rate raised to 8 per cent. These were followed by
exceptionally severe Budgets and tightening of credit restraints, but on the face of it bank lending did not respond as
readily as in the previous squeezes; for 1968 as a whole,
advances were 7½ per cent higher than in 1967. The published figures do not tell the whole story, since they include

public sector and other borrowing not subject to ceiling control, in particular fixed-rate finance for exports which has been rising rapidly. Even so, and although the rate of growth of advances was greatly reduced in 1969, by contrast with earlier periods the banks have been unable to meet the ceiling requirement since late in 1968.

In two respects, the effects of the quantitative and qualitative controls of bank lending have been similar to those noted by Radcliffe: '... the main effect of the restriction of bank credit was to drive frustrated borrowers to other sources of credit' (para. 460); and 'any severely restrictive control of their operations is certain over a period of time, to be defeated by the development of rival institutions...' (para. 504). However, the authorities have meanwhile extended their control of credit to a widening range of other institutions. The growth of sterling lending by the accepting houses and overseas and other banks since 1964, other than to U.K. local authorities and also excluding inter-bank transactions, has been no faster than that of the clearing banks themselves.

Several possible reasons for the difficulty experienced in 1968 and more especially in 1969 in bringing the total of controlled lending down to the ceiling—98 per cent of the November 1967 level—can be briefly indicated. First has been the sharp increases in wholesale and retail prices; between the ceiling base date and mid-1969 the former rose by 7·7 per cent, and the latter by 9·7 per cent.[12] Meanwhile, during 1968 the general level of economic activity was rising fairly strongly, and by the first quarter of 1969 gross domestic product was $3\frac{1}{2}$ per cent above the last quarter of 1967, after allowing for seasonal and price factors. Thirdly, the overdraft system provides a cushion for borrowers, allowing them collectively to increase their use of bank finance quite substantially within the total of agreed facilities. Again, lending by other financial intermediaries has been kept under severe restraint. Finally, and perhaps most important when comparing the present situation with previous periods when lending ceilings have

[12] Much of this price use is directly attributable to the effects of the devaluation.

13—M.I.B.

been operative, financial pressures are being exerted more effectively over the economy as a whole.

IX. PRESSURES ON BANK LIQUIDITY

For the banks themselves, the pressures on liquidity have developed to a degree not experienced for several decades, a consequence mainly of the declining availability of Treasury bills with the turn-around in the Exchequer situation. The clearing banks' holdings of Treasury bills in 1968 were on average around £100 million lower than in 1967, and fell even more steeply in 1969. This decline partly reflected a switch into call money, but the total for the banks and the discount market combined fell by £60–70 million between 1967 and 1968; the outstanding volume of Treasury bills fell more sharply, but 'other' holdings of bills outside the public sector and overseas central monetary institutions also contracted by some £100 million. No easing of the pressures arising from these movements occurred in 1969. Taking the whole period from 1959 to 1969, the Treasury bill portfolio of the clearing banks, together with money lent at call or short notice to the money market (predominantly on the security of Treasury bills), has fallen from 21·8 per cent of gross deposits to only 12·0 per cent.

At first sight it is surprising that the average liquidity ratio in 1968 was virtually the same as in 1967, and was only slightly lower in 1969, at 30·1 against 30·5 per cent. One factor has been a rise in holdings of bills other than Treasury bills; although commercial bill holdings are subject to ceiling requirements along with advances, the totals also include other public sector bills and refinance-able export credits, both outside the control. Over the preceding years, a considerable revival occurred in the use of the commercial bill, partly associated with the introduction and subsequent growth of refinanceable export credits, thus belying the judgement of Radcliffe when it spoke of 'the irreversible shrinkage in the relative supply of commercial bills' (para. 584).

A more significant factor in the maintenance of liquidity ratios in the recent past has been realizations of government securities. In the financial year 1968–9 the net reduction in portfolios was £141 million, and between November and March £200 million, and subsequently further sales have been necessary; even so, some individual banks have on occasion fallen short of the minimum ratio requirement. The ratio of investments has meanwhile been brought to an unusually low level. The banks might be prepared to see it go lower still, but ideally it should be large enough to provide a steady succession of maturities for reinforcement of liquid assets if required. The position today, however, is that early maturities have to a large extent already been realized to meet liquidity pressures, and further realizations could only be effected at substantial losses.

The effect of the changes in official policy described above therefore, has been first to bring substantial pressures on bank liquidity, and secondly to make it both difficult and expensive for the banks to restore liquidity by realization of investments. In short, although direct controls over lending are maintained, the weight of monetary and fiscal policy is increasingly bearing on liquidity. Against the fulcrum of the ratio requirements, reinforced by Special Deposits, it is this aspect that is coming to assume much greater significance in the conduct of banking operations, and the quantitative control correspondingly less.

X. IMPLEMENTATION OF MONETARY POLICY

Finally, some comments on methods of regulation of the banks for monetary purposes may be appropriate. Control has continued to be affected by 'suasion' rather than statute, in the way described by the Bank of England in a memorandum submitted to the Radcliffe Committee in 1957:

The Bank have had no formal control over other banks and no duty of inspection; the possibility that the Bank might refuse to continue to maintain an account for another bank has been historically an effective sanction. Since 1946, if the Bank think it necessary in the public interest,

they may request information from bankers and make recommendations
to them; and, if so authorized by the Treasury, may issue directions to
ensure compliance with such a request or recommendation. This power
has not been used.

It has still to be 'activated', and could well be the more
effective for that. Indeed, it may be noted that doubts have
been cast upon the customary interpretation of the powers
bestowed on the authorities by Section 4(3) of the Bank of
England Act 1946.[13]

The Bank's practice continues to be to pass on the 'requests'
of the authorities to the clearing banks, usually after consultation with them as to the feasibility or desirability of
particular forms or degrees of control. The mutual confidence
and understanding that had developed over the years under
these arrangements suffered a setback in May 1968, when a
new lending ceiling was indicated to the banks at extremely
short notice and, as they maintained, without 'adequate prior
consultation'; following discussions with the authorities they
were allowed a 'reasonable time' within which to meet the
new requirement. Likewise the special deposits arrangement,
though bankers have no doubts that if statutory force were
necessary to ensure observance, then it would be applied.

The system of control by 'suasion' which has developed is
readily adaptable to changing needs, and can be operated
more flexibly than could a formal code. But such a system also
has disadvantages, when monetary regulation must extend
beyond the relatively small number of clearing banks and
discount houses with which the authorities are able to maintain close contact. As other financial intermediaries have
grown in importance, the authorities have found it necessary
to indicate to them also criteria and levels to be observed in
their lending. However the suspicion remains, certainly in the
clearing banks, that the quantitative and qualitative controls
do not bear as hardly on some of the non-bank sources of
credit. Nor are other institutions subject to cash and liquidity
ratio requirements, or to Special Deposits, as are the clearing

[13] Woods, E. C., articles in *New Law Journal*, 27 February, 12 and 19 June,
1969 and 'How big is grandma's stick?', *Bankers' Magazine*, July 1969.

banks, although the embryonic cash deposits scheme might be regarded as a move in this direction.

Another disadvantage of the present system is that the wishes of the authorities may lack precision and be misunderstood, a danger illustrated two years ago when considerable confusion existed among the clearing banks as to what the official attitude was to mergers between them.[14]

Thus a case can be made for asking whether, in a changing situation, methods of implementing policy also need to be reconsidered.[15] The more important question, however, concerns the objective of the authorities as regards the clearing banks, in particular, following the Radcliffe prescription, that of trying to control their lending directly. Frequent resort to lending 'directives' has demonstrably weakened competition between the banks, and has stifled new initiatives. In the light especially of the recent significant change in emphasis and objectives in official policy, bringing pressures on the banks quite different—at least in degree—to anything experienced for many years, then, the traditional methods of bringing policy to bear on the clearing banks also call for serious reconsideration, by the banks themselves, perhaps, as much as by the authorities.

SELECT BIBLIOGRAPHY OF ARTICLES

Bank of England Quarterly Bulletin
'The procedure of special deposits', December 1960.
'Bank liquidity in the United Kingdom', December 1962.
'The management of money day by day', March 1963.
'The U.K. banking sector 1952–67', June 1969.

Midland Bank Review
Annual Monetary Surveys (unbroken series in May issue, 1950 onwards).
'The Radcliffe Report and the Banks', November 1959.
'Three Credit Squeezes—Similarities and Contrasts', November 1965.

[14] See Monopolies Commission report on the proposed merger of Barclays Bank, Lloyds Bank and Martins Bank, para. 48 (July 1968).
[15] See J. S. G. Wilson, 'Regulation and Control of the United Kingdom Banking and Financial Structure', *Banca Nazionale del Lavoro Quarterly Review*, June 1969.

'Banking Regulation in Britain—by "Suasion" not Statute', November 1967.
'Money Supply and the Banks', February 1969.
'Managing the Gilt-Edged Market—A Temporary Change of Emphasis?', May 1969.

Westminster Bank Review
'Background to the Banking Scene 1951–64', February 1965.
'Changes in the Banking Scene—1951–64', May 1965.

Lloyds Bank Review
Manning Dacey, W., 'Treasury bills and the money supply', January 1960.

Economica
Bell, G. L. and Berman, L. S., 'Changes in the money supply in the United Kingdom', May 1966.

Manchester School
Coppock, D. J. and Gibson, N. J., 'The volume of deposits and the cash and liquid assets ratios', September 1963.

Oxford Economic Papers
Crouch, R. L., 'A re-examination of open market operations', June 1963.

Discussion Papers

(a) P. DAVIDSON
(Rutgers—The State University, New Jersey, U.S.A.)

ANY discussion of the growth of monetary and financial institutions can focus on at least four different, but not necessarily independent aspects. These are:

1. *The efficiency of financial institutions' operations.* This is primarily a technical question, a sort of production function problem involving laws of returns.

2. *Equity considerations.* For example, is the growth and evolution of financial institutions related to price discrimination against certain borrowers or sub-market borrowers? Do bankers make overly large profits for performing a public service for which they have a semi-monopolistic franchise?

3. *Monetary effects on the real domestic sector and the international sector.* For example, how does the growth of financial institutions affect aggregate output levels? The Radcliffe Report suggests two possible mechanisms through which monetary changes operate on the real sector. These are (*a*) the interest incentive effect which recognizes that changes in the rate of discount will change the present value of any given income stream and therefore alter the demand price for capital goods, and (*b*) the general liquidity effect, or what I would call the availability of finance effect. The Radcliffe Report, in my opinion, tends to downplay the importance of the quantity of bank money in this latter effect by rolling it into the portmanteau concept of the 'whole liquidity position of the economy'. This view seems, at times, almost to disregard the fact that borrowers must have bank money if they are to make their demand-price calculations of investment projects operational in the capital goods markets. Since the ability of

businessmen significantly to increase their demand for investment goods by arranging for increased clearings of debts outside of the banking system is, in the short period, extremely
limited, any increase in the availability of bank money to
markets where there is an 'unsatisfied fringe of borrowers'
will result in a significant increase in the demand for goods.

4. *Resource allocation.* The differential growth and evolution
of financial institutions will affect the allocation of resources
not only between employment and unemployment, but also
between the consumption and investment sectors, and among
industries in each sector.

In the traditional course in monetary economics, the money
market is often assumed to operate as a 'perfect market'.
Under such a view, all potential borrowers have equal access
to the market, and given the supply of funds, it is the borrowers
with the highest expectations of profits who gain the necessary
claims to bid for real resources.

In the real world, however, the financial industry is a highly
structured, segregated, and oligopolistic community. Certain
borrowers are likely to be discriminated against, although the
magnitude of discrimination may well be different in periods
of slack demand than in periods of high demand for credit.
Legal, institutional, and customary factors including such
things as accounting rules, safety rules on portfolio composition, etc. tend to perpetuate this discrimination which not only
gives rise to some of the equity questions suggested in item 2
but also alters the allocation of resources from what it would
be in a perfect market.

Another way of viewing this aspect could be developed as
follows. In the absence of financial institutions each income
receiving unit would have to plow its savings into tangible
goods, and resource allocation would largely depend on the
units' view of what physical goods were a good store of value.
With growth of financial institutions, a mechanism is provided which permits (but does not require) the efficient transfer of command of real resources from economic units that
wish to spend less than income to units that wish to spend
more. Nevertheless, it should be made clear that such a system

does not guarantee that the abstaining households will be able to command, in the future, as much resources as they relinquish at the present time. Nor does it require that those who abstain gain title to the increment of real wealth which such abstinence permits.

Moreover if abstinence exceeds the desire of other units to spend in excess of their income, the services of the real resources will be wasted, while if the excess spending of these latter units exceeds abstinence when resources are already fully employed, financial institutions can permit some units to outbid others for resources so that some units may have involuntarily to relinquish command over real resources. These questions of voluntary and forced abstinence, the ownership of real wealth, and the ability to make economic provision for the future raise questions about equity of a different type than those in item 2 above.

I wish now to comment on five topics raised by Mr. Clark in his extremely interesting paper. My comments will be primarily concerned with items 2 and 3 above.

1. Mr. Clark indicates that monetary controls in the 'sixties have been continually tightening while the trend of the pre-Radcliffe 'fifties was that of monetary ease. This difference in trend should, *ceteris paribus*, exacerbate commercial bank policies of discriminating between types of borrowers. To the extent that this discrimination leaves large sub-markets with little or no access to credit, but with large potential profits if finance can be made available, there is an incentive for either maverick bankers or outsiders to attempt to service these potentially lucrative sub-markets. Custom and tradition being as strong as it is in the U.K., it is not surprising that the presence of these potentially profitable sub-markets has encouraged the establishment of new financial institutions, which can take advantage of arbitrage between the quoted costs of borrowing from the clearing banks and the bid prices of the borrowers discriminated against.

Nevertheless this type of arbitrage behaviour cannot go on forever without the traditional sources of credit taking some steps to avoid the complete loss of these discriminated markets, partly because these older institutions hope to salvage some segment of these sub-markets for the future when credit conditions ease. Thus the rate spread on loans and overdrafts above Bank rate will rise to discourage others from borrowing at the clearing banks in order to re-lend to one of the disadvantaged borrowers.

Furthermore, the clearing banks can stake out a claim on these discriminated sub-markets by forming subsidiaries, whereas they would break the rules of the 'money game' if they were to expand into these markets through a department of the parent bank. For example, Clark suggests that if a subsidiary buys equities, it has not violated the rule against participation in equities by clearing banks. Moreover, by the establishment of a subsidiary, overhead costs are separated from the parent operation, allowing more flexibility in the pricing and bilateral bargaining on loan transactions than might be allowed by the accounting practices of the more conventional parent organization.

2. The widespread use of the overdraft in the U.K. as compared to the fixed loan approach of the U.S. commercial banks shifts some of the risks of illiquidity from the business firms to the banks. Thus firms need less precautionary balances if they have unused overdraft facilities, while banks need larger precautionary balances. To the extent that there are economies of scale in the demand for precautionary balances, the overdraft system makes a more efficient use of funds for any given quantity of money than the fixed loan system, as far as society is concerned. Even so, from the viewpoint of the banks it means that, at any point of time, less can be lent out at interest. Since the production of bank money involves no real resources, it is not obvious that this efficiency improves welfare, except for the fact that, in my opinion, central bankers tend to pursue the wrong social objectives. Thus, the overdraft system permits the economy to expand further, for any given credit squeeze, than the fixed loan system. Given the Bank rate, however, the clearing banks are bearing the entire cost of providing this more efficient use of funds and it is therefore not surprising to find Mr. Clark indicating that the tight

monetary policy is pushing the clearing banks into preferring fixed loans to overdrafts. In addition, Clark's suggestion of regularizing compensating balances as a feature of bank loans would further push the costs of maintaining precautionary balances onto the borrowers. In a world of uncertainty, the need for precautionary balances is a necessary adjunct of a viable monetary system, but whether the banks or the borrowers should pay the costs is, at least partly, a question of equity.

If there are no tacit agreements among financial institutions, competition for inputs may raise their price and therefore ultimately increase the price of output. This is particularly likely to occur if the existing market price does not clear the market of borrowers. If the total money supply in the system is fixed by the central bank then higher rates on funds flowing into the various financial institutions merely increase the economic rents paid to the depositors. (Of course, to the extent that different rates on deposits are paid by different financial institutions, this will affect the flow of funds from one institution to another.)

Economic units keep funds in current accounts for the usual liquidity preference motives. The use of such a repository is appealing to the individual because of the negligible cost of converting from this store of value to the medium of exchange; hence it should not be necessary to pay owners of these funds in order to encourage them to maintain their current accounts. In fact, one can view the account balance as a payment to the bank for providing an asset which can serve the dual functions of money without cost and with maximum safety from loss, fire, or theft.

If, however, banks simultaneously provide an interest-bearing bank account form which, though legally requiring seven days notice, in practice permits one to move from the store of value to the medium of exchange on demand without cost, then as long as the interest payment exceeds the convenience of cheque writing (as opposed to travelling to the bank office and standing in a queue to obtain the medium of exchange), the inconvenience costs of converting from store of value to medium of exchange for deposit accounts has been overcome and the deposit account becomes a superior store of value. As Clark notes, rising interest rates on deposit accounts have produced movement in this direction. If it was not for uncertainty as to when specific payments were to become due and to legal restrictions as to who may have deposit accounts, the transfer from current accounts to deposit accounts would probably be considerably greater than the banks have so far experienced.

This will, of course, have sharp effects on bank earnings and the level of economic rents paid to depositors. It is not surprising therefore to find that such a potential adverse impact on bank earnings in this oligopolistic industry encourages tacit agreements on input prices. Of course, if the oligopoly power in the industry is too diffuse for informal agreements to bind all the producers, then, as in the U.S., government regulation may be necessary to prevent impairments to the liquidity of some financial institutions, as funds flow from one financial institution to another in response to changing competitive input price offers.

3. The growth of the Euro-dollar market has, at least for the U.S., required the Monetary Authority to tighten the monetary screw even further than otherwise in order to achieve the slackness in the domestic goods markets which the Federal Reserve believed was essential for combating inflation. Regardless of the merits or otherwise of the Federal Reserve's policy, the existence of a parallel market such as the Euro-dollar market, while not unduly hampering the Fed.'s ability to raise the prime rate, did severely constrain its ability to limit the growth in the credit supply. As long as any system of fixed exchange rates remain, therefore, the existence of such large 'parallel' markets can, as Clark notes, hamper the Monetary Authority's ability to affect real output via what Radcliffe called the general liquidity effect.

Moreover, I would agree with Clark that the existence of such markets *need not* imply the transmission of high interest rates from one country to another. If such apparent transmission occurs it is probably due to deliberate central bank policy attempting to change the nation's balance of payments by affecting the international lending balance rather than policy aimed directly at either the trade balance or the existing exchange rate. Accordingly I would blame deliberate policy rather than 'the world hunger for capital', as Clark suggests, as the mechanism of high interest-rate transmission.

4. The requirement that local authorities must behave as if they were merely another borrower in the private sector, while the national government's borrowing is (unless the masochistic views of politicians and central bankers interfere) supported by the central bank, is, as far as I am concerned, an archaic anomaly of the Dark Ages in economic thinking. Co-ordination of all governmental borrowing and taxation is such an obviously desirable social objective that I am at a loss to explain why more progress has not been made in this area. If it is in the social interest for local governments to command real resources, then the transfer of claims for resources should be effected in the most expeditious manner without, as a matter of equity, leaving a large perpetual burden of financial claims on the future.

5. The reduction in the number of clearing banks since the Radcliffe Report, even if stimulated by production economies of scale, must result in an even tighter oligopolistic structure than before, particularly if foreign and overseas banks do not compete for, or at least do not solicit, domestic loans. As the number of members of such an oligopolistic system declines, the probability increases that their individual views on what 'good' banking practices are will be similar, so that tacit agreements will more readily arise even when they are not even recognized as such by the parties involved. Furthermore, increased public scrutiny of the remaining clearing banks assures that no one bank—at least under the aegis of the parent firm—behaves unconventionally. Simultaneously, the reduction in numbers will make it easier for bankers to discourage their customers from seeking alternative sellers, lowering the effective cross-elasticity of demand among the remaining banks. Under such circumstances, the equity questions become more important and may require continual

surveillance of bank charges by the National Prices and Incomes Board.

A study of Professor Almarin Phillips reported in the *Federal Reserve Bulletin* (July 1967) showed that after adjusting for loan size, bank size, geographical region, and time (which was a proxy for monetary policy and interest rate levels), there is a significant association between the rate charged on loans by banks, and banking concentration. If this relationship carries over to the U.K., then the merging of the clearing banks should, *ceteris paribus*, increase borrowing costs. This would ultimately involve questions of equity between the borrowers and the banks which is a particularly difficult problem if there still remains a fringe of unsatisfied borrowers. The central bank can still maintain control over aggregate demand for any given set of circumstances (unless we are in a liquidity trap) by altering the quantity of credit.

Competition between the clearing banks and other financial intermediaries is, as Clark points out, quite a separate question. Nevertheless, since different financial institutions cultivate different submarkets, such competition will lead to both a reallocation of resources depending on which borrowers ultimately receive the funds and a possible redistribution of bank discrimination practices.

Discussion Papers

(b) A. B. CRAMP
(Fellow of Emmanuel College, Cambridge)

THIS comment will concentrate on J. E. Maycock's lucid summary of the impact of monetary policy on the clearing banks in the 1960s. The broad picture emerging from a decade's perspective differs little from one's impressions built up from day-to-day observation over the years. The picture shows the clearing banks operating in a straitjacket, due to the near-continuous use by the authorities of lending directives of a type visualized in the Radcliffe Report as an emergency weapon of last resort. And if, notwithstanding, deposit totals (the primary focus of interest in current monetary debate) have grown only a little less slowly than national income (p. 174), they would have grown a good deal faster had the banks been released from the advances straitjacket.

Or would they? For advances account for only half the clearers' assets. There is nothing in directives about advances that impedes expansion of the other half, of which the bulk consists of some form or another of holdings of government debt (direct, or indirect via the discount market). In the absence of 'investments directives' and 'liquid assets directives', the banks could have been prevented from securing larger increases in their government debt holdings only by policy measures directed successfully at restricting their deposit totals.

As is well known, and as Mr. Maycock reminds us, the authorities have (until very recently at least) refrained from any serious attempt to impose such restriction by the text-book ratio mechanisms. Cash ratio control has not been exercised because (p. 164) of official preference for stability of the Treasury bill rate. Liquid asset ratio control has been neutralized by expansion of 'exempted' liquid assets (p. 184) and by banks' sales of gilt-edged securities (p. 185) the authorities, of course, frequently being the purchaser. I would suggest, then, that one gap in Mr. Maycock's paper is his failure to consider explicitly why the banks have not offset the effect on their deposits of restrictions on their advances by competing for an increased share of the rather plentiful supply of government debt.

A large part of the answer surely lies in the fact that the clearers have in their own businesses (whatever may be true of their subsidiaries' operations, p. 172) behaved in a manner that can usefully be labelled 'docile'. Docility in this context refers to their adherence to the convention linking deposit rates to Bank rate, so that in competing for deposits they have (with varying degrees of official blessing and criticism, pp. 167–72) fought with one arm behind their back.

The significance of this docility is clarified by contrasting it with the 'dynamic' methods of the clearers' United States counterparts in the 1960s. One of the puzzles of the U.K. banking scene has been the apparent failure of the clearers to observe, and to draw conclusions from, the spectacularly successful competition for deposits (and lending opportunities) by the American commercial banks which at times (notably in 1966) threatened U.S. non-bank financial intermediaries with extremely severe liquidity problems.

In the U.K. the non-banks have not only avoided such problems but have thrived, for which fact Mr. Maycock presents the 'Radcliffian' explanation that their rates have risen (p. 176) and they have used the resulting deposit increments to satisfy the needs of borrowers deflected from the banks (p. 183).

However in the absence of changes in tastes or in the 'quality' of different financial assets, the non-banks could have attracted deposits by rate competition only if their rates rose relatively to those of the clearers. The performance of U.S. banks might surely have called into question the standard defence of the clearers' rate cartel—repeated by Mr. Maycock

(p. 176)—that there is no clear-cut mechanism linking gains of deposits by non-bank financial institutions with a decline in the (absolute) level of bank deposits.

Mr. Maycock gives a neutral mention (pp. 170-1) of the Prices and Incomes Board's attempt to formulate such a mechanism, the argument leading along the chain: more non-bank deposits, more non-bank credit, higher aggregate demand and inflationary pressures, official measures to reduce bank lending and deposits. The weak link in the chain, as has already been implied, is the last, for it is based on a misconception of the objectives and techniques of post-war monetary policy, which has not been directed towards (short-period) control of bank deposits.

I want to suggest that we can replace the last link in the P.I.B.'s chain with a much stronger one. The revised chain would trace the sequence: more non-bank deposits, more non-bank credit, higher aggregate demand and incomes, more savings, and (*given* the M.P.P.S.G.D.—the marginal propensity to place savings in government debt) larger non-bank private sector demand for such debt. This demand would (given the debt management policy of smoothing gilt-edged price and yield movements) be satisfied by the authorities. Hence, less government debt for the docile banks. On this view, the banks have contentedly but quite unnecessarily accepted the passive role of 'residual holders of government debt'.

It seems that Mr. Maycock's picture of the authorities' clamp-down on the banks' access to private sector debt needs to be complemented by recognition that the banks have in effect (if not in intention) limited their own access to public sector debt. And that does represent a significant modification of the overall picture he has given us.

Discussion Papers

(c) G. CLAYTON
(University of Sheffield)

THIS conference is an eloquent testimony to the upsurge of interest in monetary economics which, I cannot help reflecting, would have given a great deal of wry amusement to Sir Dennis Robertson if he were alive today. He, more than anyone else, kept alive the Marshallian tradition in monetary theory during the early post-war years when it was neither popular nor fashionable, and the only reward for his pains was a great deal of undeserved and ill-mannered ridicule.

In approaching the task of commenting on the papers delivered at this session it was originally my intention to confine my remarks mainly to Mr. Maycock's contribution, but by arrangement with Dr. A. B. Cramp I have decided to make some general remarks on the growth of British financial intermediaries since Radcliffe which is a common theme of them all. I wish to concentrate on theoretical and practical aspects and the impact of contemporary monetary policy on the efficiency of intermediation.

All three contributors have commented on the continued growth of financial intermediaries which on general grounds is not a development to be deplored since financial intermediaries are an aid to the efficient allocation of resources. Improvements in their efficiency are analogous to increases in productivity and innovation in industry and have an important influence on economic growth and welfare. At the same time, as the Radcliffe Committee pointed out, the non-bank financial intermediaries constitute a potential threat to monetary policy in that, if the monetary authorities seek to restrain the expansion of the level of money income by stabilizing the stock of bank deposits and currency, the intermediaries can prove an embarrassment by raising the income velocity of circulation.

The Radcliffe Committee, because it believed that there was no reason for supposing that there is any limit to the velocity of circulation (para. 391), saw no salvation for the monetary authorities in operating on the supply of money. Another strand in its thinking which influenced its policy prescriptions was the fear that widely fluctuating rates of interest might seriously weaken the capital and reserve positions of financial intermediaries. From this the Committee developed its emphasis on the need to influence general liquidity.

Theoretical discussion since Radcliffe has emphasized that the extent to which the activities of non-bank financial intermediaries are destabilizing depends on the elasticity of substitution between idle bank deposits, which are an element in asset-holders' wealth, and their own debt and how far they are willing to bid up the reward offered to the holders of their liabilities, which in turn depends upon the prospective return on their assets. To solve this problem adequately a rigorous general equilibrium analysis is required which has not yet been attempted in the U.K. for obvious reasons. Nevertheless we can highlight some of the major theoretical issues.

One of the most difficult and intractable problems is concerned with the practical difficulty of identifying 'equilibrium' and 'disequilibrium' situations. Our contributors have pointed both to the growth of non-bank financial intermediaries and the increase in income velocity during the 'fifties and 'sixties. *Prima facie* this establishes a case for believing that the intermediaries' activities have been responsible for the observed rise in velocity. But the evidence can be interpreted differently if it is argued that what we have been observing during the last twenty-odd years in the United Kingdom has been a reallocation by asset-holders of their portfolios involving a reduction in their relative holdings of bank deposits. It may then be concluded that the undoubted increase in income velocity reflects a long-term adjustment to a more 'normal' level of velocity, which puts the role of intermediaries in a very different light.

Another crucial problem arises from the difficulty in determining whether the growth of financial intermediaries can be attributed to substitution or income effects. When I tackled this problem in an article in the *Economic Journal* in December 1962, I suggested that the expansion of intermediary debt might simply reflect the growth in personal savings in the 'fifties and that the observed rise in income velocity could be attributed to the public switching from idle deposits into equities and fixed-interest securities. I doubt whether I would now offer this as an explanation with any greater confidence. But the substitution effect remains the key to the problem. Our contributors have provided us with firm evidence that the financial intermediaries have continued to grow relatively to the clearing banks but this growth is a function of both the income and substitution effects. Unfortunately, since we have as yet failed to undertake the necessary statistical analysis to distinguish between these effects, the only tenable position remains one of agnosticism.

Let us now turn to a consideration of the impact of monetary policy on the efficiency of intermediation during the 'sixties. Mr. Maycock has shown what a battery of qualitative and quantitative controls, supported by moral suasion, the monetary authorities have employed in recent years to curb monetary demand. The situation is not unlike that of a railway signalman who, having been informed that on his section of the line there is a train out of control through brake failure, reacts by pulling every lever in his box and finally throwing a hand-grenade out of his window in the hope that somehow it will be brought to a stop. There is little doubt that the measures adopted have had an adverse effect on the efficiency of intermediation as the Radcliffe Committee suggested it might. 'Any severely restrictive control of their (the commercial banks') operations is certain over a period of time, to be defeated by the development of rival institutions; during the interim, the community will have suffered loss by interference with the most efficient channels of lending' (para. 504).

This has been true not only of the banks but of other intermediaries such as those providers of consumer credit who, while their own activities have been restricted, have seen other bodies such as check traders able to make inroads on their business.

The efficiency of intermediation is also reduced by monopolistic and restrictive practices such as the commercial banks' cartel arrangements. Since Dr. Cramp deals with this point more extensively, I content myself with observing that I remain unconvinced by Mr. Clark's argument that the failure of the banks to compete for deposits does not mean that they lose such deposits. If new lending by the financial intermediaries augments the income flow, some of the additional flow of saving thus created will be used by the public to make additions to their holdings of financial assets. In making their decisions the public will be influenced by the relative yields of various financial assets; if the commercial banks collectively make no effort to increase the relative attractiveness of their debt, the demand for bank deposits will be less than it otherwise would be.

I also remain unconvinced by Mr. Clark's arguments in favour of the commercial banks' working through subsidiaries rather than through their own departments. In particular his suggestion that the latter policy would lead to the acquisition of inappropriate assets seems redolent of that old red-herring, the self-liquidating principle. British commercial bankers have tended to draw the wrong lessons (including the need for secrecy) from the catastrophes of the Great Depression when many banks in Europe and the United States failed while the British commercial banking system emerged unscathed. While it would be wrong to ignore the structural weaknesses of the continental and American banking systems, a major cause of the collapse was the inappropriate policies pursued by the monetary authorities. In this issue of long-term versus short-term lending by commercial banks the liquidity aspect is not important in that, if it came to such a pass that the banks were forced to liquidate large blocks of assets, the central authority would have to step in anyway. The real point is that the risks are greater in long-term finance because there is a greater possibility of eventual loss and the safeguards are of a different character if a bank is guarding against eventual loss rather than against a need for liquidity. Long-term realizability must be a criterion for judging the suitability of long-term assets. One of the lessons of the German bank failures is that they could in part be attributed to a lack of centralized control with the result that the main administration was not always aware of the extent of their commitments to given sectors of the economy. There are advantages in the managements of the banks being fully aware of the extent of both their short-term and long-term commitments and the use of subsidiaries does not ensure this. But this is a large topic and there is insufficient time to develop it further here.

The main point is that both the extreme interventionism exercised by the monetary authorities in recent years and the commercial banks' own practices have tended to impair the efficiency of financial intermediation. It is to be hoped that, once we emerge from this period of constant preoccupation with the balance of payments, the monetary authorities will move away from its present 'finger in the dike' policies of monetary intervention and experiment with policies designed to improve and strengthen market mechanisms instead of frustrating them. They might even come to rely almost entirely on open market operations for controlling the financial system—or is that too utopian for words?

SUMMARY OF THE GENERAL DISCUSSION

THE major theme of the general discussion was competition between banks and other financial intermediaries, and within the banking sector itself. To many of the academic economists there seemed little to justify the banking sector's cartel arrangements, which may be responsible for the slow growth of the clearing banks relative to non-clearing intermediaries, and which lead to mis-allocation of resources. American experience suggests that banks could provide strong competition for non-bank intermediaries, and that this might even lead to maximum deposit-rate fixing by the authorities to stop the banks from sweeping the board.

Against this it was suggested that competition could never come about while the banking system remained under the tight restraints it had experienced in the 1960s. When banks had grown through opening subsidiary companies to bid for deposits, they had experienced tighter controls on their regular business as the authorities had tried to regain control of the monetary sector. But, even when the monetary authorities are fixing bank lending and borrowing rates it is still possible for individual banks to alter their rates by varying the terms on which they make loans or the services they provide for deposit holders. In this connection the discussion raised the possibility of a move by U.K. banks to a greater concentration on 'liabilities management' rather than on asset management. Bankers justified their suggestions that the overdraft system should be replaced by fixed loans, and that holding compensating balances might be made a feature of lending, by claiming that this would give them more certainty in forecasting the level of their deposits and would release them from having to hold reserves against unexpected drawings on overdraft facilities. It was suggested that these devices merely transferred uncertainty from the banks to their depositors, but the discussion about the effects of these changes on the overall efficiency of the economic system proved inconclusive. For monetary policy purposes the switch would give more stability in the measurement of the money stock, but might add to uncertainty in trying to predict velocity.

It was doubtful whether the move to compensating balances would help bank profits because the banks' increased rate of return on the loan would be partially offset by the cost of holding reserves against the balances. Studies had suggested that the U.K. practice of levying service charges to help meet the costs associated with lending led to greater efficiency than the U.S. practice of requiring borrowers to hold part of their loan on deposit.

Competition might be brought about by widening the membership of the bankers' clearing house, and by banks looking for ways to extend the banking habit. There seemed to be no reason why the first should not be done, but it was suggested that the banking industry might be reluctant to encourage more high-cost, small-depositor business. They would respond to changes in the economy by moving towards an American 'one-stop' banking system, and would probably supply a greater range of specialized assets and liabilities to meet the demands of portfolio managers whose needs are becoming increasingly more detailed. However, the suggestion that they might grow by extending their lending on government bonds seemed implausible after the experience of bondholders since 1967, in which both the fall in capital value and the variability of prices have made bonds an unattractive asset.

Another line of discussion took up the question of the optimum controls the authorities should place on the banking system. Bankers rejected controls on their advances, even though it was pointed out that the advances ceiling might be vitiated by the squeeze on bank liquidity forecast for the near future. In place of advances control, bankers would prefer policies which operated along lines which they would follow in normal business operations, probably a required cash and liquidity ratio at levels which ordinary financial prudence would dictate. However, such control would be difficult so long as the authorities were not willing to make it expensive for banks to get cash because of possible repercussions on bond markets, and while specialized financial intermediaries could always provide cash for banks at rates below penal Bank rate. All discussants were agreed on the need for control of the supply of nominal money. However, some speakers claimed that the criteria for judging policy should be whether it was successful, without paying much regard to the allocative effects of the policy, while others stressed that the major tests of policies should be based on their effect on the institutions of the financial sector.

V

THE OPERATION OF MONETARY POLICY SINCE RADCLIFFE

A paper prepared in the Bank of England in consultation with the Treasury

Discussion Papers

(*a*) R. F. G. ALFORD
(*b*) J. R. WINTON

V

THE OPERATION OF MONETARY POLICY SINCE RADCLIFFE

A paper prepared in the Bank of England in consultation with the Treasury

I. INTRODUCTION

IF the fundamental nature of the economic difficulties confronting the United Kingdom has perhaps not altered over the past decade, the difficulties have certainly become much more severe. There have at the same time been dramatic developments in financial institutions and markets, both domestically and internationally. In these circumstances, and especially as some of the limitations of demand management through fiscal policy have been revealed, there has been considerable evolution in the methods and tactics of monetary policy. Broadly, however, the approach to policy has been similar to that of the Radcliffe Committee in that the authorities have consistently believed that it was right to pay attention to and try to understand the general financial position of all sectors of the economy and insufficient to concentrate exclusively on a single variable such as the quantity of money, however that may be defined.

This paper begins with a brief survey of some of the developments in the general economic context within which monetary policy has had to work. This is followed by a discussion of the actual operation of policy over the period—the broad approach followed, the problems and complications which have been encountered and the responses which have been made in methods and tactics. Finally, there is an attempt to assess the effects of monetary policy, both in itself and in relation to fiscal policy.

II. THE CONTEXT OF MONETARY POLICY

(a) *The Economic Problems and Objectives*

During the ten years since 1959 official policy has been particularly concerned to achieve two major economic objectives—the acceleration of the sustainable rate of growth of the economy and the rectification of the balance of payments—without sacrificing the goal of a high level of employment to which all post-war British governments have been committed. Though the Radcliffe Committee discussed both these objectives, they were, perhaps, not as acutely aware as we are today of the difficulty of pursuing both of them at the same time. Nor was the problem of the balance of payments as serious then as it became later. Indeed, the Committee looked back (para. 633) to 'a substantial surplus on current account over the past ten years' suggesting 'no fundamental lack of balance in the United Kingdom's trading position'. The repeated exchange crises had, in the Committee's view, been due not 'to any failure on the part of the United Kingdom to pay her way but to the velocity of various elements in the balance of payments and to the lack of reserves adequate to withstand the resulting pressure on them'.

In the attempts made by successive administrations since 1959 to foster an acceleration of the United Kingdom's growth rate by official policies, monetary policy was seen as having primarily a permissive role. In the earlier part of the period, when it was hoped it would be possible to provide a long-term solution to the balance of payments problem through an acceleration of the increase in national productivity, monetary policy therefore occupied a somewhat subsidiary role. Monetary measures were largely taken, as had been common in the earlier period, as supporting elements in general 'packages' of measures. Later, as a short-term conflict between the balance of payments and domestic expansion—especially expansion not centred on productive capital expenditures—became increasingly strong, economic policy had increasingly to be directed to the short-term balance of payments problem. The earlier conception of prolonged periods of relatively permissive monetary policy punctuated only occasionally by bouts of short-lived severe measures gave way to the prolonged use of stringent measures of all kinds. Moreover, as the limits of effectiveness of fiscal policies, incomes policies and exchange controls appeared to be more nearly reached, the relative emphasis placed on monetary policy increased.

(b) International Developments

Externally, the Radcliffe Committee looked back on the years of the dollar shortage, inconvertible European currencies and relatively low levels for interest rates throughout the world. Although the United States had by 1959 already moved into the position of substantial external deficit which has been maintained ever since, this major change was not yet widely recognized. The Committee suggest (para. 684) that the problem of dollar shortage might be 'more intermittent and less intractable than is sometimes supposed, and that it has already changed in character and is likely to continue to do so'; but they did not believe 'that the rest of the world, including the United Kingdom, can safely dismiss from its calculations any future difficulty in effecting settlements with the United States'. Certainly they did not foresee the problem of dollar surplus.

The major European currencies only became fully convertible in 1958 and there were a number of liberalizing moves in the next few years. As a result the 'sixties have seen an international mobility of short-term capital on a scale unprecedented since pre-war days.

The prolonged U.S. deficit and the convertibility of major currencies have had several important consequences for the operation of U.K. monetary policy. One was the enormous growth of the Euro-dollar market, which barely existed in 1959 and now amounts to some $40 billion. London is, of course, the major centre for Euro-dollar transactions, and the effects of this development on the structure of both financial institutions and financial markets in the United Kingdom are discussed briefly below. A further effect has been that both in 1966–7 and 1968–9 a restrictive U.S. monetary policy has had a substantial influence on short-term flows and on international interest rate levels. Although 'covered margins' have ceased to have the significance they previously had, they obviously remain important.

(c) The Central Government Borrowing Requirement

The period has been marked by a rapid growth in the borrowing requirement of the central government—from a position of approximate balance in 1958–9 to £1,335 million in 1967–8—and by a similar increase in the borrowing requirement of the public sector as a whole. Implicit in this trend is the problem of ensuring that public expenditure does not pre-empt an excessive share of the growth of real resources. But there are monetary problems, too, in financing a deficit for the public sector; and as the deficit grew, the means of financing it had increasingly severe implications for finance in the private sector. The Radcliffe Committee reported (in para. 528) that they could 'find no automatic rule for restricting a Government that is determined to spend'. Ten years later we are still without an automatic rule. But much effort has been, and is being, devoted to improving the statistics and the administrative techniques for keeping public spending and borrowing on course. The results are already apparent in a striking reversal since 1967–8: the central government has moved from a deficit of £1,335 million in 1967–8 to a surplus of £273 million in 1968–9. And in 1969–70 not only the central government but the whole public sector should be in a position to make a net repayment of debt. This in turn will have unfamiliar consequences for finance in the rest of the economy.

(d) Institutional Financial Developments

In 1959 the deposit banks (the London Clearing Banks, together with the Scottish and Northern Ireland Banks) accounted for 85 per cent of the total sterling deposits of the U.K. banking sector. By 1968 they had increased their deposits by about two-thirds; but their share of total sterling deposits had fallen to 75 per cent, as the sterling deposits of the accepting houses, overseas banks, and other banks trebled, from about £1,000 million to £3,000 million. Meanwhile the rapid growth of the Euro-dollar market has resulted in an increase in foreign currency deposits from a few hundred million in 1959 to about £16,000 million now. Not only has the business of existing banks in London increased, but also many overseas banks have been encouraged by the development of the Euro-dollar market to set up new offices or branches in London. The total number of banks in London has risen by more than 50 per cent since 1959. The deposit banks have, however, been inhibited from directly taking in any significant amount of foreign currency deposits by their cash and liquidity ratios which make it difficult for these banks to employ such deposits profitably—though many of them have been able to participate in the business through their subsidiaries. Their share of the U.K. banking sector's total sterling and foreign currency deposits has thus fallen to 50 per cent.

The overall growth of the accepting houses, overseas banks and other U.K. banks has had a number of important consequences for policy. Restriction of the lending of the deposit banks alone would have been increasingly inequitable and ineffective in restricting total bank credit; on the other hand, the structures of the balance sheets of the other banks differ so greatly from those of the deposit banks and from one another, that control over their lending by means of balance sheet ratios poses difficult problems, and the possibility of switching in and out of foreign currency has had implications for the balance of payments, interest rate policy, and exchange control.

(e)   *Developments of Financial Markets*

As striking as the growth of the accepting houses and over-seas banks, and very closely linked with it, has been the growth of new short-term financial markets unknown, or relatively unimportant, when the Radcliffe Report was written. The Euro-dollar market has already been mentioned. Domestically the parallel money markets—the market in sterling inter-bank funds and the market for local authority deposits (each attracting about 8 per cent of the assets of the accepting houses, overseas, and other banks)—have grown up alongside the Treasury bill market; interest rates in these markets are not in any fixed or conventional relation to Treasury bill rates. More recently, important markets first in dollar, then in sterling certificates of deposit have grown up. There has also been a strong revival of the use of commercial bills over the ten-year period.

(*f*)   *Developments in Information*

Finally, a very important change has occurred in the information available to the policy-makers. As the magnitude of this change and the extremely short period for which usable statistics have been available are often under-rated, it may be worth saying a little about it.

The approach of the Radcliffe Committee to monetary policy, with which, as has already been indicated, the authorities have been broadly in sympathy, could not be realized without a major development in statistical information on the financial positions of all the main sectors of the economy and the flows of funds between them. The Radcliffe Committee remarked that appropriate financial statistics should 'be capable of being fitted together to show the total movement of funds and not merely the flow through individual institutions' (para. 865) and this is the aim which has been kept in mind in developing the 'flow of funds' or 'sector financing' accounts.

Six sectors are now distinguished—personal, public, banking, other financial institutions, industrial and commercial companies, and overseas. These accounts have been linked to the capital accounts of the corresponding sectors derived from the national income statistics, with the aim of explaining the financial surplus or deficit of each sector—i.e. the residual after setting the sector's capital expenditure against its savings—which is what it is presumed to have lent to, or borrowed from, other sectors. Ideally, within such a framework it should be possible to decide on appropriate measures to influence the flows of funds between sectors and their effects on real expenditures. Considerable progress has in fact been made towards using the statistics, in a rough and ready way, for these purposes. The estimates of the financial surpluses and deficits themselves cannot provide any independent check on the national income estimates and forecasts, since they are derived from them; but the process of completing the sector financing tables can often provide 'plausibility checks' by bringing to light relationships between financial and real magnitudes which are implied in the national income forecasts but look unlikely in relation to past experience (e.g. between company profits and fixed investment). More directly related to the conduct of monetary policy is the assessment of the outlook for the flows of funds between sectors. Attempts are made to forecast these flows in the light of past experience, and in particular to assess the sources from which the public sector will derive whatever it will need to borrow—or to which it may be able to repay debt.

In this field, however, although we have come a long way since 1959, it is perhaps more striking how far we have still to go. The figures go back only a very small distance: annual data (with a high degree of estimation) to 1952, quarterly data only to 1963. There are many difficulties in deriving sector figures accurately from the available statistics. There are serious conceptual problems in seasonally adjusting these financial figures, so that it is only within the last year or two that it has been possible to make a sensible attempt to do so: and we are still far from satisfied with the results. Moreover, many of the relationships are likely to vary cyclically, so that in effect four or five years' figures may provide only one set of parameters.

There is considerable delay in collecting the figures: it takes at present up to four months after the end of a quarter to assemble a set of financing accounts for that quarter. But perhaps the most important barrier to intelligent use of the financial statistics lies in the large residual errors. One of the main advantages of the technique is supposed to be that it goes beyond the statistics of financial institutions as such and displays what is happening in the company and personal sectors. Yet it is just in these two sectors that the largest residual discrepancies appear. Thus on average over the four years to 1968 over £500 million a year of net lending or spending by companies remains unexplained and over £600 million a year of net borrowing or receipts by persons is similarly unaccounted for. Discrepancies of this order naturally weaken confidence in the estimates as a whole.

Of course, the errors indicated by these discrepancies may derive at least partly from the national income and expenditure accounts. But there are certain known gaps in the sector financing accounts, outstanding among which are the lack of any adequate figures of trade credit and the lack of any regular reports by companies of their transactions in financial assets/liabilities. Attempts are being made to close these gaps, which are no doubt responsible for swelling the residual discrepancies. Meanwhile, it is useful to have constantly in view a measure of the mismatch of the two sets of data.

Whatever the shortcomings of the data, however, a position has certainly been reached where much useful analysis can be undertaken with a view to determining some of the important relationships—both between financial and real variables and within the financial framework itself. We are stepping up very sharply work of this kind in the Bank and the Treasury; and we hope to learn from work done outside—for example, from the studies on the company sector at present being done at Stirling University. Indeed, we have deliberately extended this section of this paper in the hope of stimulating interest in the academic world in work in conjunction with the authorities on areas important for policy-making.

Even if it could be compiled with reliable estimates in every box, however, the complete flow-of-funds matrix is not a handy means of communicating running comment on the latest developments, nor therefore a convenient aid to short-term policy reviews. There is a parallel need for prompt and frequent indicators as to how the underlying position is developing. Interest rates and such magnitudes as the government deficit, the level of bank advances, the sale of gilts—and of course the transactions of the Exchange Equalization Account—have long been watched. More recently, however, an aggregate comprising broadly the growth of the domestic money supply plus or minus any external deficit or surplus and styled 'domestic credit expansion' (D.C.E.) which is available relatively quickly has come into use as a helpful additional indicator.[1]

Much work remains to be done on the nature of any causal inter-relationships between D.C.E. and the important real magnitudes; but there is some indication from work already carried out of some statistically significant associations, and charts comparing the movements of D.C.E. and some expenditure series have been published in the Bank's *Quarterly Bulletin*. The stress at present laid on D.C.E. is as a prompt, shorthand supplement to, rather than a replacement of, the regular 'real' and financial forecasts for the economy. Moreover, fully to interpret and draw policy significance from movements in D.C.E. it is necessary to disaggregate it and analyse developments in its constituent parts. For this, of course, the sector financing accounts are useful.

III. POLICY DEVELOPMENTS OVER THE LAST TEN YEARS

As has already been emphasized, the official approach to policy has over the whole period laid stress on influencing the

[1] See articles in *Economic Trends* for May and *Bank of England Quarterly Bulletin* for September for the detailed composition of D.C.E.

cost or availability of credit flows to the various sectors of the economy.

Developments over the last ten years in the means of giving effect to credit policy were a continuation of a process already under way before the Radcliffe Enquiry. Credit controls have gradually become more specific and direct, in that the forms of credit to which restrictions are applied, the priorities to be observed and the exemptions to be allowed have been defined in more detail (though the authorities continue to have a strong aversion to making the banks' individual decisions for them). Moreover, various forms of control have been applied to a widening range of banks and other financial institutions have been covered.

Certain areas have been subject to quite specific control by the authorities. Thus credit extended through finance houses for the purchase of cars or customer durables has been affected by variations in the regulations concerning down-payments and the terms of repayment. Hire purchase controls were used quite actively in the 1950s and despite the Radcliffe Report's verdict that they were suitable for use only for short periods at times of emergency, they have been employed for quite long periods and the terms have been changed thirteen times since 1959. Controls were reimposed in April 1960, and were tightened progressively in June 1965, February 1966, and July 1966. Following relaxations in 1967, the controls were tightened at the time of devaluation and again in November 1968, when they reached the same level as at July 1966. There has, however, been persistent criticism of this particular weapon both because of its high specificity of effect—though this can also be seen as one of its principal advantages—and also because of a steady increase in avoidance. Official recognition of the problems of controls in this area was underlined by the appointment of the Crowther Committee (see p. 227 below).

Private housebuilding is another sector which has been subject to quite specific effects from monetary policy, not because of any direct official controls over the flow of credit through the financial intermediaries concerned, but as a result of changes in the general level of interest rates brought about by the authorities. The institutional fact that building society rates are sticky and respond to movements in general rates only partially and with a lag means that raising the general level of interest rates usually produces a marked reduction in the supply of funds available for house purchase, which in turn influences the rate of housebuilding.

Apart from these two specific areas, the authorities have concentrated their efforts in monetary policy largely on influencing lending by the banking system; but they have not attempted to achieve this by acting to reduce the cash base of the system. The authorities are always prepared to deal in Treasury bills and gilt-edged stocks at a price, because they attach importance to the maintenance of an effective market in these instruments. So any holder of such government debt—and indeed of other types of government debt such as national savings—can always switch into or out of cash at will; should the debt instrument be near to maturity, at little cost. To achieve influence over the banks' lending by means of pressure on their cash must involve conscious manipulation of interest rates primarily to that end. But in the short run at least, the market's reaction to interest changes can be perverse in the sense that the public will sell as rates rise—expecting worse to come—and is generally unpredictable. The authorities' stance has generally been to decide on an interest rate policy broadly appropriate to the general aims of economic policy at the time rather than using it to enforce a particular level of cash reserves irrespective of the wider effects of such a policy.

Broadly similar considerations govern action on the liquidity ratios of the clearing banks and Scottish banks, but it has nevertheless been possible to exert some leverage by this means. This pressure has been, on occasions, reinforced by the use of the Special Deposits Scheme. Although the first impact of a call for Special Deposits is on the banks' cash position, their normal and expected reaction is to encash enough of their liquid assets to make the payment, so that the impact is immediately transmitted to their liquidity position. Use of the

Special Deposits Scheme can also cause interest rate variations —if, for example, the banks are induced to sell gilts—which are not entirely to the liking of the authorities, but at least such a response is more calculable and subject to the influence of the authorities. The Scheme, which at the time of the Radcliffe Report had been worked out but not used, was first employed in April 1960. Except for a period of about 2½ years between 1962 and 1965, some calls on the clearing banks and Scottish banks have been outstanding ever since.

One of the authorities' problems has been that monetary restraint has frequently seemed necessary at times when it would have been difficult to sell large quantities of government debt to the public at any reasonable price. So at such times the banks often obtained additional liquid assets. Moreover in the earlier years of this decade, largely as a consequence of war-time finance, they were still holding very large quantities of liquid assets and short-dated gilts.

One solution to problems of this kind might have been to require the banks to keep their total lending to the private sector within a specified ratio to their deposits (as proposed in paragraph 527 of the Radcliffe Report). A 'private sector lending ratio' may indeed appear to have substantial advantages over a liquidity ratio, because it would be simpler in appearance and because it might be thought to be more certain in its effect. There are several reasons why the device has not been adopted. First, there are, of course, seasonal variations in lending to the private sector, so that the prescribed ratio would have to look forward to the next seasonal peak—and so look too relaxed for the intervening months— or be varied frequently in an attempt to follow the seasonal pattern. In either case it would be difficult to give the changes any clear and decisive impact. And there would be no safety-valve (such as is provided with a liquidity ratio by sales of gilt-edged). This looks at first sight like an advantage; but the practical result would probably be that the banks would fail to maintain the prescribed lending ratio, because they do not have 'instant' control over their advances and deposits. There are obvious embarrassments in prescribing a minimum ratio between quantities that are liable to large random fluctuations.

In recent years the situation has improved in one respect: the proportion of government debt in the banks' total assets has considerably declined during the past decade leaving the banks less scope for cushioning the impact of restraint by switching their lending from the public to the private sector. The problems of controlling both the credit base and monetary liquidity more generally, on the other hand, have not become significantly easier. The major difficulty is that circumstances which call for the dampening of economic activity tend to be unfavourable to government financing in non-liquid form particularly through sales of gilt-edged. Obviously the task may become more difficult at times when the central government needs to raise large amounts of new finance as it did, for example, during the bulge in public sector capital investment programmes in the middle 1960s. But even with the central government in overall surplus as at present, the position of the authorities remains vulnerable because of the constant need to refinance maturing debt.

With gilt-edged maturities currently at a rate of around £1,500 million a year, a primary official objective must continue to be that described in the *Bank of England Bulletin* in June 1966, that is 'to maintain market conditions that will maximize, both now and in the future, the desire of investors to hold British government debt'. This long-term objective obviously affects the authorities' choice of tactics in a particular short-run situation. Because the market response to a moderate price change for gilt-edged has been found to be unstable and often perverse in the short term, the movement of interest rates required to achieve adequate liquidity absorption through debt operations may be so large that a rapid or seemingly arbitrary adjustment could permanently damage the willingness of investors to hold gilt-edged, compounding the difficulties of monetary management in the future. What can be achieved at any given time is essentially a matter of judgement of the state of market expectations and of the effects upon them of alternative courses of action, both in the long and the short run, and both within and outside the gilt-edged field. This means that there can be no simple code of conduct for debt management but that each situation must be assessed in the light of the complex of circumstances then prevailing and the current aims of policy, including the need to preserve the attractiveness of the market in the longer term.

In some cases official judgement has favoured moderating considerably any movements of interest rates; in other situations, however, where the market was tending to move in a manner considered to be an appropriate adjustment to current conditions, official intervention has been on a very limited scale, allowing market forces to be much more fully reflected in prices. In the last years of the period, as greater weight has been placed on monetary policy, there has been a greater flexibility in policy on interest rates and a greater willingness to allow upward pressures on rates in the market to take effect; and this has given more scope for flexible tactics in debt management.

To allow the authorities to adapt their tactics to market conditions more readily, two changes of technique have recently been introduced in official dealings in the gilt-edged market. In July of this year it was made known that the authorities would no longer announce the price at which they were prepared to sell tap stocks, but would instead consider bids made by the market. Some two months earlier it was announced that the official buying price for stocks within three months of maturity would for the time being not be tied to the Treasury bill rate, but that the Government Broker remained ready to receive offers of such stock.

In practice during the past ten years the level of interest rates has fluctuated considerably, and there is little evidence that a more active approach would have been more effective. For example, even with yields at the historically high levels of the recent past, it was not at all clear that official sales of stock would have been increased in the short term by lowering prices still further, and the long-term effects of such tactics would certainly have been harmful. In short, official operations in gilt-edged continue to be constrained both by the underlying market situation and by long-term concern for the maintenance of a broad market.

For much of the ten-year period the circumstances required more severe restraint on credit than could be achieved by acting on liquidity and ratios. It was therefore necessary to have recourse to direct forms of control—the imposition of lending ceilings. Direct requests to the deposit banks to restrict the level of their advances had been made at times in the 1950s. A similar request was made in July 1961, in association with a call for Special Deposits. However, it was no longer possible, on grounds of either equity or efficiency, to restrict ceilings to deposit banks alone, and on this occasion the request was addressed to all groups of banks and to a wide range of financial institutions. The terms of the request were fairly general (. . . that the recent rate of increase in advances should be greatly reduced). Lending ceilings were reimposed in 1965 when all banks and hire purchase finance houses were asked to restrict their lending to an annual rate of increase of 5 per cent in the twelve months to March 1966. Specific ceilings of this general kind have been in force for most of the time since then. The quantitative ceilings have been accompanied by qualitative guidance—again, not a new development—on the direction of lending. This guidance has always accorded priority to export finance.

The increased importance of banks other than the deposit banks has made it appropriate to devise a form of control over their lending, analogous to Special Deposits, for use when moderate, rather than severe, restraint is necessary. Because of the wide diversity in the balance sheet structures of the accepting houses, overseas banks, etc., it would have been difficult to devise a mechanism which, like Special Deposits, worked simply by its effect on the banks' liquidity. The Cash Deposits Scheme was therefore designed so that it could be made to impinge, if necessary, on the banks' earnings as well as on their liquidity. It provides for the banks to make cash deposits with the Bank of England calculated as a percentage of certain of their deposit liabilities in sterling (together with foreign currency deposits to the extent that they have been switched into sterling). The Bank would normally treat all participating banks alike and would pay a market rate of interest, linked to the Treasury bill rate, on all Cash Deposits. But they reserve a right in exceptional cases to treat banks individually; and also to pay a lower rate of interest than the Treasury bill rate. These penalty aspects of the scheme would not necessarily be invoked; their mere existence should help to reinforce any official guidance to the banks on their lending. However, this Scheme has not yet been used because it has continued to be necessary to exercise tighter control through ceilings.

Problems have also arisen of influencing lending by other financial institutions, particularly finance houses. As has been pointed out above, hire purchase terms control, imposed by the Board of Trade, gives some measure of control over parts of the credit. But terms control applies to only certain goods and certain forms of lending and in any case has been subject to increasing avoidance. Direct requests by the Bank of England for the observance of ceilings over lending were therefore extended beyond the banking sector to include the members of the Finance Houses Association and larger non-members in 1965. At present they are being asked to bring their lending down to 98 per cent of its level at end-October 1967. Within this ceiling, the finance houses have been asked not to grant personal loans for the purchase of goods subject to terms control on easier terms than would apply to a hire purchase agreement.

As with the banks, the Bank rely on the voluntary co-operation of the finance houses for the implementation of ceiling control. Again as with the banks, there are obvious objections to ceiling control as a method of restricting credit—such as arbitrary choice of a base date, and curtailment of competition between controlled institutions. There is also the inescapable problem of the borderline (which has to be drawn somewhere) between institutions to which requests for credit restriction are directed and those to which they are not. But although check-traders, small finance houses, and other institutions are not at present covered by ceiling controls, the

Bank find that limiting their requests to members of the F.H.A. and to larger non-members covers the bulk of finance house lending, while avoiding the complexities that any significant extension of the present coverage would involve. It is also true that institutions not receiving the Bank's requests do not generally finance themselves to any significant extent by taking deposits or borrowing on the capital market, but have to rely on sources of finance already controlled. As noted above, the authorities are aware of the shortcomings of ceiling control for finance houses, and have been considering alternative methods of control for some time. The views of the Crowther Committee on Consumer Credit are expected to be received during 1970.

The Bank send copies of the notices or letters issued to the banks and finance houses on credit restraint to the British Insurance Association, the National Association of Pension Funds, the Building Societies Association, and to institutions such as I.C.F.C. and F.C.I. These institutions are asked to bear the Bank's objectives closely in mind, but are not asked to keep to ceilings on their lending.

IV. THE EFFECTS OF MONETARY POLICY

Preceding sections of this paper have attempted to describe briefly the changes in the context in which monetary policy has been operating over the past ten years and developments in the tactics and methods employed. It is reasonable to ask in conclusion what the result has been. What can monetary policy be said to have achieved? In fact, it is very difficult to answer such questions. Even the wider question of the effects of economic policy, comprising fiscal, monetary, incomes, industrial, regional, and external policies, cannot be given a simple answer, for these, too, are inseparable from social and foreign policies. In one sense, economic policy may be said quite simply to have failed, in that none of the economic problems facing the United Kingdom in 1959 can be said to have been solved and some of the most important of them have become more severe. But the explanation cannot be sought wholly in economic events and policies, still less in the narrower range of monetary policies. It would be necessary to analyse and relate the various objectives, not all of them economic and many of them conflicting, which the authorities were aiming to achieve at various times throughout the period. Such a discussion would lead far beyond the bounds of this paper.

When one attempts to measure and distinguish the effects of monetary and other policies the difficulties are even greater. Almost invariably moves in the monetary field have been taken in conjunction with fiscal measures ('packages'). Moreover, the role of expectations is, in the authorities' view, much greater than is normally assumed in academic and journalistic comment. Changes in the climate of expectations—whether brought about by events outside the United Kingdom, by events within the country but outside the control of the policy-makers, or by the timing and manner of the announcement and implementation of policy measures—can often act either to negate or greatly to reinforce the tactics of the authorities. This is particularly important in relation to sales of government stock, but has much wider application. The winter of 1966–7 provides a striking example. All the indications were that there would be extreme financial stringency at this time when the first impact of S.E.T. (the once-for-all 'forced loan' to H.M.G.) on companies was being felt. In fact, as a result of the package of measures taken in July 1966, augmented by the radical change in expectations that this engendered, there was a marked weakening of demand and financial supply constraints were barely felt.

Certain effects of monetary policy can, however, be fairly clearly demonstrated. A substantial tightening or easing of terms control can be seen to be followed by marked changes in spending on the goods involved. Probably the most striking example of this occurred in 1966. Consumers' expenditure on durable goods fell from £492 million[2] in the second quarter of 1966 to £429 million in the third quarter and £405 million in

_____

[2] At 1963 prices, seasonally adjusted.

the fourth quarter. This change in terms was, however, part of the 'package' of measures announced in July, which included higher purchase tax and an increase in Bank rate; the fall in spending cannot be attributed solely to a change in hire purchase terms. Similarly, private housebuilding has on occasions been severely affected by variations in the available flow of mortgage finance, as occurred, for example, during the mortgage 'famine' in 1965, when lending by the societies was sharply reduced, and the number of houses started for private owners fell from 64,000 in the last quarter of 1964 to 48,000 a year later. On business investment, despite the enormous amount of work that has been done, the evidence remains inconclusive as to the effects of either the cost or the availability of funds, though there is perhaps some support for the *a priori* expectation that investment would be affected. What does seem clear, however, is that the timing of any effect is very uncertain and that the lags as well as being variable tend to be rather long. On consumption, the evidence remains even more sketchy. However, there seem grounds for believing that really tight control of bank lending can, both directly and through its indirect effects on stock market values, exert some effect on consumers' expenditure.

Much will depend on the concurrent severity of fiscal and incomes policy. Following a fiscal year (1968–9) in which the central government was able to make net repayments of debt for the first time for a number of years, it is expected that in 1969–70 the central government surplus will more than offset the borrowing requirements of the local authorities and public corporations, enabling the public sector as a whole to repay debt for the first time certainly since the statistical series began in 1952 and almost certainly since before the war. These surpluses and the current ceilings on credit together form much the most severe monetary restraint that has been imposed for a long time.

In general, it remains the authorities' belief that fiscal and monetary policy work—and must work—jointly. Without monetary restraint, fiscal restraint will either be largely ineffective or—if it is made effective in a conjunctural sense—

is likely to have damaging longer run effects on incentives or the provision of public services. Likewise with a large public sector deficit, monetary restraint to be effective at all will have to be so severe as to risk drastic and unpredictable consequences for the whole financial system. The lesson is perhaps not to expect too much of any one arm of economic policy, especially for 'fine tuning'. As we learn more we should be able to refine our techniques and predict better their effects; but, at least in the present state of our knowledge, it looks unlikely that we shall ever be able to rely primarily on monetary policy for short-term stabilization of the economy and the balance of payments.

Discussion Papers

(a) R. F. G. ALFORD

(*Reader in Economics, London School of Economics*)

IN the 1960s the role of monetary policy has been recognizably on the lines recommended in the Radcliffe Report. The intention, at any rate, of the authorities appears to have been that monetary and budgetary policy should work together as follows:

1. The authorities take a view upon the appropriate general level of interest rates and take action to establish this level, though leaving market rates free to move within its neighbourhood.
2. They use budgetary policy (which in this context means policy on income and expenditure of the whole public sector) to directly influence domestic expenditure.
3. If these together are insufficient, they resort to the policy of obstructing capital market channels, through such measures as hire purchase terms controls and controls on bank lending to the private sector, as a further means of holding down spending.

Each of these arms of policy has its problems of timing, effectiveness, undesired consequences and political acceptability; these need not be rehearsed here.

The following diagram shows a highly simplified schema of an open macro-economic system:

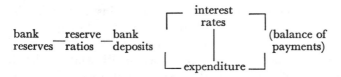

In terms of this schema, the strategy of the U.K. authorities has been to act directly upon interest rates through Bank rate and operations in the gilt-edged market, and directly upon domestic expenditure through budgetary policy and obstruction measures. Since interest rates and income or expenditure are the usual arguments in the demand function for bank deposits, with this strategy of management the volume of domestic bank deposits is demand determined by the U.K. private sector, and given reserve ratios, so is the volume of bank reserves. This may be compared with the textbook version of the management of the U.S. system, in which control over bank reserves is the means of influencing bank deposits and so expenditure. These two different strategies lead to chains of causation passing through the monetary system in opposite directions. This offers impressive scope for misunderstanding between those implicitly thinking in terms of one system and those implicitly thinking in terms of the other. The choice between these (and other) strategies is a matter of political attitudes and the technical efficiency of the different measures in local circumstances.

It has been suggested that the U.K. authorities should make more use of the quantity of money as a policy instrument for influencing aggregate expenditure. This implies some new strategy which has not been clearly specified as yet, and the debate at present is not upon the relative effectiveness of budgetary policy and policy acting through the quantity of money, but rather upon the feasibility in U.K. conditions of controlling bank deposits through operations by the monetary authorities in the gilt-edged market. The Bank of England's case against such a policy rests upon the instability of the private sector's demand for gilt-edged, which could make it impossible to influence bank deposits with any degree of precision.

It is not clear whether the assertion of instability in the demand for gilt-edged is based upon market feel or quantitative investigation. But even if demand for gilt-edged were to be quite well explained by such factors as wealth and the level, expected rate of change and expected variance of interest rates on gilt-edged and its competing assets, the presence of strong expectations could mean that the authorities would find themselves commonly faced with sales of gilt-edged which, for the purpose of controlling bank deposits, came only in two sizes—too big or too small.

Further, even a given level of sales of gilt-edged may have an unreliable effect on bank deposits and hence spending. Consider the simplified situation in which the financial surplus of the private sector is zero and it is making zero net purchases of public sector debt. Net sales of gilt-edged to the private sector must then mean equal net reduction in private sector holdings of other forms of public sector debt. We then have the following possibilities:

1. Net sales of gilt-edged go to transactors who in effect pay for them by running down their holdings of other forms of public sector debt, with no effect upon bank deposits.
2. Net sales go to transactors who pay for them by running down their bank deposits; bank deposits and bank holdings of public sector debt fall equally.
3. As in 2 above, but the change in bank asset structure creates a disequilibrium which puts pressure on the banks to reduce their lending to the private sector.

Cases 1 and 2 show the private sector switching to a new equilibrium situation; there is no induced change in expenditure arising from the change in deposits under 2. If switching of this kind is induced by the authorities leading the private sector to expect (correctly) a fall in rates, then the authorities to this extent are simply offering the private sector an upward ride on the gilt-edged escalator, encouraging it to speculate successfully at the expense of the authorities, with no useful effects on bank deposits. The fact that private sector holdings of gilt-edged, at market prices, now form a significantly smaller proportion of their holdings of total public sector debt than ten years ago (due chiefly to the growth of local authority debt) could conceivably have increased the likelihood of the outcome under case 1.

In case 3 there would be effects on private sector expenditure through induced change in bank deposits and bank lending to the private sector. But, the private sector need not readily give in to a squeeze of this kind; for example rates in the private sector could rise to the point at which some existing holders of public debt would be persuaded to sell it back to the authorities who would have to pay for it with deposits acquired by selling to the banks acceptable forms of public sector debt, offsetting (though not necessarily symmetrically) the switches induced by the authorities which initiated the squeeze through the banks. In other words, the authorities might try to induce changes in the form and location of the public sector debt in order to secure effects upon expenditure as under case 3; but the private sector could induce counter-switching to offset this, reducing the effects to those of cases 1 or 2. In these circumstances, operations by the authorities in the gilt-edged market would ultimately be able to achieve little more than interest rate effects upon private sector expenditure.

Turning briefly now to D.C.E., this appears to be the product of a view which sees the quantity of money as the chief source of change in an open economy—not perhaps the most useful model for the U.K. Whether it is a relevant magnitude for policy appears still to be under investigation; some might think this should have been established before it was given such a prominent position. This is however less important than might have been expected since D.C.E. evidently has to be taken apart to discern its policy implications, perhaps a further reason for wondering why (apart from being a counter in international monetary politics) it was ever put together in the first place.

If the D.C.E. target is taken seriously, it is a feedback mechanism imposed upon the U.K. economy, and as such it may or may not in fact be a stabilizing influence. If more countries had D.C.E. targets (including perhaps D.C.E. floors for persistent creditors), the interaction between them would raise further interesting possibilities. Clearly D.C.E. is only one of a whole range of possible feedback mechanisms which could be used. One amongst many alternatives would be to move interest rates upwards as the balance of payments deteriorated, and vice versa. Then instead of domestic credit expansion we could have domestic interest rate expansion—D.I.R.E. for short—and it might then be convenient to refer to this as a D.I.R.E. arrangement with D.I.R.E. consequences.

Discussion Papers

(b) J. R. WINTON
(*Economic Adviser, Lloyds Bank*)[1]

THERE is little new in the paper presented by the Bank of England whose message seems to be that 'Radcliffe is alive, well, and living in Threadneedle Street'. The paper is too brief in its comments on hire purchase controls which have had an increasingly selective impact on the economy, and provides little new evidence about the operations of the Bank in the gilt-edged market. In this connection, it would be easier to identify the important turning points of the market if the authorities could provide monthly statistics of gilt-edged transactions.

To bankers, credit control has seemed like a tourniquet, and it is remarkable that they have been able to slow down the growth of their lending as much as they have. The Special Deposits that have been collected seem to have little relevance as a lending control while the advances 'ceiling' is in effect, and bankers tend to treat them as a fine. Certainly, there has been a change from the Radcliffe view of Special Deposits as a flexible instrument of monetary control. If the authorities are going to call for Special Deposits in times of monetary stringency, they should consider placing deposits with commercial banks in times of monetary ease.

The Bank of England paper does not take enough account of the change in the government financing position which threatens to produce a virtual disappearance of the Treasury bill by mid-1970. In general, monetary policy instruments should follow the lines that commercial banks would advocate for their own business, emphasizing control by reserve ratios rather than rules about the growth of advances, which are not part of banking tradition.

[1] This summary of Mr. Winton's remarks has been prepared by the editors.

SUMMARY OF THE GENERAL DISCUSSION

THE discussion on the Bank of England paper was mostly concerned with trying to clarify the attitude of the authorities to the D.C.E. concept, their views on the bond market, and the particular type of policy they favoured.

In a previous discussion, it had been argued that the adoption of D.C.E. was an indication of the authorities' failure to provide an explanation of the link between their activities in the monetary sector and the level of economic activity. It was suggested that the authorities did not seem to have worked out the behaviour links they must be assuming if they thought that the D.C.E. statistic was important. The presenters of the paper explained that the application of the D.C.E. concept to U.K. conditions had developed out of discussions with members of the staff of the I.M.F. The U.K. authorities regarded D.C.E. as a potentially useful additional index of economic performance; but it could be only one of the indices used. More work needed to be done on its linkages with economic activity, which might be pretty loose (though there was preliminary evidence of positive relationships). Other discussants suggested that D.C.E. should be refined to take account of changes in the proportion of high-powered to other money in the overall amount.

In explaining their attitude to the bond market the presenters of the paper re-emphasized the extreme difficulty of making statements which could be tested by empirical research. The nature of the market, which operated within a framework of expectations about the policy reactions of the authorities, meant that it was impossible to subject it to the type of 'experiment' which would prove or disprove theories of behaviour. Similarly, it would be wrong to use evidence from market behaviour under conditions where market operators knew the authorities had an interest in stabilizing rates to conclude that the market could operate efficiently if this stabilization framework were withdrawn. However, most discussants agreed, as did the authorities, on the need for more measurement and analysis in this field.

Some discussants suggested that there was a stable demand for money which could be used in determining policy. Another aspect must be the relative costs of different policies. For the banks the amount of bank deposits was seen to be determined by the level of constraints on bank lending and some of them felt that the most efficient policy for them to live under would be where the authorities controlled the credit base and the banks kept to fixed reserve requirements. In the discussion it was apparent that bankers were worried about the effects of the authorities not being in full control of the credit-base supply, which threw the onus of stabilization onto the institutions.[1] It was argued that, because the authorities had interest rates as their principal policy variable and sought to achieve their aims for interest rates while fostering the maximum demand for gilt-edged in the long run, the supply of reserves could not be under control at the same time. The presenters of the paper and some discussants thought that interest rates should remain the principal policy variable; but many other discussants thought it was desirable to take the supply of money as the principal policy variable. The desirability of independent borrowing by the local authorities in financial markets was also questioned by a number of discussants.

The session concluded with a discussion of the role of monetary policy in the next few years. It seemed likely that there would be a greater reliance on monetary policy which would take account of developments in empirical and theoretical work on the financial sector. There was need for more research, particularly into aspects of the short-term determinants of economic activity. However, even if there were more success in achieving policy goals in the next few years

[1] This point has been made in a useful comment submitted by P. K. Marks (Midland Bank).

than in the 1960s, this might not provide conclusive proof of the superiority of monetary policies. Devaluation, the turn-round from financial deficit to surplus in the government sector, and the margin of unused capacity now present in the economy have provided a better background for the successful application of policy.

VI

A BIBLIOGRAPHY OF ARTICLES
RELATING TO THE U.K. FINANCIAL
SYSTEM PUBLISHED BETWEEN 1958
AND 1968–1969

D. R. CROOME *and* P. J. NICHOLLS

VI

A BIBLIOGRAPHY OF ARTICLES RELATING TO THE U.K. FINANCIAL SYSTEM PUBLISHED BETWEEN 1958 AND 1968–1969

D. R. CROOME *and* P. J. NICHOLLS

(*Dept. of Economics, Queen Mary College London*)

I. INTRODUCTION

THIS bibliography attempts to collect material referring to the U.K. financial sector published as articles in British journals from 1958 to 1968–9. Because of the large area covered, the compilers have had to put limits on the nature of the material they have included. In general, material which normally would be catalogued as a separate book, paper, or monograph is excluded. Although all the journals surveyed have their own indexes, there is no co-ordinated index of articles currently published which has the same scope, or is as up to date as this bibliography.

The journals surveyed are almost exclusively published in England; a check on foreign-published journals suggested that they contained little of direct relevance to the subject of this bibliography. All publications covered are listed in Section II, but several received less attention than others. In particular, the *Journal of the Institute of Bankers* and the *Transactions of the Manchester Statistical Society* were not examined exhaustively. The articles and books referred to in the papers presented by Professor Johnson, Professor Walters, and **Mr.** Maycock to the 'Radcliffe—Ten Years After Conference', give important additions to these lists.

The bibliography is arranged under subject headings, and articles have been allocated to sections after reading them through to determine their major area of concentration. Within each section the articles are grouped by topic and arranged chronologically. Generally, a brief note is appended to describe or evaluate the contribution made by the articles to the topic. These notes also attempt to give some cross-referencing between subjects.

The compilers would like to thank Professor W. Newlyn, Mr. R. F. G. Alford and Dr. M. Miller for suggesting improvements, and Joan Faller and Carol Croome for their secretarial help.

II. LIST OF JOURNALS COVERED IN THIS BIBLIOGRAPHY

Journal	Abbreviation
Applied Statistics	*AS*
Banca Nazionale Del Lavoro Quarterly Review	*BNL*
Bank of England Quarterly Bulletin	*BEQB*
The Banker	*Ba*
The Bankers' Magazine	*BM*
Barclays Bank Review	*BBR*
Bulletin of the Oxford Institute of Economics and Statistics	*BOIES*
District Bank Review	*DBR*
Economic Journal	*EJ*
Economica	*Ec*
The Economist	*Est*
Hill, Samuel Occasional Papers	*HS*
Journal of Economic Studies	*JES*
Journal of Industrial Economics	*JIE*
Journal of the Institute of Bankers	*JIB*
Journal of the Royal Statistical Society	*JRSS*
Kyklos	*Ky*
Labour Research	*LR*
Lloyds Bank Review	*LBR*
Manchester School of Economic and Social Studies	*MS*
Midland Bank Review	*MBR*
Moorgate and Wall Street Review	*MW*

National and Grindlays Bank Review	*NGBR*
National Institute Economic Review	*NIER*
National Provincial Bank Review	*NPBR*
National Westminster Bank Review	*NWBR*
Oxford Economic Papers	*OEP*
The Scottish Bankers' Magazine	*SBM*
Scottish Journal of Political Economy	*SJPE*
Three Banks Review	*TBR*
Transactions of the Manchester Statistical Society	*TMSS*
Weltwirtschaftliches Archiv	*Welt*
Westminster Bank Review	*WBR*
Yorkshire Bulletin of Economics	*YB*

III. METHOD OF INDEXING ARTICLES INCLUDED IN THIS BIBLIOGRAPHY

The major arrangement of articles in Section V is by the subject they primarily refer to. A list of subject categories is given in Section IV.

Articles are listed by title within each category. The complete reference gives:

   (i) Number of the reference within the subject category,

  (ii) Full title of the article,

 (iii) Full name of the author,

 (iv) Name of the journal, abbreviated as noted in Section II,

  (v) Volume number of the journal, and/or

 (vi) Number of the journal edition,

(vii) Month and year of publication,

(viii) Page reference.

Brief notes are appended to many of the topics. In these notes particular articles are referred to by the numbers they have in the subject category. Also, topics which have a close relationship with other areas of the bibliography are italicized.

Articles which contain useful bibliographies are denoted by the abbreviations: MSR (Major Source of References) and FRG (Further Reference Given).

An index of articles arranged alphabetically by author is given in Section VI. After each author's name, his publications are noted by reference to their position in the subject bibliography.

IV. LIST OF SUBJECT CATEGORIES

V. BIBLIOGRAPHY ARRANGED BY SUBJECT

A.i.a

THE U.K. FINANCIAL STRUCTURE—FINANCIAL INTERMEDIARIES
AND MARKETS

Domestic Banks

  Domestic Banks—Statistics

1. British Monetary Statistics. H. G. JOHNSON, *Ec* xxvi, Feb. 1959, 1–17.
   Parallels the *Radcliffe Committee's* re-examination and criticism of pre-
   1960 statistics of the *money supply*.
2. Banking, Finance, and the National Income Accounts. J. R. WINTON,
   BM clxxxix, no. 1393, Apr. 1960, 311–20.
3. More Light on British Banking. *MBR* Aug. 1961, 14–19.
   Examines statistical developments initiated by the *Radcliffe Report*.
4. Banking Statistics. *BEQB* iii, no. 4, Dec. 1963, 285–94.
   Explains *BEQB* coverage of the U.K. banking sector especially the
   definition of net deposits in the *money supply*.
5. Swings and Roundabouts in Bank Figures. *MBR* Feb. 1965, 19–24.
6. Seasonal Adjustment of Banking Statistics: London Clearing Banks.
   BEQB iii, no. 2, June 1963, 95–7.
7. Seasonal Adjustment of Banking Statistics. *BEQB* iii, no. 3, Sept. 1963,
   196–8.
8. Seasonal Adjustment of the London Clearing Banks' Deposits and
   Advances. *BEQB* vi, no. 1, Mar. 1966, 46–50.
   Introduction (6), development (7), and revision (8) of techniques to
   eliminate seasonality in banking statistics.
9. What Advance in Advances?: Difficulties in Seasonal Adjustment.
   J. I. MASON, *Ba* cxiii, Sept. 1963, 621–30.
10. Seasonal Adjustment of the British Bankers' Association Analysis of
    Advances. *BEQB* vi, no. 3, Sept. 1966, 257–62.

11. New Classification of Bank Advances. *BEQB* vii, no. 1, Mar. 1967, 48–51.

Development (10, 11) and criticism (9) of statistical techniques used in estimating changes in the critical area of *bank lending* to the *private sector*.

12. Bank Clearings as a Measure of Economic Activity. *BEQB* v, no. 1, Mar. 1965, 32–8.

Successful test of simple relation between clearings and National Expenditure, quarterly from 1956–64.

13. The following publications provide the major statistical sources for the U.K. domestic banking sector:

Bank of England Quarterly Bulletin
   (i) Analysis of Financial Statistics from 1960. Coverage widened especially after 1963.
   (ii) Statistical Annex.

Financial Statistics, H.M.S.O. monthly from 1962.

Bankers Magazine—annual survey of bank profits.

A.i.b

U.K. Domestic Banks—General

1. The Radcliffe Report and the Banks. *MBR* Nov. 1959, 3–9.

Useful summary of the *Radcliffe Committee's* recommendations.

2. An Appraisal of Recent (1960) Developments in British Banking. Lord PIERCY, *BM* clxxxix, no. 1391, Feb. 1960, 102–10.

3. Background to the Banking Scene—1951–64. *WBR* Feb. 1965, 23–36.

4. Changes in the Banking Scene—1951–64. *WBR* May 1965, 29–39.

5. Banking Survey. *Ba* 119, Mar. 1969, 203–14:
   1. The Banks and the Government.
   2. From the Chairman.
   3. Clearing Bank Complexities.

   Relates banking developments to the changing economic environment and *financial policies* of the 1950s (2) and '60s (3, 4, 5,).

6. Commercial Banks Portfolio Behaviour. F. P. BRECHLING and G. CLAYTON, *EJ* lxxv, June 1965, 290–316.

Important theoretical-empirical study of models of U.K. bank behaviour and implications for *financial policy* and the *money supply*.

7. Bank Liquidity in the U.K. *BEQB* ii, no. 4, Dec. 1962, 248–55.

8. Banks and their Competitors (FRG). A. B. CRAMP, *Ba* cxiii, Feb. 1963, 89–96.

9. Should the Banks Bid for Deposits? W. KING, *Ba* cxii, Dec. 1962, 761–72:
   1. Implications of the Freeing.

2. The Banks and their Competitors.
3. Could the Banks Compete?
4. Competition in Practice.
10. More Economical Banking? M. GASKIN, *Ba* cviii, May 1958, 334–38.
11. Jones Points the Way. *Est* (supp.), 10 June 1967, ix–x.
12. The Report on Bank Charges—I. A. JONES, *BM* cciv, Aug. 1967, 61–4.
13. The Report on Bank Charges—II. H. G. JOHNSON, *BM* cciv, Aug. 1967, 64–8.
14. The Report on Bank Charges—III. T. C. GORDON, *BM* cciv, Aug. 1967, 68–71.
15. The Report on Bank Charges—IV. G. MAYNARD, *BM* cciv, Aug. 1967, 71–4.
16. Deposit Rates After Mr. Jones. F. W. PAISH, *Ba* 117, Oct. 1967, 845–9.
17. The Bank Mergers. L. BARAGWANATH, *Ba* 118, Apr. 1968, 216–21.
18. Monetary Policy and the Mergers. E. W. DAVIS and E. NEVIN, *BM* ccv, Apr. 1968, 221–5.
19. Merging for What? *Est* (supp.), 15 June 1968, xi–xv.
20. The Monopolies Commission Report. M. ARTIS, *BM* ccvi, Sept. 1968, 128–35.
21. Monopolies Epilogue. P. E. SMART, *BM* ccvi, Sept. 1968, 143–4.
22. Why Not Two Clearers? J. R. HARROLD, *BM* ccvi, Sept. 1968, 139–43.
   Discussion of problems in the clearing-bank sector. These have related especially to the competition of non-clearing bank intermediaries (8, 9), bank charges, and deposit rates (10–15) and the competitive structure of the industry (16–22).

23. Cheques and Credit Cards: More Competition between the Banks. A. N. BANK, *BM* cci, Feb. 1966, 85–9.
24. (1) A Reader's Guide of Credit Cards. (2) Are Credit Cards Inflationary? M. WARD, *Ba* 116, July 1966, 444–54.
25. The Case for the Credit Card. J. THOMSON, *Ba* 116, July 1966, 444–54.
26. Credit Transfer Scheme. R. HINDLE, *BM* clxxxviii, no. 1385, 93–7.
27. The New Credit Transfer Service. B. C. SHARP, *Ba* cxi, Mar. 1961, 180–5.
28. What's Happening to Credit Transfers? *Est*, 30 June 1962, 1340–4.
   Mainly factual descriptions of new credit instruments and processes developed to extend commercial banks conventional deposit facilities.

29. The Banks and their Properties. P. GALVIN, *Ba* cxiv, Oct. 1964, 640–5.
30. Clearing Banks as Issuers. G. PULAY, *Ba* cxv, Nov. 1965, 724–8.

31. Bankers as Retailers. *Est* (supp.), 15 June 1968, xxviii–xxxii.
    Factual descriptions of aspects of miscellaneous bank activities
    including selling insurance (31).

32. The Value of Banking Studies. G. CLAYTON, *BM* ccii, Sept. 1966,
    167–72.

33. Some Comparisons Between Banking in the U.S.A. and U.K.
    H. W. AUBURN, *BM* clxxxvl, no. 1374, 193–7.

34. Banking Comparisons in the U.S. and U.K. Sir R. HAWTREY,
    BM clxxxvi, no. 1374, Sept. 1958, 197–8.

35. Banking History and Economic Development: Seven Systems.
    S. G. CHECKLAND, *SJPE*, 15 June 1968, 144–66.
    Comparative banking studies (33–35) and their usefulness (32).

36. The Bankers' Clearing House. E. A. YOUNG, *JIB* 80 and 81:
    I. Oct. 1959, 375–81.
    II. Dec. 1959, 464–71.
    III. Feb. 1960, 66–72.
    IV. June 1960, 196–204.

37. A valuable annual survey of the British Banking Sector appears in a
    June issue of *The Economist* each year (except 1959 and 1961).

A.i.c

Scottish Banks

1. The State of Scottish Banking Statistics. M. GASKIN, *BM* clxxxv,
   no. 1371, June 1968, 493–7.

2. Radcliffe on the Scottish Banks. M. GASKIN, *SJPE*, 7 Feb. 1960,
   65–8.

3. More Light on Scottish Banking. *Est*, 18 June 1960, 1260–3.

4. The Changing Face of Scottish Banking: Scottish Banks Under the
   Microscope. I. W. MACDONALD, *Ba* cx, Apr. 1960, 250–64.

5. The Changing Face of Scottish Banking: Electronics and the Future.
   J. LETHAM, *Ba* cx, Apr. 1960, 250–64.

6. The Changing Face of Scottish Banking: The Fruits of Freedom.
   F. S. TAYLOR, *Ba* cx, Apr. 1960, 250–64.

7. The Changing Face of Scottish Banking: The Bank Balance Sheets
   Analysed. *Ba* cx, Apr. 1960, 250–64.

8. Are Scots Banks Fully Lent? F. S. TAYLOR, *Ba* cxi, Apr. 1961,
   271–9.

9. Two Challenges for Scots Banks. F. S. TAYLOR, *Ba* cxiii, Apr. 1963,
   270–5.

10. Banking on Growth. F. S. TAYLOR, *Ba* cxiv, Apr. 1964, 247–51.
    Descriptions of developments in Scottish banking from their treat-
    ment by the *Radcliffe Committee* to the mid '6os. *Bank competition* (6),
    technical efficiency (5), and contribution to lending facilities (8, 9) are
    discussed.

11. The Scottish Banks' Interest Rates. M. GASKIN, *SJPE*, 5 Feb. 1958, 67–74.
12. Monetary Policy and the Scottish Banks. M. GASKIN, *SJPE*, 5 Oct. 1958, 202–18.
    Interesting comparison of the *English* and Scottish *banking systems* and their respective position relative to *monetary policy*.
13. The references given under A.i.a.13 also give separate coverage for Scottish banking statistics. Note also
    The Banker—yearly articles on the position of Scottish banks.

A.i.d

Bank Technical Efficiency

1. Banking Systems of the Future. R. HINDLE, *BM* clxxxvi, no. 1374, Sept. 1958, 179–88.
2. Electronics in Banking: An Interim Survey. J. D. COWEN, *Ba* cix, Jan. 1959, 31–40.
3. New Methods in Banking. R. HINDLE.
   A comprehensive fourteen part survey appearing in the *Bankers' Magazine* between 1959 and 1961 under the following titles:
   New Methods in Banking. clxxxviii, no. 1388, Nov. 1959, 341–7.
   Input and Output. clxxxix, no. 1392, Mar. 1960, 230–5.
   Voucher Handling and Reading Techniques. clxxxix, no. 1393, Apr. 1960, 321–7.
   Coding Vouchers. clxxxix, no. 1394, May 1960, 429–33.
   Full Electronic Accounting System. cxc, no. 1398, Sept. 1960, 171–3.
   A Computer System. cxc, no. 1399, Oct. 1960, 247–50.
   Semi-Electronic Equipment. cxc, no. 1400, Nov. 1960, 325–30.
   Development of Semi-Electronic Equipment. cxc, no. 1401, Dec. 1960, 403–8.
   An Interim Report. cxci, no. 1402, Jan. 1961, 29–30.
   New Developments in Computers. cxci, no. 1404, Mar. 1961, 226–9.
   Centralization and Communications. cxci, no. 1405, Apr. 1961, 311–15.
   Service to Customers. cxcii, no. 1408, July 1961, 24–8.
   Division of Responsibility. cxcii, no. 1411, Oct. 1961, 259–62.
   The Branch of the Future. cxcii, no. 1412, Nov. 1961, 335–8.
4. Electronics in Banking: The Phase of Action. J. D. COWEN, *Ba* cxi, Jan. 1961, 24–30.
5. Thoughts on Electronics in Banking. *TBR* 52, Dec. 1961, 19–27.
6. Electronic Aids to Banking. R. HINDLE, *BM* cxciii, no. 1415, Feb. 1962, 109–12.

7. Automatic Bank Systems: The Lessons from America. R. HINDLE, *BM* cxiv, Dec. 1962, 423–6.
8. Into the Computer Age. A. W. BROOKS, *Ba* cxiii, Mar. 1963, 172–7.
9. Progress Report on Automation. R. HINDLE, *BM* cxcix, Oct. 1965, 247–51.
10. The New Look in Bank Systems. R. HINDLE, *BM* cc, Nov. 1965, 301–5.
11. Computer Systems. R. HINDLE.

Four part survey of computer systems, appearing in the *Bankers' Magazine* under the following titles:
Computer Systems—The Next Generation. ccii, Nov. 1966, 391–6.
Computer Systems—The Goal. cciii, Jan. 1967, 7–12.
Automation—A New Generation in Systems. cciv, Aug. 1967, 76–9.
The Inter-Bank Computer Bureau. ccv, June 1968, 354–6.

12. Efficiency of the Banks. *Ba* 117, June 1967, 486–517:
    1. What the Prices and Incomes Board Report Says.
    2. Progressive Steps.
    3. Why the Banks have Gone in for Automation. R. VINE.
    4. Problems and Solutions. D. SIMPSON.
    5. The Future. S. DIXON-CHILDE.
13. Banking on Computers. *Est* (supp.), 10 June 1967, xxiii–xxvii.
14. Computer Banking—A New Perspective. I. A. EDMONDS, *Ba* 117, Dec. 1967, 1041–7.
15. The Cashless Revolution. F. W. GIBSON, *WBR* Feb. 1968, 20–30.
    Implications of the possible 'next-step' in monetary evolution.
16. Banking Automation in the 1970s. C. H. PETERSON, Jr. *Ba* 119, Jan. 1969, 44–7.
17. The Inter-Bank Research Organization. R. HINDLE, *BM* ccvii, June 1969, 349–53.
18. Bank Automation, Progress, and Problems. C. B. HOWLAND, *Ba* 119, July 1969, 689–95.

A.ii.a

Financial Intermediaries other than Domestic Banks
  London Money Markets—General

1. Freedom of the City. W. M. CLARKE, *NPBR* 45, Feb. 1959, 9–14.
2. London's Money Brokers. R. F. G. ALFORD, *Ba* cix, June 1959, 380–9.
3. The City and the Radcliffe Report. C. F. COBBOLD, *BM* clxxxviii, no. 1389, 418–20.
4. Lombard Street after Radcliffe. *Est*, 19 Sept. 1959, 945–7.
5. The Changing Money Market (London). *Est*, 30 June 1962, 1331–5.

6. London—Europe's Financial Centre. J. R. Colville, *Ba* 116, July 1966, 459–69.
7. London's Many Money Markets. M. S. Mendelsohn, *Ba* 117, May 1967, 411–17.
8. London as a Money Magnet. *Est* (supp.), 10 June, 1967, xv–xix.
9. Changes in British Banking; The Growth of a Secondary System. J. Revell, *HS* 3.
10. Recent Developments in London's Money Markets—The Clearing Banks and Discount Houses. *MBR* Aug. 1969, 3–8.
11. Prospects for the City. E. V. Morgan and J. H. Dunning, *Ba* 118, May 1968, 384–90.
12. The U.K. Banking Sector, 1952–67. *BEQB* 9, no. 2, June 1969, 176–200.

    Descriptive accounts of post-*Radcliffe* developments, especially in the short-term money markets. Articles 7, 9, and 12 provide major summaries of money market organization.

13. Institutional Investors and the Stock Exchange. J. G. Blease, *DBR* 151, Sept. 1964, 38–64.
14. The Financial Institutions. *BEQB* 5, no. 2, June 1965, 132–55.

    Useful summaries concentrating especially on developments in long-term capital markets.

15. British Financial Intermediaries in Theory and Practice. G. Clayton, *EJ* lxxii, Dec. 1962, 869–86.

    An attempt to provide a theoretical base to review developments since the *Radcliffe Report*.

16. The New Money Markets. J. S. G. Wilson, *LBR* 64, Apr. 1962, 31–45.

    An interesting theoretical/descriptive look at the growth of money markets in five Commonwealth countries.

A.ii.b

Overseas Banks and Accepting Houses

1. The Overseas and Foreign Banks in London. *BEQB* i, no. 4, Sept. 1961, 18–23.
2. New Banking Statistics: Accepting Houses and Overseas Banks in London. *BEQB* ii, no. 4, Dec. 1962, 267–9.
3. British Overseas Banks: No Place Like Home. M. S. Mendelsohn, *Ba* 118, Oct. 1968, 880–4.
4. Foreign Banks in London: A Survey. *Ba* 118, Oct. 1968, 895–925.
5. Foreign Banks in London: Why the American Banks Come to London. L. S. Thornton, *Ba* 118, Oct. 1968, 895–925.
6. Foreign Banks in London: A European Pioneer in the City. G. de Miramon, *Ba* 118, Oct. 1968, 895–925.

7. Foreign Banks in London: U.S. Banks in London: Then and Now. C. J. BRIDGE, *Ba* 118, Oct. 1968, 895–925.
8. Overseas and Foreign Banks in London: 1962–8. *BEQB* 8, no. 2, June 1968, 156–65.
   Statistical descriptions (1, 2, and 8) and explanations (3–7) of the reasons for the rapid growth of non-U.K. based banks in London.

A.ii.c

Merchant Banks

1. Merchant Banks. T. M. RYBCZYNSKI and S. F. FROWEN. *BM* cxcii, no. 1408, July 1961, 1–10.
2. Merchant Banks in Britain and the New Europe. J. F. CHOWN, *MW* 3, Spring 1962, 52–72.
3. Fresh Fields for Merchant Banks. D. MONTAGU, *Ba* cxv, Sept. 1965, 612–17.
   Description of the evolution of merchant banks from pre-1914 (1) and their place in the contemporary money market (2, 3). Some description of merchant banks as *acceptance houses*.

A.ii.d

Trustee Savings Banks and Giro

1. The Growth of the Trustee Savings Banks. J. E. M. COLLOFF, *BM* cxcviii, Sept. 1964, 213–20.
   Uses statistics from the Trustee Savings Bank Year Book to explain the growth pattern of these banks.

2. No Service to Giro. J. HUNSWORTH, *BM* cxcviii, Nov. 1964, 347–50.
3. Living with the Giro. A. BAMBRIDGE, *Ba* cxv, Sept. 1965, 579–84.
4. Giro for the Million. J. F. FULLER, *BM* cci, June 1966, 394–8.
5. National Giro Starts Up. J. GRADY, *Ba* 118, Oct. 1968, 874–9.
6. The National Giro. R. HINDLE, *BM* ccvi, Nov. 1968, 245–8.
   Description (4, 5, 6) and discussion of the relationship of the banking system and the Giro.

A.ii.e

Finance Houses and Hire Purchase; Factoring

1. U.K. Finance Companies: The Uses and Sources of Funds, 1949–58. N. RUNCIE, *BM* clxxxvii, no. 1383, June 1959, 455–64.
2. U.K. Finance Companies: A Study of Profits, 1949 to 1958. N. RUNCIE *BM* clxxxviii, no. 1386, Sept. 1959, 189–99.
3. Hire Purchase Revisited. J. BATES, *BM* cxcii, no. 1410, Sept. 1961, 195–200.

4. Sources of Funds of Hire Purchase Finance Companies, 1958–62. *BEQB* ii, no. 4, Dec. 1962, 256–62.
5. Estimates of Hire Purchase and Its Finance, 1948–57. J. K. S. GHANDHI, *BOIES* 28, no. 4, Nov. 1966, 247–59.
   Primarily descriptive accounts of H.P. and financing providing statistics to evaluate relation of hire purchase and *financial controls* (5).
6. The Banks in Hire Purchase. *Ba* cviii, Sept. 1958, 561–8.
7. Hire Purchase and the Banks (FRG). J. A. BATES, *BM* clxxxvi, no. 1376, Nov. 1958, 361–7.
8. The Banks and Hire Purchase. P. J. GREAVES, *NPBR* 45, Feb. 1959, 1–8.
9. Bringing Finance Houses into the Market Place? *Est* (supp.), 10 June 1967, xxvii–xxviii.
10. Banks and Factors: Partners in Finance? R. A. PILCHER, *Ba* 118, Feb. 1968, 147–51.
11. (1) Hire Purchase Today. (2) The Banks and Hire Purchase. M. TURNER, *Ba* 118, Sept. 1968, 807–19.
    Problems and opportunities of bank involvement with H.P. credit institutions and implications for *financial policy* (9).

A.ii.f

Investment and Unit Trusts

1. Investment Trusts and Unit Trusts. *BEQB* i, no. 4, Sept. 1961, 29–30.
2. British Investment and Unit Trusts since the War (MSR). J. C. GILBERT, *TB* 14, no. 1, May 1962, 3–13.
3. British Investment and Unit Trusts since 1960. J. C. GILBERT, *TB* 17, no. 2, Nov. 1965, 117–29.
4. British Investment and Unit Trusts and the Finance Act, 1965. J. C. GILBERT, *TB* 18, no. 2, Nov. 1966, 86–94.
5. Unit Trusts Today. P. J. NAISH, *BM* ccv, Feb. 1968, 88–9.
6. Unit Trusts—A Survey: Equity Linked Assurance and Tax Relief. E. PALAMOUNTAIN, *Ba* 119, Apr. 1969, 329–50.
7. Unit Trusts—A Survey: The Banks and the Unit Trusts. F. W. HOLDER, *Ba* 119, Apr. 1969, 329–50.
8. Unit Trusts—A Survey: The Unit Trust Phenomenon: Will it Last? E. DUNCAN, *Ba* 119, Apr. 1969, 329–50.
9. Investment Trusts and Unit Trusts: Assets and Transactions, 1960–67. *BEQB* 9, no. 1, Mar. 1969, 62–73.
   Statistics (1, 2, 3, 9) and description of unit and investment trust development. Their problems are discussed (2, 3, 4) and their relationship to *banks* (5) and *insurance* (6).

A.ii.g

Building Societies

1. Building Societies. A. STEWART, *NPBR* 46, May 1959, 1–8.
2. Building Societies in a New Age. G. LEE, *Ba* cix, May 1959, 315–23.
3. Building Societies in 1965. J. R. L. POTTER, *NPBR* 72, Nov. 1965, 1–7.
4. Building Societies: A Review. Living with High Interest Rates. G. J. ANDERSON, *Ba* 119, May 1969, 437–51.
5. Building Societies: A Review. Looking to the Future. S. W. G. MORTON, *Ba* 119, May 1969, 437–51.
   General description of the development (1) and present position of building societies.
6. Building Societies' Reserves Against Losses. J. MOREH, *BM* cciii, May 1967, 293–7.
   Critical review and proposal for restructuring building society asset structure.
7. Investment in Building Societies—I. J. MOREH, *BM* ccv, May 1968, 279–86.
8. Investment in Building Societies—II. J. MOREH, *BM* ccv, June 1968, 343–8.
   Examination of how building society deposits may provide competition for the growth of *bank* liabilities.
9. Building Societies and the Bank Rate. G. LEE, *Ba* cxi, May 1961, 326–33.
10. Finance for Housing. *MBR* Feb. 1963, 3–10.
11. Housing Mortgages in an Inflationary and Growing Economy. G. MILLS, *BOIES* 27, no. 2, May 1965, 135–49.
12. Building Society Mortgages and the Housing Market. M. WRAY, *WBR* Feb. 1968, 31–45.
    The general flow of funds into mortgages (9, 10) especially from building societies (11). A proposal for an equity-linked building society mortgage is discussed (10).

A.ii.h

Insurance Funds

1. Life Assurance Summarized. P. STEDDINGS, *BM* clxxxviii, no. 1385, Aug. 1959, 105–9.
2. British Insurance—An Outline. K. A. USHERWOOD, *NPBR* 49, Feb. 1960, 1–9.
3. No Ceiling for Life Assurance? W. NURSAW, *Ba* cxii, Mar. 1962, 174–8.
   Description of the development (1, 2) and prospects (3) for life insurance.

4. Insurance Companies and the Finance of Industry. G. CLAYTON and W. T. OSBORN, *OEP* 10, Feb. 1958, 84–97.
5. Insurance Companies and the Capital Market. G. CLAYTON and W. T. OSBORN, *TBR* 37, Mar. 1958, 21–35.
6. Life Assurance Funds and the Capital Market. G. L. REES and W. HORRIGAN, *MS* xxvii, no. 2, May 1959, 203–9.

> The particular contribution of insurance companies to the finance of the *industrial sector*, including major empirical studies of the position in the late 1950s (4, 6).

A.ii.i

I.C.F.C., etc.

1. The Role of the Industrial and Commercial Finance Corporation in Scotland's Economic Development. G. DAVIES, *BM* ccii, Sept. 1966, 161–5.
2. The Industrial and Commercial Finance Corporation: A Progress Report. G. W. MURPHY and D. PRUSMANN, *MS* i, Sept. 1968, 223–50.
3. The Regional Significance of I.C.F.C. G. DAVIES, *JIE* xvi, no. 2, Apr. 1968, 126–46.
4. F.C.I. and the Capital Market. I. HICKS and R. HOUGHTON, *JIE* vi, no. 2, Feb. 1958, 149–60.

> Studies concentrating on the role of F.C.I. and I.C.F.C. in *financing the industrial sector*, especially *small business* (2) and the regions.

A.ii.j

The Discount Market

1. The Functioning of the London Discount Houses. H. F. GOODSON, *JIB* 83, Apr. 1962, 82–100.
2. The Commercial Banks and the London Discount Market. C. W. LINTON, *JIB* 83, June 1962, 165–75.
3. The London Discount Market's Changing Role. W. KING, *JIB* 83, Aug. 1962, 224–40.
4. The Mechanics of Block Discounting. D. W. C. KITCHING, *BM* cxcv, no. 1430, May 1963, 361–6.
5. Innovation in the Discount Market. A. J. BUCHANAN, *SBM* lix, May 1967, 13–18.
6. The London Discount Market: Some Historical Notes. *BEQB* 7, no. 2, June 1967, 144–56.
7. What Future for the Discount Houses? *Est* (supp.), 15 June 1968, xxxvi–xxxix.

> Descriptions of the work of the discount houses (1), their history (6), and prospects (3, 7). The discount market is related to the *general money market* (4, 5), and the *banks* (2).

A.ii.k

Domestic Credit Instruments, Not Elsewhere Noted

1. Commercial Bills. *BEQB* i, no. 5, Dec. 1961, 26–31.
2. The Resurgence of the Commercial Bill. R. LAW, *BM* cc, Dec. 1965, 341–7.
   Statistics (1) and comment (2) on the growth of commercial bill business in the 1960s and its financial policy implications.
3. A New System for Savings Deposits. F. POLLAK, *BM* cciv, Dec. 1967, 304–7.
   Discussion of a scheme linking the benefits of deposits with premium bonds.

A.ii.l

International Credit Instruments, Not Elsewhere Noted

1. Dollar Deposits in London. P. EINZIG, *Ba* cx, Jan. 1960, 23–7.
2. Overseas Money in London. *Est*, 18 June 1960, 1263–4.
   General descriptions of the market.
3. Statics and Dynamics of the Euro-Dollar Market. P. EINZIG, *EJ* lxxi, Sept. 1961, 592–5.
4. Euro-Dollars. P. A. MANSON, *SBM* liv, no. 213, May 1962, 16–20.
5. Credit Creation through Euro-Dollars? G. L. BELL, *Ba* cxiv, Aug. 1964, 494–502.
6. Shake Up in Euro-Dollars. *Est* (supp.), 19 June 1965, xiii–xiv.
7. Euro-Dollars—Tonic or Toxic? B. READING, *BM* cciv, Oct. 1967, 233–7.
8. Euro-Dollars: The Problem of Control. E. W. CLENDENNING, *Ba* 118, Apr. 1968, 321–9.
9. That Controversial Euro-Dollar Market. I. O. SCOTT, Jr., *NWBR* Aug. 1969, 2–22.
   Selected articles particularly linking Euro-dollars with London *money markets, banks,* and U.K. *financial policy.*
10. The Eurobond Market. *BBR* xliv, no. 1, Feb. 1969, 3–5.
11. Unit of Account Bonds: Their Meaning and Function. J. C. INGRAM, *MW* 5, Autumn 1964, 65–80.
12. London Dollar Certificates of Deposit. P. EINZIG, *BNL* xix, no. 79, Dec. 1966, 328–45.
13. Sterling Certificates of Deposit. *BBR* xliii, no. 3, Aug. 1968, 47–9.
14. Sterling Certificates of Deposit (figures). *Est*, 4 Jan. 1969, 54–6.
    Useful descriptions and statistics of new international financial instruments.

A.ii.m

The Gold Market

1. The London Gold Market. *BEQB* iv, no. 11, Mar. 1964, 16–21.
2. Gold over a Decade: Supplies and Marketing since 1954. *MBR* Nov. 1964, 3–9 (a sequel to an article in *MBR* Feb. 1955).
3. What Future for London's Gold Market? *Est* (supp.), 15 June 1968, xx–xxviii.

> Descriptions of the history (2), organization (1), and prospects for the gold market.

The references given under A.i.a.13 also give separate coverage for capital markets, etc.

> Note also:
> *Bankers' Magazine*—yearly analysis of building societies.
> *The Banker*—annual review of foreign banks in London (starting from 1968).

A.iii

The Bank of England

1. The Functions and Organization of the Bank of England. *BEQB* vi, no. 3, Sept. 1966, 233–45.
2. The Bank of England as Registrar. *BEQB* iii, no. 1, Mar. 1963, 22–9.
3. The Overseas Work of the Bank of England. *BEQB* vii, no. 4, Dec. 1967, 374–8.
4. The Bank of England as Registrar: 1968. *BEQB* viii, no. 3, Sept. 1968, 262–70.
5. Bank, City, and Public. *Ba* cviii, Mar. 1958, 161–83.
6. The Bank Rate Tribunal Evidence: A Symposium 'An Economist's View of the Bank Rate Tribunal Evidence'. E. DEVONS, *MS* xxvii, no. 1, Jan. 1959, 1–16.

> The Bank of England and its relation to the public as described in evidence to the Bank Rate Tribunal.

B.i

U.K. SECTOR FINANCING

General

1. Financial Statistics to Date. T. M. RYBCZYNSKI, *BM* cxcv, no. 1426, Jan. 1963, 5–11.

> Suggestions for improving statistical coverage for financial flows.

2. The Wealth of the Nation. J. REVELL, *MW* 7, Spring 1966, 57–89.
   A summary inventory of the balance sheets of major macro-sectors, based on the author's book of the same title.
3. Flow-of-Funds Accounts. A. HOLMES, *BM* cxcvi, no. 1436, Nov. 1963, 305–11.
4. Flow of Funds in the U.K. L. BERMAN, *JRSS* 3, 1965, 321–60.
5. a. Money and the Social Accounts (1). F. SETON, *BM* cxcix, Jan. 1965, 7–15.
   b. Money and the Social Accounts (2). F. SETON, *BM* cxcix, Sept. 1965, 198–205.
6. Sector Financing: 1960–62. *BEQB* iii, no. 3, Sept. 1963, 184–95.
7. Sector Financing: 1961–63. *BEQB* iv, no. 2, June 1964, 109–17.
8. Sector Financing: 1962–64. *BEQB* v, no. 2, June 1965, 121–31.
9. Sector Financing: 1965. *BEQB* vi, no. 2, June 1966, 128–40.
10. Sector Financing Accounts: 1952–66. *BEQB* vii, no. 4, Dec. 1967, 360–73.
    The theory (3), methods of presentation (4), and statistics of the flow of funds approach to social accounting. Ref. B.i.4 is especially useful.

B.ii.a

Government Finance

Government Finance—General

1. Is the National Debt a Burden? J. E. MEADE, *OEP* 10, June 1958, 163–83.
   A serious error in this article is corrected in 'Is the National Debt a Burden?: A Correction', by J. E. Meade, *OEP* 11, Feb. 1959, 109–10.
2. The Logic of National Debt Policy. J. WISEMAN, *WBR* Aug. 1961, 8–15.
3. The National Debt. *BBR* xxxvii, no. 2, May 1962, 28–30.
4. Is the National Debt a Burden? E. J. MISHAN, *Ba* cxiii, Sept. 1963, 601–12.
5. The New Treasury. *BBR* xxxviii, no. 4, Nov. 1963, 70–2.
   Theoretical aspects of the National Debt (1, 2, 4) and U.K. debt management experience, except the *financial policy* aspects.
6. Distribution of the National Debt.
   An annual series in the *BEQB*. Particular references to major statistical changes and links with other series are noted in the following list:
   • Distribution of the National Debt. ii, no. 2, June 1962, 106–11.
     Links series with Radcliffe Report estimates for 1937–57, and gives description of statistical methods.

- Distribution of the National Debt, 1962. iii, no. 1, Mar. 1963, 30–1.
- Distribution of the National Debt: March 1963. iv, no. 1, Mar. 1964, 34–6.
  Describes extended method of analysis.

- Distribution of the National Debt: March 1964. v, no. 1, Mar. 1965, 46–9.
- Distribution of the National Debt: March 1965. vi, no. 1, Mar. 1966, 40–5.
- Distribution of the National Debt: March 1966. vii, no. 1, Mar. 1967, 43–7.
- Distribution of the National Debt: March 1967. viii, no. 1, Mar. 1968, 41–7.
- Distribution of the National Debt: March 1968. ix, no. 1, Mar. 1969, 53–61.
  Comparison of U.K. national debt distribution with that in other countries, and over the last 30 years.

B.ii.b

Central Government Finance—Methods

1. Exchequer and Central Government Finance. *BEQB* vi, no. 1, Mar. 1966, 29–36.
   Important descriptions of the statistical link between the Budget accounts and other financial statistics.

2. The Effects of the National Loans Act 1968 on Central Government Accounts. *BEQB* viii, no. 3, Sept. 1968, 280–1.

3. The Treasury Bill: The Story of an Economist's Invention. *MBR* Feb. 1961, 3–9.
4. The Treasury Bill. *BEQB* iv, no. 3, Sept. 1964, 186–93.
5. The Treasury Bill Tender in the U.K. A. D. BAIN, *JES* i, no. 1, Winter 1965, 62–71.
6. The U.K. and U.S. Treasury Bill Markets. *BEQB* v, no. 4, Dec. 1965, 327–38.
   Useful descriptions and analysis of the Treasury bill mechanism, other than its *monetary policy* aspect.

7. Living with the Inelastic Bond Market. B. TEW, *BNL* xi, no. 47, Dec. 1958, 511–19.
8. What Price Gilt-Edged? E. G. ELLINGER, *Ba* 116, Apr. 1966, 231–7.
9. Gilt-Edged—Can the Budget Help? E. V. MORGAN, *Ba* 116, Aug. 1966, 530–6.
10. Official Transactions in the Gilt-Edged Market. *BEQB* vi, no. 2, June 1966, 141–8.

11. Turnover in British Government Stocks. *BEQB* viii, no. 1, Mar. 1968, 48–51.
12. Managing the Gilt-Edged Market—A Temporary Change of Emphasis? *MBR* May 1969, 3–5.
    Statistics (10), methods (11), and problems in managing the government bond market, except the direct *monetary policy* aspects.

13. Non Marketable Debt and the Exchequer. *MBR* Nov. 1962, 3–9.
14. Tax Reserve Certificates. *BEQB* ii, no. 3, Sept. 1962, 176–85.
15. Tax Reserve Certificates. *BEQB* viii, no. 4, Dec. 1968, 391–401.

B.ii.c

Local Authority Finance—Methods

1. Local Authorities' Borrowing. *BBR* xxxviii, no. 3, Aug. 1963, 50–2.
2. Local Authorities and the Capital and Money Markets. *BEQB* vi, no. 4, Dec. 1966, 337–47.
3. Local Authorities in the Capital Market. H. R. PAGE, *TBR* 71, Sept. 1966, 26–37.
4. Local Authority Finance: Changing Attitudes to Borrowing. *BBR* xlii, no. 4, Nov. 1967, 72–5.
    General descriptive articles on the size and growth of this sector.

5. Local Authority Borrowing, 1955–60. H. COWEN, *LBR* 57, July 1960, 18–33.
6. Borrowing by Local Authorities; Further Sources of Funds. *MBR* Nov. 1961, 3–11.
7. The Practice and Problems of Local Authority Borrowing. H. R. PAGE, *TMSS* (61–62 Session), 14 Feb. 1962.
8. New Sense in Local Borrowing. R. BIRD, *Ba* cxiii, Dec. 1963, 819–23.
9. Reforming Local Authority Finance. R. J. CLARK, *WBR* Aug. 1965, 38–48.
    Articles dealing especially with the relation of local government to *central government* finance and the implications for *financial policy*.

10. Radcliffe and the P.W.L.B. *LR* xlviii, no. 12, Dec. 1959, 190.
11. Trustee Banks and Local Authorities: 'Special' Finance through P.W.L.B. C. L. LAWTON, *Ba* cxiii, Apr. 1963, 243–50.
12. Whys and Wherefores of Local Bonds. P. K. MARKS, *BM* cxcviii, Aug. 1964, 99–103.
13. New Deal in Municipal Finance. *BBR* xxxix, no. 3, Aug. 1964, 45–7.
    With special reference to the development of local authority bonds.

B.iii.a

Overseas Sector

Export Credit

1. *BEQB*

   General notes and articles describing U.K. export credit facilities have appeared under the following titles:

   - Re-Financing of Medium-Term Export Credits. i, no. 2, Mar. 1961, 15–16.
   - Finance for Exports. i, no. 3, June 1961, 21–9.
   - Finance for Exports. ii, no. 1, Mar. 1962, 23–4.
     The previous article examines the authorities' replies to criticisms of the export credit mechanism (N.B. B.iii.a. 12 and 13).
   - Help for Exports. v, no. 1, Mar. 1965, 30–1.
   - Improvements in Export Finance. vi, no. 2, June 1966, 149–50.
   - Improvements in Export Finance. vii, no. 4, Dec. 1967, 379–80.

2. Medium-Term Finance for Exports. N. MOMTCHILOFF, *BM* clxxxvi, no. 1375, Oct. 1958, 257–63.
3. Finance for Overseas Development and Export Credits. L. ARCHIBALD and M. A. B. HAMLYN, *BM* clxl, no. 1396, July 1960, 3–12.
4. The Finance of Exports. A. TUKE, *BBR* xxvi, no. 3, Aug. 1961, 45–7.
5. Refinance Facilities for Export Credits. *Ba* cxi, Mar. 1961, 170–4.
6. The Early History and Development of Export Credit Insurance in Great Britain, 1919–1939. D. H. ALDCROFT, *MS* xxx, no. 1, Jan. 1962, 69–85.
7. Export Finance from the Banks. *MBR* Aug. 1962, 10–20.
8. Medium and Long-Term Credit Granted by U.K. Exporters to Countries Outside the Sterling Area. *BEQB* iii, no. 1, Mar. 1963, 32–4.
9. Finance for Exports. *NPBR* 62, May 1962, 14–20.
10. The Finance of Exports. W. E. MINCHINTON, *DBR* 148, Dec. 1963, 35–51.
11. Economic Aid, Credit Insurance, and Exports. *BBR* xxix, no. 4, Nov. 1964, 72–5.
    The history, status, and techniques of export credit. There are links with the general *banking* system, the *balance of trade* and comparisons with other countries (2, 11).

12. The Problems of Financing Medium-Term Credit for Exports of Capital Goods. E. A. YOUNG, *JIB* lxxix, Feb. 1958, 41–9.
13. Export Credits—Where Britain Lags. P. BAREAU, *Ba* cx, Dec. 1960, 785–9.
14. A British Export Bank? The Case For. A. D. P. EDWARDS, *Ba* 118, Dec. 1968, 1122–9.

15. A British Export Bank? The Case Against. S. Cook, *Ba* 118, Dec. 1968, 1122–9.
16. U.K. Restrictions on Short Term Credit Overseas. T. M. Rybczynski, *Ba* 119, June 1969, 513–22.
    Criticisms and suggestions for improvement of export credit facilities.

B.iii.b

U.K. International Portfolio Investment and Aid

1. *BEQB*
   A series of statistical estimates of U.K. Overseas Portfolio Investments for the years:
   (i) 1958–1960. i, no. 3, June 1961, 30–2.
   (ii) 1959–1961. ii, no. 2, June 1962, 103–5.
   (iii) 1960–1962. iii, no. 2, June 1964, 118–20.
   (iv) 1961–1963. iv, no. 2, June 1964, 118–20.

2. Britain the Good Neighbour. *BBR* xxxv, no. 2, May 1960, 25–7.
3. Capital Flows. *BBR* xxxix, no. 1, Feb. 1964, 1–4.
4. Capital for Overseas. *LR* liii, no. 3, Mar. 1964, 39–41.
5. Problems of Capital Export. *LR* liv, no. 1, Jan. 1965, 5–6.
6. Government Spending Overseas: 1. How It has Risen. R. Fry, *Ba* 118, June 1968, 493–505.
7. Government Spending Overseas: 2. How Others Compare with the U.K. W. A. P. Manser, *Ba* 118, June 1968, 493–505.
   Primarily statistical surveys of long-term capital and aid flows from the U.K.

8. The Impact of Post-War Capital Movements. A. R. Conan, *WBR* Aug. 1963, 2–13.
9. Capital Movements in the Twentieth Century. J. H. Dunning, *LBR* 72, Apr. 1964, 17–42.
10. Overseas Lending and Internal Fluctuations, 1870–1914. A. G. Ford, *YB* 17, no. 1, May 1965, 19–31.
11. Long-Term Capital Movements. A. G. Kemp, *SJPE* 13, Feb. 1966, 136–59.
    Historical accounts of changes in long-term capital flows and their economic impact.

12. International Investment: The Role of Security Markets. *BEQB* iii, no. 2, June 1963, 106–17.
    Description of the relation between overseas investment and the U.K. capital market.

13. Does Foreign Investment Pay? J. H. Dunning, *MW* 5, Autumn 1964, 5–36.

14. Aid and the British Balance of Payments. A. KRASSOWSKI, *MW* 6, Spring 1965, 24–44.
15. The Importance of Overseas Investments. J. A. CLAY, *MW* 6, Spring 1965, 85–92.
16. A Reply (to Article B.iii.b.15). J. H. DUNNING, *MW* 6, Apr. 1965, 93–9.
17. The Role of Overseas Investment in the U.K. Balance of Payments. A. F. B. WILLIAMS, *WBR* May 1965, 14–23.
18. British Direct Investment in Western Europe. J. II. DUNNING and D. C. ROWAN, *BNL* xviii, no. 73, June 1965, 127–56.
19. The Attack on Portfolio Investment. D. SACHS, *Ba* cxv, June 1965, 384–8.
20. The Problem of Direct British Private Investment Overseas (MSR). D. C. ROWAN, *BM* cc, Nov. 1965, 293–9.
21. Further Thoughts on Foreign Investment. J. H. DUNNING, *MW* 7, Autumn 1966, 5–37.
22. Investment Overseas. B. SWEET-ESCOTT, *Ba* 116, Aug. 1966, 526–9.
23. Second Thoughts on Reddaway. E. V. MORGAN, *Ba* 117, July 1967, 600–4.
24. Capital Movements in Europe; The Approach to Liberalisation. *MBR* Aug. 1967, 12–22.
25. The Reddaway Report—A Rejoinder. W. A. P. MANSER, *WBR* Feb. 1968, 66–71.
26. Professor Reddaway's Last Word? W. A. P. MANSER, *NWBR* Feb. 1969, 40–52.
27. Review of the Final Reddaway Report. E. V. MORGAN, *Ba* 119, Jan. 1969, 28–43.
28. Reddaway Vindicates Overseas Investment; Effects on Exports and Balance of Payments. *NGBR* 15, no. 1, Feb. 1969, 4–8.
   A selection of articles with special reference to the financial aspects of U.K. involvement in international capital flows, including comments on the Reddaway Report on 'Effects of U.K. Direct Investment Overseas'.

B.iv

Personal Sector

1. The 1955 Savings Survey. M. J. ERRITT and J. L. NICHOLSON, *BOIES* 20, no. 2, May 1958, 113–52.
   Analysis of C.S.O. survey and comparison with 1952, '53, and '54 investigation.
2. Thrift in Fashion. *DBR* 126, June 1958, 30–9.
   Discusses reasons for the rise in the average savings propensity in the late 'fifties.

3. Personal Saving in the National Economy. *MBR* Nov. 1958, 3–7.
4. The Financial Surplus of the Private Sector, 1952–59. *BEQB* i, no. 1, Dec. 1960, 21–9.
5. The Financial Surplus of the Private Sector, 1960. *BEQB* i, no. 3, June 1961, 14–16.
6. The Financial Surplus of the Private Sector, 1961. *BEQB* ii, no. 2, June 1962, 112–15.
7. Personal Saving. *DBR* 149, Mar. 1964, 38–44.
8. Personal Saving and Financial Investment: 1951–65. *BEQB* vi, no. 3, Sept. 1966, 246–56.
   Important analysis based on Sector Finance Tables. See B.i.
9. Personal Saving and the Capital Market. E. V. MORGAN, *DBR* 163, Sept. 1967, 3–18.

B.v.a

Industrial, Commercial, and Agricultural Sector
Capital Markets and Company Finance—General

1. Comments on Company Finance. R. F. HENDERSON, *LBR* 51, Jan. 1959, 20–33.
2. Corporate Investment in Equities. *MBR* Feb. 1959, 3–8.
3. The Employment of Savings; Limitations on 'Institutional Investment'. *MBR* Nov. 1960, 9–16.
4. Equities and Growth. T. WILSON, *LBR* 54, Oct. 1959, 14–31.
5. On the Structure of the Capital Market. M. J. FARRELL, *EJ* lxxii, Dec. 1962, 830–44.
6. Company Finance—Too Much Equity? A. J. MERRETT, *Ba* cxiii, June 1963, 391–9.
7. U.K. Security Markets: The New Transfer System and the Reintroduction of Bearer Securities. *BEQB* iv, no. 4, Dec. 1964, 270–5.
8. Company Finance in the U.K. J. BATES, *BM* cxcix, Nov. 1965, 337–42.
9. Company Finance: 1952–65. *BEQB* 7, no. 1, Mar. 1967, 29–42.
10. The E.E.C. and the London Capital Market: The Opportunities. G. D. NEWBOULD, *NPBR* 79, Aug. 1967, 8–11.
11. Developing the Domestic Capital Markets. G. D. NEWBOULD, *Ba* 117, Jan. 1967, 46–53.
12. The English Capital Market before 1914. A. K. CAIRNCROSS, *Ec* xxv, May 1958, 142–6.
13. The English Capital Market before 1914—A Reply. A. R. HALL, *Ec* xxv, Nov. 1958, 339–43.
    General, descriptive articles on aspects of company finance, the role of *financial intermediaries* (3), different types of capital issues (1, 4, 6–8), and patterns of *relative interest rates* (5), receive attention.
    Article B.v.a.9. is a useful summary based on Sector Finance Tables (see B.i.).

B.v.b

Capital Markets and Company Finance—New Issues

1. The Role of the Stock Exchange in Raising New Capital. E. T. STEER, *BM* clxxxvii, no. 1378, Jan. 1959, 20–4.
2. Capital Issues on the U.K. Market. *BEQB* i, no. 5, Dec. 1961, 35–7.
3. Some Aspects of the Provincial New Issue Market. J. K. S. GHANDHI, *BOIES* 26, no. 3, Aug. 1964, 239–63.
4. Sources of Funds from Rights Issues and their Cost. S. K. EDGE, *JES* i, no. 1, Winter 1965, 30–50.
5. The Comparative Efficiency of Methods of Issue. A. J. MERRETT and G. D. NEWBOULD, *MS* xxxiv, no. 1, Jan. 1966, 1–14.
6. Capital Issues in the U.K. *BEQB* vi, no. 2, June 1966, 151–6.
7. Equity Placings on the New Issue Market. G. W. MURPHY and D. F. PRUSMANN, *MS* xxxv, no. 2, May 1967, 167–84.
   Descriptive and empirical (4, 5, 7) reports on the new issue market.
8. New Capital Issues. *MBR* Feb. (annually).
   An important source of statistics and commentary on the previous years volume of new issues.

B.v.c

Finance of Small Business and Innovations

1. The Finance of Small Business. J. A. BATES, *BOIES* 20, no. 2, May 1958, 153–86.
2. The Radcliffe Evidence—III: Medium- and Long-Term Finance for Small Business. S. FROWEN, *BM* clxl, no. 1398, Sept. 1960, 159–66.
3. A Comment (on B.v.c.2). A. A. SHENFIELD, *BM* clxl, no. 1400, Nov. 1960, 333.
4. The Finance of Small and Big Business (FRG). J. BATES, *BM* cxci, no. 1405, Apr. 1961, 291–8.
5. The Macmillan Gap—Thirty Years After. J. BATES, *Ba* cxi, July 1961, 470–9.
6. Financing the Small Business: A Rejoinder to Dr. Bates. Lord PIERCY, *Ba* cxi, Oct. 1961, 690–3.
7. Financing Innovation: Role of Specialized Agencies. K. GROSSFIELD, *Ba* cxi, Nov. 1961, 758–63.
8. The Macmillan Gap in Britain and Canada. J. BATES, *BM* cxciii, no. 1416, Mar. 1962, 203–9.
9. The Finance of Innovations. J. BATES, *BM* cxciv, no. 1420, July 1962, 1–6.
10. Financing Technical Development. Sir J. BENN, *Ba* cxiii, Oct. 1963, 706–13.
    Articles describing progress in an area highlighted by the *Radcliffe Report*. Several articles contrast the position in Britain with other countries (note esp. 8).

B.v.d

Finance of Agriculture

1. Long-Term Credit for Farmers. S. G. STURMEY, *Ba* xviii, Dec. 1958, 787–93.
2. Lending to Farmers. S. HOOPER, *Ba* cxiii, May 1963, 334–40.
3. Finance for Farming. *MBR* Feb. 1965, 3–10.
4. Long-Term Finance for Farmers. M. BUTTERWICK, *Ba* 116, June 1966, 396–402.
   Descriptive accounts of channels of finance open to farmers, especially those related to bank business.

B.v.e

Company Finance—Miscellaneous

1. Undisclosed Non-Recourse Finance: New Strength for Company Coffers. M. A. B. HAMLYN, *MW* 3, Autumn 1962, 39–48.
2. Finance for Shipbuilding. *BEQB* 7, no. 2, June 1967, 157–8.

C.i.a

MONEY, CREDIT, AND INTEREST RATES

Money and Liquidity

Theoretical Discussions

1. Radcliffe under Scrutiny: What is this Liquidity? F. PAISH, *Ba* cix, Oct. 1959, 583–604.
2. Radcliffe under Scrutiny: Another Look at 'Liquidity'. H. B. ROSE *Ba* cx, Mar. 1960, 160–7.
3. (1) Verdict on Money. (2) New Light on Liquidity. *Est*, 19 Mar. 1960, 1123–5.
4. Radcliffe under Scrutiny: 'General Liquidity'. J. ROBINSON, *Ba* cx, Dec. 1960, 790–5.
5. The Radcliffe Report and the Quantity of Money. H. EDEY, *BM* clxl, no. 1401, 381–7.
6. The Liquidity of Money. G. SCHMOLDERS, *Ky* 13, no. 3, 1960, 346–60.
7. Two Views on Money. A. B. CRAMP, *LBR* 65, July 1962, 1–15.
8. Radcliffe's Victorian Forebears: Liquidity and Money Supply. A. B. CRAMP, *Ba* cx, Sept. 1960, 593–9.
   Articles discussing general, theoretical analysis of the money-liquidity relation developed in the *Radcliffe Report*.

C.i.b

U.K. Statistics, Not Elsewhere Described

1. Radcliffe under Scrutiny: The New Data—and their Uses. C. T. SAUNDERS, *Ba* cix, Dec. 1959, 723–30.
2. Analysis of Financial Statistics. *BEQB* v, no. 1, Mar. 1965, 16–29.
3. The Note Circulation. *BEQB* v, no. 1, Mar. 1965, 39–45.
4. The Identification of Money. P. A. Cox, *JES* 3, no. 3/4, Dec. 1968, 27–30.
5. Money Supply and Turnover. *MBR* Aug. 1969, 16.
   Descriptions of statistical problems in estimating the *money supply*, including *statistics on bank deposits.*

C.ii.a

The Demand for Money
Theoretical Discussions

1. The Public's Preference for Cash. F. BRECHLING, *BNL* xi, no. 47, Sept. 1958, 377–93.
2. Idle Balances and the Motives for Liquidity. A. J. L. CATT, *OEP* 14, June 1962, 124–37.
3. Keynes's Finance Motive. P. DAVIDSON, *OEP* 17, Mar. 1965, 47–65.
4. Keynes's Finance Motive: A Comment. G. HORWICH, *OEP* 18, July 1966, 242–51.
5. The Importance of the Demand for Finance. P. DAVIDSON, *OEP* 19, July 1967, 245–53.
6. A Case Study in Mathematical Programming of Portfolio Selections. N. R. PAINE, *AS* (Series C) 15, no. 1, 1966, 24–36.
7. The Encashment Function and the Non-Speculative Demand for Money. T. P. LIANOS, *YB* 19, no. 1, May 1967, 62–8.
   Theoretical analyses which seem to be based mainly on U.K. experience or have direct connection with discussion of U.K. monetary issues.

C.ii.b

Empirical Work on U.K. Experience

1. Who Holds Britain's Cash? E. V. MORGAN, *Ba* cix, Mar. 1959, 171–6.
2. Demand for Money in the U.K., 1877–1961: Some Preliminary Findings. N. J. KAVANAH and A. A. WALTERS, *BOIES* 28, no. 2, May 1966, 93–116.
3. The Demand for Money: A Cross-Section Study of British Business Firms (particular reference to the work of A. H. Meltzer in the U.S.A.). L. De ALESSI, *Ec* xxxiii, Aug. 1966, 288–302.

4. Lags and the Demand for Money (FRG). A. A. WALTERS, *JES* 2, no. 1, Spring 1967, 3–22.
5. The Demand for Money in Britain. Quarterly Results 1951 to 1967. D. FISHER, *MS* xxxvi, no. 4, Dec. 1968, 329–44.

C.iii
The Velocity of Money and Money Multipliers

1. Short-Term Fluctuations in the Velocity of Circulation of Money in the U.K., 1954–61. C. DRAKATOS, *BM* cxiv, Dec. 1962, 408–15.
2. Monetary Multipliers in the U.K.: 1880–1962. A. A. WALTERS, *OEP* 18, Nov. 1966, 270–83.
   Studies closely linked to *empirical work on the demand for money.*

C.iv.a
The Level and Structure of Interest Rates
Theoretical Discussions

1. Inflation and the Bank Rate. C. KENNEDY, *OEP* 12, Oct. 1960, 269–73.
2. Interest Rates and Asset Prices (Review Article on R. Turvey *Interest Rates and Asset Prices*, London 1960). B. TEW, *Ec* xxviii, Nov. 1961, 427–31.
3. Inflation and the Bank Rate: A Postscript. R. J. BALL, *OEP* 14, June 1962, 196–9.
4. Recent Theories Concerning the Nature and Role of Interest. G. L. S. SHACKLE, *EJ* lxxi, June 1961, 209–54.
5. A Theory of Interest Rates or Asset Prices? C. V. BROWN, *SJPE* 12, Nov. 1965, 297–308.
   Theoretical discussions which seem to have special relevance to U.K. experience. C.iv.a.4 is a useful survey, and C.iv.a.5 suggests a new approach for the presentation of this subject.

C.iv.b
Empirical Studies in the U.K.

1. The Future of the Rate of Interest. J. R. HICKS, *TMSS* (Session 1957–58), 12 Mar. 1958.
2. Some Econometric Analyses of the Long-Term Rate of Interest in the U.K., 1921–61. R. J. BALL, *MS* xxxiii, no. 1, Jan. 1965, 45–96.
3. Some Statistical Analyses of the Long-Term Rate of Interest in the U.K., 1948–63. J. L. FORD and T. STARK, *BOIES* 27, no. 4, Nov. 1965, 287–97.
   Empirical studies, especially looking at the influence of financial institutions on interest rate levels (3).

4. Analysis of 'The Reverse Gap'. *MBR* May 1960, 3–8.
5. Meiselman on the Structure of Interest Rates: A British Test. J. A. G. GRANT, *Ec* xxxi, Feb. 1964, 51–71.
6. The Structure of Interest Rates: A Comment. D. FISHER, *Ec* xxxi, Nov. 1964, 412–19.
7. Expectations, the Term Structure of Interest Rates, and Recent British Experience. D. FISHER, *Ec* xxxiii, Aug. 1966, 319–29.
8. The Structure of Interest Rates and Recent British Experience: A Comment (on C.iv.b.7). A. BUSE, *Ec* xxxiv, Aug. 1967, 298–308.
9. Reply (to C.iv.b.8). D. FISHER, *Ec* xxxiv, Aug. 1967, 309–13.
10. Yield Curves and Representative Yields on British Government Securities. *BEQB* 7, no. 1, Mar. 1967, 52–6.

> Statistics (10) and empirical analysis, especially linking U.K. experience with U.S. theory and empirical work (5–9).

D.i.a

FINANCIAL POLICY AND TECHNIQUES

General Aspects

U.K. Economic Management

1. In the Event of a Slump. H. JOHNSON, *DBR*, no. 126, June 1958, 18–29.
2. Can We Control the Economy? C. F. CARTER, *DBR*, no. 128, Dec. 1958, 3–17.
3. Fiscal Policy and Monetary Policy as Instruments of Economic Control:
   1. The Needs of the Case. J. C. R. Dow, *WBR* May 1960, 7–11.
   2. The Possibilities of Fiscal Policy. J. C. R. Dow, *WBR* Aug. 1960, 3–15.
   3. The Choice of Measures for Different Situations. J. C. R. Dow, *WBR* Nov. 1960, 2–14.
4. Unemployment and the Economists in the 1920s. K. HANCOCK, *Ec* xxvii, Nov. 1960, 305–21.
5. The U.K. Economy 1951–1961: Performance and Prospect. G. HUTTON, *LBR* no. 61, July 1961, 1–25.
6. The Management of the British Economy (Review article on J. C. R. Dow, *The Management of the British Economy*, London 1964). F. W. PAISH, *LBR*, no. 76, Apr. 1965, 1–17.
7. The British Economy, 1945–60 (Review article on J. C. R. Dow, *The Management of the British Economy*, London 1964). A. R. PREST, *MS* xxxiii, no. 2, May 1965, 141–7.
8. Are Monetary and Fiscal Policies Enough? R. F. HARROD, *EJ* lxxiv, Dec. 1964, 903–14.

9. How Fast Can Britain Grow? A. MADDISON, *LBR*, no. 79, Jan. 1966, 1–14.
10. Monetary-Fiscal Policy for Growth and the Balance-of-Payments Constraint. G. K. SHAW, *Ec* xxxiv, May 1967, 198–202.
11. How the Economy Works. F. W. PAISH, *LBR*, no. 88, Apr. 1968, 1–30.

> Articles referring to the general theoretical (5, 10, 12), institutional (2, 6–9, 11), and policy aspects of economic control, especially in the U.K.

D.i.b

Theory and Problems of Financial Policy

1. Progress, Prices, and the Pound. F. W. PAISH, *DBR* 125, Mar. 1958, 1–17.
2. The Control of Bank Credit: Monetary Policy And Central Bank Organization. A. T. PEACOCK, *SBM* l, no. 197, 1958, 7–40.
3. Advancing from Steam Banking. J. E. WADSWORTH, *BM* clxxxvi, no. 1372, July 1958, 11–14.
4. The Dilemma of Central Banking. R. S. SAYERS, *JIB* lxxix, June 1958, 160–70.
5. The Radcliffe Report and Domestic Monetary Policy. R. ALFORD and H. ROSE, *London and Camb. Econ. Bull.*, Dec. 1959.
6. Monetary Management in Modern Times: Some Aspects of the Radcliffe Report. H. G. HODDER, *NPBR* 49, Feb. 1960, 10–16.
7. New Tasks for Central Bankers. A. JASAY, *BNL* xiii, no. 54, Sept. 1960, 282–97.
8. Monetary Thought and Monetary Policy in England. R. S. SAYERS, *Ba* cx, Oct. 1960, 671–83.
9. Monetary Thought and Monetary Policy in England. R. S. SAYERS, *EJ* lxx, Dec. 1960, 710–24.
10. How Does Monetary Policy Work? B. A. CORRY, *BM* cxci, no. 1402, Jan. 1961, 15–22.
11. Money Still Under Review. H. ROSE, *Ba* cxi, Feb. 1961, 98–106.
12. Alternative Views of Central Banking. R. S. SAYERS, *Ec* xxviii, May 1961, 111–24.
13. Monetary Policy and the Banks. D. J. ROBERTS, *NPBR* 57, Feb. 1962, 1–5.
14. Monetary Techniques—An International Comparison. B. V. GESTRIN, *Ba* 119, Apr. 1969, 318–26.
15. Current Issues in Monetary Policy. H. JOHNSON, *BM* ccvi, Nov. 1968, 251–7.

> Articles mostly deriving from the *Radcliffe Report's* treatment of the nature and aims of monetary policy in general.

16. Monetary Survey. Annual Monetary Survey. *MBR* May.

> A useful review of the annual developments of monetary policy.

D.i.c

The Macro-Economic Background

1. Policy for Expansion and the Money Weapon. Sir R. Harrod, *DBR*, no. 130, June 1959, 3–20.
2. Money, Trade, and Employment. A. N. Shimmin, *DBR*, no. 131, Sept. 1959, 3–14.
3. The Cost Push Theory of Inflation and Tight Money Policy. W. P. Egle, *Welt* 86, no. 2, 1961.
4. Monetary Policy and Economic Growth. M. Niveau, *BM* cxcii, no. 1410, Sept. 1961, 172–84.
5. Money, Liquid Assets, Velocity, and Monetary Policy. G. Garvey, *BNL* xvii, no. 71, Dec. 1964, 324–38.
6. Imported Inflation and Monetary Policy. I. O. Scott, Jr. and W. S. Schmidt, *BNL* xvii, no. 71, Dec. 1964, 390–403.
7. Imported Inflation and Monetary Policy: A Comment (on D.i.b.6). P. M. Oppenheimer, *BNL* xviii, no. 73, 191–7.
8. Imported Inflation and Monetary Policy: A Reply (to D.i.b.7). I. O. Scott, Jr. and W. S. Schmidt, *BNL* xviii, no. 73, June 1965, 197–200.
9. The Lags in Monetary Policy: An Assessment of Alternative Approaches (FRG). V. Argy, *BNL* xviii, no. 73, June 1965, 157–67.
10. The Timeliness of the Effects of Monetary Policy: The New Evidence from Econometric Models. W. H. White, *BNL* xxi, no. 86, Sept. 1968, 276–303.

   Selected articles discussing the relation of monetary policy to major macro-economic variables, with special reference to U.K. problems.

D.i.d

The Radcliffe Report

1. The Radcliffe Report on the Working of the Monetary System: A Preliminary Survey. Sir R. Hawtrey, *BM* clxxxviii, no. 1386, Sept. 1959, 171–3.
2. Radcliffe under Scrutiny: A Post-Mortem on 'Freedom'? T. Balogh, *Ba* cix, Oct. 1959, 583–604.
3. The Radcliffe Report. *LR* xlviii, no. 11, Nov. 1959, 169–71.
4. The Radcliffe Report. *Est*, 22 Aug. 1959, 553–8:
   1. The Monetary Mechanism.
   2. Improving the System.
   3. Sterling.
5. The Radcliffe Report. *Est*, 29 Aug. 1959, 658–661:
   4. The Bank England.
   5. New Financing Institutions?
   6. Figuring it Out.
6. Radcliffe Evidence Appraised. *Est*, 26 Mar. 1960, 1233–7:
   1. How Monetary Policy has Evolved.

2. Argument on Gilt-Edged.

3. The Bank of England.

7. The Radcliffe Report: A Short Guide. *NIER* 5, Sept. 1959, 18–21.

8. The Radcliffe Report. R. V. ROOSA. *LBR* 54, Oct. 1959, 1–13.

9. The Radcliffe Report. P. BAREAU, *JIB* 80, Oct. 1959, 334–47.

10. The Radcliffe Report. Sir O. HODSON, *Ba* cix, Sept. 1959:

    1. No Verdict on Money. 491–6.

    2. The Report Analyzed. 497–534.

    3. No Clear Guidance. 542–6.

11. The Radcliffe Report on the Working of the Monetary System: A Preliminary Survey. Sir R. HAWTREY, *BM* clxxxviii, no. 1386, Sept. 1959, 171–3.

12. The Report of the Radcliffe Committee. Sir R. HAWTREY, *BM* clxxxviii, no. 1387, Oct. 1959, 251–261.

13. Radcliffe Report: An Important Document. *WBR* Nov. 1959, 1–2.

14. Radcliffe Report: An American Impression. A. I. BLOOMFIELD, *WBR* Nov. 1959, 15–20.

15. Radcliffe Report: In Search of Guidance. J. S. G. WILSON, *WBR* Nov. 1959, 7–15.

16. The Radcliffe Committee Report. *SBM* li, no. 203, Nov. 1959, 123–248.

17. A Squeak from Aunt Sally. Sir D. ROBERTSON, *Ba* cix, Dec. 1959, 718–22.

18. Radcliffe Report: A Socratic Scrutiny. W. T. NEWLYN, *BM* clxxxix, no. 1390, Jan. 1960, 21–6.

19. Monetary Policy in Action: The Radcliffe Evidence. *Ba* cx, Apr. 1960, 223–40:

    1. The Governor on Bank Rate.

    2. Funding Policy and Interest Rates.

    3. Banks' Sales of Gilts.

    4. The Government Broker Explains.

20. The Radcliffe Evidence. *Ba* cx, May 1960, 323–36:

    1. How the 'Special Deposits' Plan Originated.

    2. Treasury on Need to Control Money Supply.

    3. Mr. Cobbold on Dangers of Coercion.

    4. Effects on Policy Clearing Banks.

    5. Threat to Gilt-Edged and Funding Policy.

21. The Working of the Radcliffe Monetary System. A. E. JASAY, *OEP* 12, June 1960, 170–80.

22. Radcliffe under Scrutiny: Now for its Critics. A. DAY, *Ba* cx, June 1960, 404–9.

23. Radcliffe Report: Professor Sayers Explains. *Est*, 3 Sept. 1960, 924.

24. Radcliffe Revisited. Sir T. WILSON, *Ba* cx, Oct. 1960, 647–51.

General articles on the Radcliffe Report, including summaries (4–7) and discussions of its theoretical contributions (8, 21).

D.ii.a

Techniques of Financial Control

Regulation of the Money Supply

1. Monetary Policy and Bank Deposits: 1. Monetary Policy in Theory. L. C. WRIGHT, *SBM* lii, no. 208, Feb. 1961, 186–211.
2. Monetary Policy and Bank Deposits: 2. Monetary Policy in Practice —1960. F. CASSELL, *SBM* lii, no. 208, Feb. 1961, 186–211.
3. Monetary Policy and Bank Deposits: 3. The Future of Bank Deposits. F. S. TAYLOR, *SBM* lii, no. 208, Feb. 1961, 186–211.
4. The Creation of Bank Money: A Comparative Study. V. V. BHATT, *BM* cxcii, no. 1412, Nov. 1961, 322–8.
5. The Creation of Bank Money; A Comment (on D.ii.a.4). P. R. NARVEKAR, *BM* cxcv, no. 1428, Mar. 1963, 201–5.
6. The Volume of Deposits and the Cash and Liquid Assets Ratio. D. J. COPPOCK and N. J. GIBSON, *MS* xxxii, no. 3, Sept. 1963, 203–22.
7. The Supply of Money and its Control. W. T. NEWLYN, *EJ* lxxiv, June 1964, 327–46.
8. The Inadequacy of 'New Orthodox' Methods of Monetary Control. R. L. CROUCH, *EJ* lxxiv, Dec. 1964, 916–34.
9. Mr. Crouch on 'New Orthodox' Methods of Monetary Control— Comment (on D.ii.a.8). B. TEW, *EJ* lxxv, Dec. 1965, 859–60.
10. Mr. Crouch on 'New Orthodox' Methods of Monetary Control— Comment (on D.ii.a.8). W. T. NEWLYN, *EJ* lxxv, Dec. 1965, 857–9.
11. Mr. Newlyn's and Professor Tew's Comments: A Reply (to D.ii.a.9 and 10). R. L. CROUCH, *EJ* lxxv, Dec. 1965, 860–3.
12. The Inadequacy of 'New Orthodox' Methods of Monetary Control (reconciliation of views in D.ii.a.8 and 11). W. T. NEWLYN and R. L. CROUCH, *EJ* lxxvii, Sept. 1967, 655–6.
13. Control of the Money Supply: A Rejoinder (to D.ii.a.12). A. B. CRAMP, *EJ* lxxvii, Sept. 1967, 666–7.
14. Control of the Money Supply: A Reply (to D.ii.a.13). W.T. NEWLYN, *EJ* lxxvii, Sept. 1967, 665–6.
15. Whatever Happened to Credit Control? *Est* (supp.), 19 June 1965, vii–x.
16. Control of the Money Supply. A. B. CRAMP, *EJ* lxxvi, June 1966, 278–87.
17. Are Open-Market Operations Effective? K. K. F. ZAWADZKI, *OEP* 17, Mar. 1965, 100–10.
18. Depreciation Realized on Security Sales by the London Clearing Banks: 1952–58. J. F. CHANT, *BOIES* 29, no. 2, May 1967, 171–84.
19. Technical Controls over Bank Deposits in Britain. A. N. McLEOD, *OEP* 18, July 1966, 177–92.
20. The Genesis of Bank Deposits: New English Version. R. L. CROUCH, *BOIES* 27, no. 3, Aug. 1965, 185–99.

21. The Genesis of Bank Deposits: New English Version—A Comment (on D.ii.a.19). J. M. PARKIN, *BOIES* 29, no. 1, Feb. 1967, 79–84.
22. The Genesis of Bank Deposits: Reply to Mr. Parkin (to D.ii.a.20). R. L. CROUCH, *BOIES* 29, no. 1, Feb. 1967, 85–6.
23. The Control of Bank Deposits. A. B. CRAMP, *LBR* 86, Oct. 1967, 16–35.
24. Financial Theory and Control of Bank Deposits. A. B. CRAMP, *OEP* 20, no. 1, Mar. 1968, 98–108.
25. Money Supply Theory and the U.K.'s Monetary Contraction, 1954–56. R. L. CROUCH, *BOIES* 30, no. 2, May 1968, 143–52.
   Articles concerned with debate between the alleged proponents (7, 9, 10, 13, 14, 23, 24) of the so-called 'new orthodox' explanation of control of the money supply derived from the *Radcliffe Report* and their critics (6, 8, 10, 20, 22, 25). A reconciliation of views is attempted in later articles (15, 17–19).

26. Open-Market Operations Versus Reserve-Requirement Variation. J. ASCHHEIM, *EJ* lxix, Dec. 1959, 697–704.
27. Open-Market Operations Versus Reserve-Requirement Variation: Comment (on D.ii.a.26). R. GOODE and J. GURLEY, *EJ* lxx, Sept. 1960, 616–18.
28. Open-Market Operations Versus Reserve-Requirement Variation: Comment (on D.ii.a.26). R. C. POTTER, *EJ* lxx, Sept. 1960, 618–20.
29. Open-Market Operations Versus Reserve-Requirement Variation: A Reply (to D.ii.a.27, 28). J. ASCHHEIM, *EJ* lxx, Sept. 1960, 620–2.
30. Open-Market Operations and the Portfolio Policies of the Commercial Banks. C. A. THANOS, *EJ* lxxi, Sept. 1961, 566–71.
31. The Relative Security-Market Impact of Open-Market Sales and 'Equivalent' Reserve-Requirement Increases (comment on D.ii.a.30). H. N. GOLDSTEIN, *EJ* lxxii, Sept. 1962, 597–610.
32. The Relative Security-Market Impact of Open-Market Sales and 'Equivalent' Reserve-Requirement Increases: A Rejoinder (to D.ii.a.31). C. A. THANOS, *EJ* lxxii, Dec. 1962, 999–1005.
33. A Note on Open-Market Operations Versus Variations in Reserve-Requirements. D. C. ROWAN, *EJ* lxxii, June 1962, 471–7.
34. Open-Market Operations Versus Reserve-Ratio Requirements—Another Viewpoint. A. J. FITZGIBBONS, *EJ* lxxii, Dec. 1962, 994–9.
35. Restrictive Open-Market Operations Versus Reserve-Requirement Increases: A Reformulation J. ASCHHEIM, *EJ* lxxiii, June 1963, 254–66.
36. Monetary Control Through Open-Market Operations and Reserve-Requirement Variations. A. D. BAIN, *EJ* lxxiv, Mar. 1964, 137–46.
37. Open-Market Operations and Reserve-Requirement Variations Again. A. D. BAIN, *EJ* lxxvi, Dec. 1966, 935–7.
38. A Re-examination of Open-Market Operations. R. L. CROUCH, *OEP* 15, June, 1963, 81–94.
   A major theoretical debate, with applications to U.K. financial policy.

39. Changes in Money Supply in the U.K. G. L. Bell and L. S. Berman, *Ec* xxxiii, May 1966, 148–65.
40. Changes in the Money Supply in the U.K., 1954–64 (comment on D.ii.a.39). D. K. Sheppard, *Ec* xxxv, Aug. 1968, 297–302.
41. Bank Credit and Gold in the U.K. W. J. Busschau, *EJ* lxviii, June 1968, 271–8.
42. The Management of Money Day by Day. *BEQB* iii, no. 1, Mar. 1963, 15–21.
    Important descriptive article on monetary technique.

D.ii.b
Special Deposits Schemes

1. The Procedure of Special Deposits. *BEQB* i, no. 1, Dec. 1960, 18.
2. The Background of Special Deposits. P. Bareau, *DBR*, no. 136, Dec. 1960, 23–38.
3. Special Deposits as an Instrument of Monetary Policy. N. J. Gibson, *MS* xxxii, no. 3, Sept. 1964, 239–59.
4. Control of Bank Lending: The Cash Deposits Scheme. *BEQB* 8, no. 2, June 1968, 166–170.
   Descriptions and analysis (3) of special deposit schemes.

D.ii.c
Regulation of Bank Rate and Other Interest Rates

1. Horsley Palmer on Bank Rate. A. B. Cramp, *Ec* xxvi, 341–9.
2. Interest Rates and Monetary Policy. J. E. Wadsworth, *BM* cxcvi, no. 1437, Dec. 1963, 380–7.
3. Bank Rate. A. A. Walters, *BM* cc, July 1965, 7–11

D.ii.d
Control of Trade Credit

1. Trade Credit and Monetary Policy. F. P. Brechling and R. G. Lipsey, *EJ* lxxiii, Dec. 1963, 618–41.
2. Trade Credit and Monetary Policy: A Reconciliation (comment on D.ii.d.1). W. H. White, *EJ* lxxiv, Dec. 1964, 935–45.
3. Trade Credit and Monetary Policy: A Rejoinder (to D.ii.d.2). R. G. Lipsey and F. P. Brechling, *EJ* lxxvi, Mar. 1966, 165–7.
4. Monetary Theory and Trade Credit, An Historical Approach. M. S. Levitt, *YB* 16, no. 2, Nov. 1964, 88–96.
5. Some Observations on Trade Credit and Monetary Policy. A. N. McLeod, *EJ* lxxiv, Sept. 1964, 729–34.
6. Trade Credit: A Case Study. J. B. Coates, *JIE* xiii, no. 3, June 1965, 205–13.

7. Trade Credit and Monetary Policy: A Study of the Accounts of 50 Companies. J. B. COATES, *OEP* 19, Mar. 1967, 116–32.
   Empirical evidence on the relation of monetary policy and trade credit.

D.ii.e

Control of General Liquidity and Non-Bank Intermediaries

1. Radcliffe Under Scrutiny: A Case for Financial Controls? B. TEW, *Ba* cx, Jan. 1960, 28–33.
2. The Radcliffe Evidence—II: Financial Institutions and Monetary Policy. H. B. ROSE, *BM* clxl, no. 1396, July 1960, 14–25.
3. The Control of Liquidity and the Radcliffe Committee. L. J. HUME, *BNL* xiii, no. 55, Dec. 1960, 372–5.
4. Competition in Lending and Monetary Policy. M. V. POSNER, *Ba* cxi, Mar. 1961, 190–6.
5. Non-Bank Credit and Monetary Policy. R. F. HENDERSON and J. O. N. PERKINS, *Ba* cxi, Aug. 1961, 543–7.
6. Radcliffe under Scrutiny: Money Substitutes and Monetary Policy. A. LAMFALUSSY, *Ba* cxi, Jan. 1961, 44–50.
7. Financial Intermediaries and Monetary Policy. A. B. CRAMP, *Ec* xxix, May 1962, 143–51.
8. Monetary Policy and Financial Intermediaries: The Hire Purchase Finance Houses. M. J. ARTIS, *BOIES* 25, no. 1, Feb. 1963, 11–46.
9. The Control of Non-Bank Financial Intermediaries. T. M. PODOLSKI, *BM* ccvii, Jan. and Feb. 1969.
   Articles mostly derived from the *Radcliffe Committee* discussion of liquidity control. D.ii.e.6,7 are especially useful.

D.ii.f

Direct Credit Control

1. The Control of Bank Credit: 2. Is Bank Lending Inflationary? I. SMITH, *SBM* l, no. 197, May 1958, 7–40.
2. The Control of Bank Credit: 3. Liquidity and the Rationing of Bank Advances. I. STEWART, *SBM* l, no. 197, May 1958, 7–40.
3. The Control of Bank Credit: 4. The 1958 Budget. *SBM* l, no. 197, May 1958, 7–40.
4. The Control of Bank Credit: 5. The Scottish Banks and the Credit Squeeze. *SBM* l, no. 197, May 1958, 7–40.
5. The Control of Bank Credit: 6. Direct Controls on Bank Credit: Qualitative and Quantitative. *SBM* l, no. 197, May 1958, 7–40.
6. Capital Issues Control: Dead or Dormant? *MBR* Feb. 1960, 3–8.
7. Bank Advances as an Object of Policy. Sir O. FRANKS, *LBR*, no. 59, Jan. 1961, 1–14.

8. Credit Control and Asset Structure. L. C. WRIGHT, *SJPE* 9, Nov. 1962, 244–52.
9. Banking Regulation in Britain—By Suasion Not Statute. *MBR* Nov. 1967, 12–20.
10. How Big is Grandmother's Big Stick? *BM* ccvii, June 1969, 1–2.

D.ii.g

Debt Management

1. Government Debt Policy and the Banking System. *MBR* Feb. 1958, 3–7.
2. Gilt-Edged and the Money Supply. F. W. PAISH. *Ba* cix, Jan. 1959, 17–25.
3. Treasury Bills and the Money Supply. W. M. DACEY. *LBR* no. 55, Jan. 1960, 1–16.
4. Radcliffe Report: Monetary Policy and Debt-Management Reconciled? S. I. KATZ, *BNL* xiii, no. 53, June 1960, 149–70.
5. Easy Budgets and Tight Money. J. M. BUCHANAN, *LBR*, no. 64, Apr. 1962, 17–30.
6. Funding Policy and the Gilt-Edged Market. E. V. MORGAN, *LBR*, no. 66, Oct. 1962, 40–53.
7. Exchequer Financing and Bank Deposits: What the Statistics Show, 1959–64. A. E. HOLMANS, *Ba* cxiv, Sept. 1964, 565–74.
8. The Futility of Funding. R. L. CROUCH, *BM* cc, July 1965, 1–6.
9. The Futility of Funding: A Comment. G. MAYNARD, *BM* cc, Sept. 1965, 143–5.

> Problems of debt management (2, 4, 6, 8). Note that there is a close connection with the '*new orthodox*' *method of discussion* (D.ii.a.6–25).

D.iii.a

Impact of Financial Control

General

1. Thoughts on the Crisis. L. ROBBINS, *LBR*, no. 48, Apr. 1958, 1–26.
2. New Credit Measures and the Balance of Payments. Sir R. HAWTREY, *BM* clxxxvi, no. 1373, Aug. 1958, 91–6.
3. An Obituary of the Credit Squeeze. H. SPEIGHT, *BM* clxxxvii, no. 1382, May 1959, 375–83.
4. Some Aspects of Monetary Policy in England, 1952–58. D. WILLIAMS, *YB* 12, no. 2, Nov. 1960, 96–110.
5. The Economic Prospect. A. SHONFIELD, *WBR* Feb. 1961, 2–9.
6. Three Credit Squeezes; Similarities and Contrasts. *MBR* Nov. 1965, 3–12.

> The progress of monetary policy. D.iii.a.6 is especially useful and complements the *MBR* annual review of monetary developments.

7. External Aspects of Monetary Policy: Some Reflections on the Radcliffe Committee's Report. J. S. G. WILSON, *JIB* 81, Aug. 1960, 235–45.

8. Credit Restriction and the Supply of Exports. R. J. BALL, *MS* xxix, no. 2, May 1961, 161–72.

9. Credit Policy and the Regional Problem. M. GASKIN, *BM* clxl, no. 1398, Sept. 1960, 151–8.

10. The U.K. Economic Position—A Guide to the Sources. R. F. G. ALFORD, *BM* cxcv, no. 1428, Mar. 1963, 215–21 (Addendum in *BM* cxcv, no. 1430, May 1963, 409).
    Particularly useful for general data on monetary policy.

D.iii.b

Money Supply Changes

1. The Finance of Inflation. H. B. ROSE, *LBR* no. 47, Jan. 1958, 1–16.

2. Money's Role. *Est*, 22 Aug. 1959, 507–9.

3. Is the Money Supply Important? Sir R. HARROD, *WBR* Nov. 1959, 3–7.

4. How Much Does Money Matter. A. B. CRAMP, *BM* cxcii, no. 1411, Oct. 1961, 242–7.
    Mainly relating to the *Radcliffe Report* treatment of the money supply.

5. The Quantity of Money, Gross National Product, and the Price Level: Some International Comparisons. A. E. HOLMANS, *SJPE* 8, Feb. 1961, 28–44.

6. The Money Supply Debate: 1. How the Argument has Revived. *Ba* 118, Dec. 1968, 1094–115.

7. The Money Supply Debate: 2. Taxes, Money, and Stabilization. M. FRIEDMAN, *Ba* 118, Dec. 1968, 1094–115.

8. The Money Supply Debate: 3. 'L'impasse' in Britain. H. WINCOTT, *Ba* 118, Dec. 1968, 1094–115.

9. The Money Supply Debate: 4. Too Much Liquidity. F. W. TOOBY, *Ba* 118, Dec. 1968, 1094–115.

10. Walters on Money (Review article on A. A. Walters *Money in Boom and Slump*, London 1969). P. R. HERRINGTON, *BM* ccvii, July 1969, 5–17.

11. The Chicago School of Thought. L. HARRIS, *BM* ccvii, July 1969, 5–17.

12. The Money Supply: Revival of a Fashion. M. CRAWFORD, *MW* Spring 1969, 16–30.

13. Two Aspects of the Monetary Debate. M. J. ARTIS and A. R. NOBAY, *NIER* no. 49, Aug. 1969, 33–51.

14. The Money Supply Question. P. G. GSCHWINDT DE GYOR, *NWBR* Aug. 1969, 61–8.

> Useful summaries of U.K. aspects of the revived interest in economic control via the money supply. Note especially the symposiums (6–9 and 10–11) and the discussion of Domestic Credit Expansion in 13.

D.iii.c

Interest Rates

1. Bank Rate: Progress and Prospects. Sir R. HAWTREY, *BM* clxxv, no. 1369, Apr. 1958, 285–91.
2. Vindicating Bank Rate. *Est* (supp.), 14 June 1958, 4–8.
3. Bank Rate Vindicated? Evidence Before the Radcliffe Committee. W. H. WHITE, *BM* clxxxvii, no. 1385, Aug. 1959, 98–104.
4. Radcliffe Under Scrutiny: What Role for Interest Rates? E. V. MORGAN, *Ba* cix, Oct. 1959, 583–604.
5. Radcliffe Under Scrutiny: Control by 'Stickiness' of Rates? J. SPRAOS. *Ba* cix, Nov. 1959, 674–80.
6. The Radcliffe Evidence—I: Stocks of Commodities, Fixed Capital and the Interest Rate. Sir R. HAWTREY, *BM* clxxxix, no. 1394, May 1960, 410–18.
7. Inventory Investment and the Rate of Interest. W. H. WHITE, *BNL* xiv, no. 57, June 1961, 141–83.
8. Money Liquidity and Interest Rates. E. V. MORGAN, *LBR*, no. 61, July 1961, 26–38.
9. The Rate of Interest and the Timing of Capital Projects. A. MERRETT and A. SYKES, *MS* xxix, no. 3, Sept. 1961, 233–48.
10. English Policy on Interest Rates, 1958–62. R. S. SAYERS, *BNL* xv, no. 61, June 1962, 111–26.
11. Bank Rate, the British Balance of Payments, and the Burden of Adjustment, 1870–1914. A. G. FORD, *OEP* 16, Mar. 1964, 24–39.
12. High Interest Rates—Who Benefits? *LR* liv, no. 3, Mar. 1965, 36–7.
13. Interest Rates, Investment Decisions, and External Financing. R. E. KRAINER, *OEP* 18, Nov. 1966, 304–12.
14. A New High for Interest Rates. *BBR* xlii, no. 4, Nov. 1967, 69–71.
15. Are Interest Rates Too High? W. A. ELTIS, *LBR*, no. 93, July 1969, 27–35.

D.iii.d

Lending Controls

1. Hire-Purchase Controls and Fluctuations in the Car Market. J. R. CUTHBERTSON, *Ec* xxviii, May 1961, 125–36.

2. A Note on the effect of Hire-Purchase Control on the Sales of Private Motor Cars in the U.K. from February, 1952 to December, 1960. P. GALAMBOS, *YB* 14, no. 1, May 1962, 37–45.
3. Hire-Purchase Controls and Replacement Cycles. J. K. S. GHANDHI, *BNL* xv, no. 62, Sept. 1962, 289–99.
4. Hire-Purchase Controls and the Demand for Cars (criticism of D.iii.d.1). A. SILBERSTON, *EJ* lxxiii, Mar. 1963, 32–53.
5. Hire-Purchase Controls and the Demand for Cars: A Comment (on D.iii.d.4). J. R. CUTHBERTSON, *EJ* lxxiii, Sept. 1963, 553–6.
6. Hire-Purchase Controls and the Demand for Cars: A Reply. A SILBERSTON, *EJ* lxxiii, Sept. 1963, 556–8.
7. Hire-Purchase Contracts for Cars. *BEQB* v, no. 3, Sept. 1965, 241–7.
8. Hire-Purchase Contracts for Cars (carries forward data in D.iii.d.7). *BEQB* 7, no. 3, Sept. 1967, 268–75.
9. Hire-Purchase Controls and the Demand for Cars. M. ALI, *JES* i, no. 1, Winter 1965, 88–97.
10. Hire-Purchase Controls and the Demand for Cars in the Post War U.K. A Comment (on D.iii.d.9). A. SILBERSTON, *JES* i, no. 2, Summer 1966, 93–7.
11. A Rejoinder (to D.iii.d.10). M. ALI, *JES* i, no. 2, Summer 1966, 98–9.
12. The Cost of Motor Vehicle Hire-Purchase. A. D. BAIN, *JIE* xiv, no. 2, Apr. 1966, 124–42.
    Statistical descriptions (7, 8), theory, and empirical work on a key sector's reaction to direct control of lending facilities.

E.i

MONETARY ASPECTS OF THE U.K. INTERNATIONAL POSITION

General

1. Notes on Balance-of-Payments Estimates. A. HAZLEWOOD, *BOIES* 23, no. 4, Nov. 1961, 393–9.
2. Unrecorded Movements in the U.K. Balance of Payments: The 'Balancing Item'. *BEQB* ii, no. 1, Mar. 1962, 16–22.
3. The U.K. Balance of Payments Accounts. T. M. KLEIN, *EJ* lxxiv, Dec. 1964, 946–53.
4. The Balance of Payments: Methods of Presentation (FRG). *BEQB* iv, no. 4, Dec. 1964, 276–86.
5. Which Balance of Payments. *WBR* Nov. 1965, 26–36.
    Selected, useful accounts of statistical problems in presenting balance of payments figures, especially *monetary* flows.
6. The U.K. as Creditor Country. A. R. CONAN, *WBR* Aug. 1960, 16–22.

7. *BEQB.* A regular series of statistics and comments on the U.K. net external financial position has appeared as follows:
   - New Series of External Liabilities and Claims in Sterling. iii, no. 2, June 1963, 98–105.
   - An Inventory of U.K. External Assets and Liabilities: End 1962. iv, no. 1, Mar. 1964, 23–33.
   - An Inventory of U.K. External Assets and Liabilities: End 1964. v, no. 4, Dec. 1965, 339–45.
   - An Inventory of U.K. External Assets and Liabilities: End 1966. vii, no. 3, Sept. 1967, 261–7.
   - An Inventory of U.K. External Assets and Liabilities: End 1967. viii, no. 3, Sept. 1968, 271–9.
8. Britain's Debts to Foreign Bankers. *LR* lvii, no. 9, Sept. 1968, 152–3.
9. British Gold and Currency Reserves. E. J. BROSTER, *BM* ccvi, Dec. 1968, 313–17.

10. Inflows and Outflows of Foreign Funds. *BEQB* ii, no. 2, June 1962, 93–102.
11. Monetary Movements and the International Position of Sterling. P. M. OPPENHEIMER, *SJPE* 13, Feb. 1966, 89–135.
12. Short-Term Capital Flows. P. M. OPPENHEIMER, *Ba* 117, Aug. 1967, 670–7.
13. Monetary Movements in the U.K. Balance of Payments. *BEQB* 8, no. 1, Mar. 1968, 34–40.
    Statistics (10, 13) and *monetary policy* (11, 12) implications of international monetary flows.

14. U.K. Balance-of-Payments, 1946–55. J. MITCHELL, *BOIES* 20, no. 1, Feb. 1958, 29–51.
15. The British Balance of Payments, 1957–58. S. FROWEN, *BM* clxxxv, 1370, May 1958, 395–403.
16. The Problem of Living Within our Foreign Earnings Further Considered. A. ROBINSON, *TBR* 28, June 1958, 3–16.
17. The Balance of Payments. D. WILLIAMS, *NPBR* 53, Feb. 1961, 15–19.
18. Factors in the Balance of Payments Problem. A. R. CONAN, *WBR* May 1961, 2–11.
19. The British Balance of Payments. Sir R. HARROD, *Welt* 88, no. 2, 1962, 151–65.
20. The Treasury and Stagnation. W. SCAMMELL, *BM* cxciii, no. 1417. Apr. 1962, 295–301.
21. Towards a Balance. *BBR* xxxix, no. 4, Nov. 1964, 67–8.
22. The Unsolved Balance of Payments Problem. A. R. CONAN, *WBR* Nov. 1963, 2–12.
23. Britain's Overseas Payment Deficit. *LR* liii, no. 10, Oct. 1964, 155–7,
24. U.K. Balance of Payments—The Weak Spot. W. A. P. MANSER, *WBR* May 1965, 24–8.

25. Balance-of-Payments: The Cost. *LR* lvi, no. 6, June 1967, 93–4.
26. Balance-of-Payments: The Problem not Solved. *LR* lvi, no. 11, Nov. 1967, 174–7.
27. Inflation and the Balance-of-Payments in the U.K., 1962–67. F. W. PAISH, *SJPE* 15, Nov. 1968, 213–26.
    Selected articles of description and commentary on the balance of payments with particular reference to its monetary aspects.

E.ii

Invisible Earnings

1. Britain's Invisible Earnings. J. MITCHELL, *Ba* cviii, May 1958, 327–31.
2. The City's Invisible Earnings. A. VICE, *BM* clxxxvi, no. 1375, 264–6.
3. The Fall in Britain's Invisible Earnings. R. S. GILBERT, *NIER* 12, Nov. 1960, 45–52.
4. Invisibles in the Balance of Payments. *BEQB* i, no. 5, Dec. 1961, 17–25.
5. The City's Earnings. G. CYRIAX, *MW* 6, Autumn 1965, 73–9.
6. Invisible Earnings. A. E. HOLMANS, *SJPE* 13, Feb. 1966, 42–64.
7. The City and the Pound; Yesterday, Today, and Tomorrow. W. F. CRICK, *Ba* 117, Aug. 1967, 700–7.
8. The Importance of Invisibles. P. BAREAU, *Ba* 117, Nov. 1967, 927–32.
9. Leads and Lags on Invisible Trade. P. EINZIG, *Ba* 118, Jan. 1968, 41–7.
10. The Role of Invisible Trade in the U.K. Balance of Payments, 1952–66. F. N. BURTON and P. GALAMBOS, *NPBR* 21, no. 82, May 1968, 9–15.
11. Is the City Good for the Country. C. G. TETHER, *BM* ccv, June 1968, 331–9.
12. Britain's Invisible Balance. M. PANIC, *LBR* 89, July 1968, 12–30 (see The Report of the Committee on External Earnings: London 1967).
13. The Overseas Earnings of U.K. Financial Institutions. *BEQB* 8, no. 4, Dec. 1968, 402–7.
    Descriptive articles on invisible earnings, stressing especially the difficulties of estimating their volume.

E.iii

Sterling as an International Currency

1. Lifebelts for Sterling? A. C. L. DAY, *BM* clxxxv, no. 1369, Apr. 1958, 296–300.

2. The Position of Sterling: Background Material. *MBR* Aug. 1960, 8–13 and 16 (Note: 'Sterling in the World Today', *MBR* Feb. 1956).
3. The Status of the Key Currencies: A Comparative Study. A. R. CONAN, *WBR* May 1962, 14–26.
4. The Pound at Home and Abroad. Sir R. HARROD, *Ky* 15, no. 3, 1962, 671–4.
5. Britain and the E.E.C.—Monetary and Financial Problems. J. T. L. DELAGAVE, *WBR* Nov. 1962, 2–18.
6. The Pound and the Dollar in the 1960s. A. R. CONAN, *WBR* May 1963, 2–13.
7. Sterling as a Key Currency. *MBR* Aug. 1963, 3–12.
8. Britain's Debts and World Liquidity. F. HIRSCH, *Ba* cxv, Oct. 1965, 649–58.
9. Financing World Trade. *Est* (supp.), 18 June 1966, x–xvi.
10. Being a Reserve Currency. *LR* lv, no. 9, Sept. 1966, 153–5.
11. Retrospect on Sterling: The Crises of 1964 and 1965. D. W. PEARCE, *BM* ccii, Nov. 1966, 337–43.
12. Sterling and the Common Market. M. STAMP, *Ba* 116, Dec. 1966, 844–52.
13. Sterling in Europe—A British View. R. FRY, *Ba* 117, Mar. 1967, 216–19.
14. Exports Can Hurt Sterling—An Economic Paradox. P. EINZIG, *Ba* 117, June 1967, 518–25.
15. The Role of Sterling. Sir R. HARROD, *DBR* 160, Dec. 1966, 2–19.
16. The Declining Use of Sterling as a Trading Currency. P. EINZIG, *WBR* May 1958, 2–10.
17. Sterling after Basle. P. BAREAU, *Ba* 118, Oct. 1968, 869–73.
    Articles with particular reference to the use of sterling in international trade.

18. Central Bank Co-operation. *BBR* xxxvi, no. 2, May 1961, 26–9.
19. Offsetting Hot Money Flows: A Survey of Expediency in Recent Years. *MBR* Aug. 1962, 3–9.
20. Co-operation Between Central Banks. R. S. SAYERS, *TBR* 59, Sept. 1963, 3–25.
21. Monetary Interdependence. *BBR* xxxix, May 1964, 29–31.
22. Twenty Years of Inter-Central Banking Co-operation. *BBR* xli, no. 4, Nov. 1966, 69–72.
    The role of the Bank of England in international monetary relations, especially policy implications.

E.iv

The Sterling Area

1. British Monetary Policy and the Overseas Sterling Area. R. G. OPIE, *WBR* Feb. 1958, 9–13.

2. Is the Sterling Area Worth While? *DBR* 125, Mar. 1958, 30–40.
3. The Future of the Sterling Area (Major symposium of thirteen articles). *BOIES* 21, no. 4, Nov. 1959, 211–375.
4. Europe and the Sterling Area: 1. The Impact of Britain's Entry. J. O. N. PERKINS, *Ba* cxii, May 1962, 306–12.
5. Europe and the Sterling Area: 2. Changing with the Times. J. O. N. PERKINS, *Ba* cxii, June 1962, 382–6.
6. Overseas Sterling Holdings. *BEQB* iii, no. 4, Dec. 1963, 264–78.
7. Is the Sterling Area Disintegrating? H. A. SPENGLER, *Ba* cxiv, Jan. 1964, 17–22.
8. The Sterling Area Balance of Payments. D. G. BADGER, *BM* cxcviii, Oct. 1964, 277–88.
9. Reconstructing the Sterling Area. A. R. CONAN, *Ba* 188, May 1968, 429–36.
10. Funding the Sterling Balances. M. CRAWFORD, *Ba* 118, July 1968, 607–13.
11. The Burden of the Sterling Area. R. G. HOLLOWAY, *BM* ccvi, July 1968, 6–11.
    Selected articles on the statistics (6, 8), problems (2, 3, 11), and prospects of the Sterling Area.

F.i

MONETARY ASPECTS OF U.K. EXTERNAL ECONOMIC POLICY

The Rate of Exchange

1. Sterling Convertibility. R. HARROD, *BM* clxxxvi, no. 1376, Nov. 1958, 345–9.
2. Case for the Status Quo. *Ba* cviii, Apr. 1958, 229–35.
3. Case for an Official Peg. J. SPRAOS, *Ba* cviii, Apr. 1958, 225–8.
4. Case for Official Support. A. E. JASAY, *Ba* cviii, Apr. 1958, 228–9.
5. The Return to Convertibility. R. TRIFFIN, *BNL* xii, no. 48, Mar. 1959, 3–57.
6. The Implications of Convertibility. Sir R. HAWTREY, *BM* clxxxvii, no. 1381, Apr. 1959, 281–7.
7. New Light on the 1931 Crisis. E. V. MORGAN, *Ba* cxiii, Feb. 1963, 104–9.
8. Lessons and Legacies: 1931–61. *Est*, 17 Jun. 1961, 1263–84.
9. The 1931 Financial Crisis. D. WILLIAMS, *YB* 15, no. 2, Nov. 1963, 92–110.
    The problems of convertibility, illustrated by reference to earlier periods of convertibility (5, 7, 8). Techniques of exchange-rate management (2–4).
10. The Alleged Case Against Devaluation. D. J. COPPOCK, *MS* xxxiii, no. 3, Sept. 1965, 285–312.
11. The Case Against Devaluation. R. J. BALL, *BM* cciii, Apr. 1967, 230–5.

12. Should the Pound be Devalued? M. Scott, *BM* cciii, Apr. 1967, 225–30.
13. Exchange Rate Policy and the Future. J. Williamson, *MW* 8, Spring 1967, 5–23.
14. Devaluation and Doubt. I. Macleod, *Ba* 118, Jan. 1968, 15–22.
15. Devaluation—for the Record. *MBR* Feb. 1968, 15–18.
16. Devaluation: Some Echoes of 1931. *BBR* xliii, no. 1, Feb. 1968, 3–6.
17. Sterling Devaluation: The Case Remains. R. N. Cooper, *BM* ccvi, Dec. 1968, 306–10.
    Articles with special reference to problems of and prospects for devaluation.
18. Exchange Rate Flexibility. J. E. Meade, *TBR* 70, June 1966, 3–27.
    Important analysis of schemes for flexible exchange rates.
19. The Case for a Floating Pound. Sir R. Hawtrey, *BM* ccvii, June 1969, 343–8.

F.ii

Other Aspects of Control

1. Bank Rate or Forward Exchange. A. E. Jasay, *BNL* xi, no. 44, Mar. 1958, 56–73.
2. Forward Exchange: The Case for Intervention. A. E. Jasay, *LBR* 50, Oct. 1958, 35–45.
3. Speculation, Arbitrage, and Sterling. J. Spraos, *EJ* lxix, Mar. 1959, 1–21.
4. Speculation, Arbitrage, and Sterling: A Comment. A. E. Jasay, *EJ* lxix, Sept. 1959, 590–2.
5. The Forward Market in Gold. P. Einzig, *Ba* cix, Apr. 1959, 225–30.
6. The Forward Pound, 1951–59. B. Reading, *EJ* lxx, June 1960, 304–19.
7. Exchange Control in Britain Today. *MBR* Feb. 1964, 3–9.
8. The Remnants of Exchange Control. *BBR* xxxv, no. 3, Aug. 1960, 45–7.
9. Some Recent Changes in Forward Exchange Practices. P. Einzig, *EJ* lxx, Sept. 1960, 485–95.
10. The Relations between Practice and Theory of Forward Exchange. P. Einzig, *BNL* xv, no. 62, Sept. 1962, 227–39.
11. Some Recent Developments in Official Forward Exchange Operations. P. Einzig, *EJ* lxxiii, June 1963, 241–53.
12. The Role of Commercial Banks in Foreign Exchange Speculation. B. Cutilli, *BNL* xvi, no. 65, June 1963, 216–31.
13. What Bankers Know, or Ought to Know, about Foreign Exchange Theory. P. Einzig, *BNL* xvii, no. 70, Sept. 1964, 296–315.

14. The U.K. Exchange Control: A Short History. *BEQB* 7, no. 3, Sept. 1967, 245–60.
15. The Exchange Equalization Account: Its Origins and Development. *BEQB* 8, no. 4, Dec. 1968, 377–90.
16. The Potential Volume of Forward Exchange Facilities. P. EINZIG, *BNL* xxi, no. 87, Dec. 1968, 397–414.
    Theoretical analyses (3, 4, 10), *monetary policy* implications (1, 11, 12, 15), and descriptions of markets and techniques in forward exchange.
17. Controls on Import Credit? L. S. PRESSNELL, *Ba* 116, Nov. 1966, 795–8.
18. The Fallacy of Import Controls. P. EINZIG, *Ba* 118, Aug. 1968, 701–5.
19. Import Restrictions as a Weapon of Balance of Payments Policy. P. M. OPPENHEIMER, *NWBR* Nov. 1968, 23–36.
20. Credit Restrictions and Import Deposit Scheme. *BEQB* 8, no. 4, Dec. 1968, 358–9.
    Discussion of methods of U.K. external financial policy.

G

MONETARY HISTORY NOT OTHERWISE NOTED

1. Does Money Always Depreciate? R. G. LIPSEY, *LBR*, no. 58, Oct. 1960, 1–13.
    Data on price changes from the thirteenth century throws doubt on the historical 'law of rising prices'.
2. Notes on the Working of the Gold Standard Before 1914. A. G. FORD, *OEP* 12, Feb. 1960, 52–76.
3. The Causes of the Great Depression. D. J. COPPOCK, *MS* xxxix, no. 3, Sept. 1961, 205–32.
4. The Gold Standard and Deflation: Issues and Attitudes in the 1920s. L. J. HUME, *Ec* xxx, Aug. 1963, 225–42.
5. The Working of the Gold Standard. W. SCAMMELL, *YB* 17, no. 1, May 1965, 32–45.
6. The Gold Standard in its Heyday. L. MARINI, *Ba* cxv, Mar. 1965, 166–76.
7. The Truth About Gold. A. G. FORD, *LBR* no. 77, July 1965, 1–18.
    Useful additions to the discussion of the effects of *money supply* changes and the U.K. external position and policy.
8. Montagu Norman and Banking Policy in the 1920s. D. WILLIAMS, *YB* 11, no. 1, July 1959, 38–55.
9. Lord Norman: A New Interpretation (semi-review of A. Boyle, *Montagu Norman*, London, 1967). Sir T. GREGORY, *LBR*, no. 88, Apr. 1968, 31–51.
10. Montagu Norman in the Per Jacobson Diaries. E. E. JUCKER-FLEETWOOD, *NWBR* Nov. 1968, 52–71.

VI. INDEX OF ARTICLES ARRANGED BY AUTHOR

Checkland, S. G. A.i.b.35
Chown, J. F. A.ii.c.2
Clark, R. J. B.ii.c.9
Clarke, W. M. A.ii.a.1
Clay, J. A. B.iii.b.15
Clayton, G. A.i.b.6,32; A.ii.a.15; A.ii.h.4,5
Clendenning, E. W. A.ii.l.8
Coates, J. B. D.ii.d.6,7
Cobbold, C. F. A.ii.a.3
Colloff, J. E. M. A.ii.d.1
Colville, J. R. A.ii.a.6
Conan, A. R. B.iii.b.8; E.i.6,18,22; E.iii.3,6; E.iv.9
Cook, S. B.iii.a.15
Cooper, R. N. F.i.17
Coppock, D. J. D.ii.a.6; F.i.10; G.3
Corry, B. A. D.i.b.10
Cowen, H. B.ii.c.5
Cowen, J. D. A.i.d.2,4
Cox, P. A. C.i.b.4
Cramp, A. B. A.i.b.8; C.i.a.7,8; D.ii.a.13,16,23,24; D.ii.c.1; D.ii.e.7; D.iii.b.4
Crawford, M. D.iii.b.12; E.iv.10
Crick, W. F. E.ii.7
Crouch, R. L. D.ii.a.8,11,12,20,22,25,38; D.ii.g.8
Cuthbertson, J. R. D.ii.d.1; D.iii.d.5
Cutilli, B. F.ii.12
Cyriax, G. E.ii.5

Dacey, W. M. D.ii.g.3
Davidson, P. C.ii.a.3,5
Davies, G. A.ii.i.1,3
Davis, E. W. A.i.b.18
Day, A. C. L. D.i.d.22; E.iii.1
De Alessi, L. C.ii.b.3
Delacave, J. T. L. E.iii.5
Devons, E. A.iii.6
Dixon-Childe, S. A.i.d.12
Dow, J. C. R. D.i.a.3(1–3)
Drakatos, C. C.iii.1
Duncan, E. A.ii.f.8
Dunning, J. H. A.ii.a.11; B.iii.b.9,13,16,18,21

Edey, H. C.i.a.5
Edge, S. K. B.v.b.4
Edmonds, I. A. A.i.d.14

Edwards, A. P. D. B.iii.a.14
Egle, W. P. D.i.c.3
Einzig, P. A.ii.l.1,3,12; E.ii.9; E.iii.14,16; F.ii.5,9,10,11,13,16,18
Ellinger, E. G. B.ii.b.8
Eltis, W. A. D.iii.c.15
Erritt, M. J. B.iv.1

Farrell, M. J. B.v.a.5
Fisher, D. C.ii.b.5; C.iv.b.6,7,9
Fitzgibbons, A. J. D.ii.a.34
Ford, A. G. B.iii.b.10; D.iii.c.11; G.2,7
Ford, J. L. C.iv.b.3
Franks, Sir O. D.ii.f.7
Friedman, M. D.iii.b.7
Frowen, S. F. A.ii.c.1; B.v.c.2; E.i.15
Fry, R. B.iii.b.6; E.iii.13
Fuller, J. F. A.ii.d.4

Galambos, P. D.iii.d.2; E.ii.10
Galvin, P. A.i.b.29
Garvey, G. D.i.c.5
Gaskin, M. A.i.b.10; A.i.c.1,2,11,12; D.iii.a.9
Gestrin, B. V. D.i.b.14
Ghandhi, J. K. S. A.ii.e.5; B.v.b.3; D.iii.d.3
Gibson, F. W. A.i.d.15
Gibson, N. J. D.ii.a.6; D.ii.b.3
Gilbert, J. C. A.ii.f.2,3,4
Gilbert, R. S. E.ii.3
Goldstein, H. N. D.ii.a.31
Goode, R. D.ii.a.27
Goodson, H. F. A.ii.j.1
Gordon, T. C. A.i.b.14
Grady, J. A.ii.d.5
Grant, J. A. G. C.iv.b.5
Greaves, P. J. A.ii.e.8
Gregory, Sir T. G.9
Grossfield, K. B.v.c.7
Gschwindt de Gyor, P. G. D.iii.b.14
Gurley, J. D.ii.a.27

Hall, A. R. B.v.a.13
Hamlyn, M. A. B. B.iii.a.3; B.v.e.1
Hancock, K. D.i.a.4
Harris, L. D.iii.b.11
Harrod, Sir R. F. D.i.a.8; D.i.c.1; D.iii.b.3; E.i.19; E.iii.4,15; F.i.1

Harrold, J. R. A.i.b.22
Hawtrey, Sir R. A.i.b.34; D.i.d.1,11,12; D.iii.a.2; D.iii.c.1,6; F.i.6,19
Hazlewood, A. E.i.1
Henderson, R. F. B.v.a.1; D.ii.e.5
Herrington, P. R. D.iii.b.10
Hicks, I. A.ii.i.4
Hicks, J. R. C.iv.b.1
Hindle, R. A.i.b.26; A.i.d.1,3,6,7,9,10,11,17; A.ii.d.6
Hirsch, F. E.iii.8
Hodder, H. G. D.i.b.6
Hodson, Sir O. D.i.d.10
Holder, F. W. A.ii.f.7
Holloway, R. G. E.iv.11
Holmans, A. E. D.ii.g.7; D.iii.b.5; E.ii.6
Holmes, A. B.i.3
Hooper, S. B.v.d.2
Horrigan, W. A.ii.h.6
Horwick, G. C.ii.a.4
Houghton, R. A.ii.i.4
Howland, C. B. A.i.d.18
Hume, L. J. D.ii.e.3; G.4
Hunsworth, J. A.ii.d.2
Hutton, G. D.i.a.5

Ingram, J. C. A.ii.l.11

Jasay, A. E. D.i.b.7; D.i.d.21; F.i.4; F.ii.1,2,4
Johnson, H. G. A.i.a.1; A.i.b.13; D.i.a.1; D.i.b.15
Jones, A. A.i.b.12
Jucker-Fleetwood, E. E. G.10

Katz, S. I. D.ii.g.4
Kavanagh, N. J. C.ii.b.2
Kemp, A. G. B.iii.b.11
Kennedy, C. C.iv.a.1
King, W. A.i.b.9; A.ii.j.3
Kitching, D. W. C. A.ii.j.4
Klein, T. M. E.i.3
Krainer, R. E. D.iii.c.13
Krassowski, A. B.iii.b.14

Lamfalussy, A. D.ii.e.6
Law, R. A.ii.k.2
Lawton, C. L. B.ii.c.11
Lee, G. A.ii.g.2,9

Letham, J. A.i.c.5
Levitt, M. S. D.ii.d.4
Lianos, T. P. C.ii.a.7
Linton, C. W. A.ii.j.2
Lipsey, R. G. D.ii.d.1,3; G.1

MacDonald, I. W. A.i.c.4
Macleod, I. F.i.14
Maddison, A. D.i.a.8
Manser, W. A. P. B.iii.b.7,25,26; E.i.24
Manson, P. A. A.ii.l.4
Marini, L. G.6
Marks, P. K. B.ii.c.12
Mason, J. I. A.i.a.9
Maynard, G. A.i.b.15; D.ii.g.9
McLeod, A. N. D.ii.a.19; D.ii.d.5
Meade, J. E. B.ii.a.1; F.i.18
Mendelsohn, M. S. A.ii.a.7; A.ii.b.3
Merrett, A. J. B.v.a.6; B.v.b.5; D.iii.c.9
Mills, G. A.ii.g.11
Minchinton, W.E. B.iii.a.10
Miramon, G. de A.ii.b.6
Mishan, E. J. B.ii.a.4
Mitchell, J. E.i.14; E.ii.1
Momtchiloff, N. B.iii.a.2
Montagu, D. A.ii.c.3
Moreh, J. A.ii.g.6,7,8
Morgan, E. V. A.ii.a.11; B.ii.b.9; B.iii.b.23,27; B.iv.9; C.ii.b.1; D.ii.g.6; D.iii.c.4,8; F.i.7
Morton, S. W. G. A.ii.g.5
Murphy, G. W. A.ii.i.2; B.v.b.7

Naish, P. J. A.ii.f.5
Narvekar, P. R. D.ii.a.5
Nevin, E. A.i.b.18
Newbould, G. D. B.v.a.10,11; B.v.b.5
Newlyn, W. T. D.i.d.18; D.ii.a.7,10,12,14
Nicholson, J. L. B.iv.1
Niveau, M. D.i.c.4
Nobay, A. R. D.iii.b.13
Nursaw, W. A.ii.h.3

Opie, R. G. E.iv.1
Oppenheimer, P. M. D.i.c.7; E.i.11,12; F.ii.19
Osborn, W. T. A.ii.h.4,5

Page, H. R. B.ii.c.3,7
Paine, N. R. C.ii.a.6
Paish, F. W. A.i.b.16; C.i.a.1; D.i.a.6,11; D.i.b.1; D.ii.g.2; E.i.27
Palamountain, E. A.ii.f.6
Panic, M. E.ii.12
Parkin, J. M. D.ii.a.21
Peacock, A. T. D.i.b.2
Pearce, D. W. E.iii.11
Perkins, J. O. N. D.ii.e.5; E.iv.4,5
Peterson, C. H., Jr. A.i.d.16
Piercy, Lord. A.i.b.2; B.v.c.6
Pilcher, R. A. A.ii.e.10
Podolski, T. M. D.ii.e.9
Pollak, F. A.ii.k.3
Posner, M. V. D.ii.e.4
Potter, J. R. L. A.ii.g.3
Potter, R. C. D.ii.a.28
Pressnell, L. S. F.ii.17
Prest, A. R. D.i.a.7
Prusmann, D. F. A.ii.i.2; B.v.b.7
Pulay, G. A.i.b.30

Reading, B. A.ii.l.7; F.ii.6
Rees, G. L. A.ii.h.6
Revell, J. A.ii.a.9; B.i.2
Robbins, L. D.iii.a.1
Roberts, D. J. D.i.b.13
Robertson, Sir D. D.i.d.17
Robinson, A. E.i.16
Robinson, J. C.i.a.4
Roosa, R. V. D.i.d.8
Rose, H. B. C.i.a.2; D.i.b.5,11; D.ii.e.2; D.iii.b.1
Rowan, D. C. B.iii.b.18,20; D.ii.a.32
Runcie, N. A.ii.e.1,2
Rybczynski, T. M. A.ii.c.1; B.i.1; B.iii.a.16

Sachs, D. B.iii.b.19
Saunders, C. T. C.i.b.1
Sayers, R. S. D.i.b.4,8,9,12; D.iii.c.10; E.iii.20
Scammell, W. M. E.i.20; G.5
Schmidt, W. S. D.i.c.6,8
Schmolders, G. C.i.a.6
Scott, I. O., Jr. A.ii.l.9; D.i.c.6,8
Scott, M. F.i.12
Seton, F. B.i.5

Shackle, G. L. S.   C.iv.a.4
Sharp, B. C.   A.i.b.27
Shaw, G. K.   D.i.a.10
Shenfield, A. A.   B.v.c.3
Sheppard, D. K.   D.ii.a.40
Shimmin, A. N.   D.i.c.2
Shonfield, A.   D.iii.a.5
Silberston, A.   D.iii.d.4,6,10
Simpson, D.   A.i.d.12
Smart, P. E.   A.i.b.21
Smith, I.   D.ii.f.1
Speight, H.   D.iii.a.3
Spengler, H. A.   E.iv.7
Spraos, J.   D.iii.c.5; F.i.3; F.ii.3
Stamp, M.   E.iii.12
Stark, T.   C.iv.b.3
Steddings, P.   A.ii.h.1
Steer, E. T.   B.v.b.1
Stewart, A.   A.ii.g.1
Stewart, I.   D.ii.f.2
Sturmey, S. G.   B.v.d.1
Sweet-Escott, B.   B.iii.b.22
Sykes, A.   D.iii.c.9

Taylor, F. S.   A.i.c.6,8,9,10; D.ii.a.3
Tether, C. G.   E.ii.11
Tew, B.   B.ii.b.7; C.iv.a.2; D.ii.a.9; D.ii.e.1
Thanos, C. A.   D.ii.a.30,32
Thomson, J.   A.i.b.25
Thornton, L. S.   A.ii.b.5
Tooby, F. W.   D.iii.b.9
Triffin, R.   F.i.5
Tuke, A.   B.iii.a.4
Turner, M.   A.ii.e.11

Usherwood, K. A.   A.ii.h.2

Vice, A.   E.ii.2
Vine, R.   A.i.d.12

Wadsworth, J. E.   D.i.b.3; D.ii.c.3
Walters, A. A.   C.ii.b.2,4; C.iii.2; D.ii.c.3
Ward, M.   A.i.b.24
White, W. H.   D.i.c.10; D.ii.d.2; D.iii.c.3,7

Williams, A. F. B.   B.iii.b.17
Williams, D.   D.iii.a.4; E.i.17; F.i.9; G.8
Williamson, J.   F.i.13
Wilson, J. S. G.   A.ii.a.16; D.i.d.15; D.iii.a.7
Wilson, T.   B.v.a.4
Wilson, Sir T.   D.i.d.24
Wincott, H.   D.iii.b.8
Winton, J. R.   A.i.a.2
Wiseman, J.   B.ii.a.2
Wray, M.   A.ii.g.12
Wright, L. C.   D.ii.a.1, D.ii.f.8

Young, E. A.   A.i.b.36; B.iii.a.12

Zawadzki, K. K. F.   D.ii.a.17

PARTICIPANTS IN THE 'RADCLIFFE REPORT—TEN YEARS AFTER' CONFERENCE

Organizing Committee

Professor H. G. Johnson (London School of Economics): Chairman
Mr. D. R. Croome (Queen Mary College London): Secretary
Mr. J. C. Hopwood (Manager, Market Intelligence Dept., National Westminster Bank Ltd.): Treasurer
Professor G. Maynard (University of Reading)
Dr. L. S. Pressnell (London School of Economics)
Mr. L. Harris (London School of Economics)

Emeritus Professor R. S. Sayers
Professor N. J. Gibson (Ulster)
Mr. J. V. Glass (Ulster)
Professor A. D. Bain (Stirling)
Professor E. T. Nevin (Swansea)
Professor W. T. Newlyn (Leeds)
Professor G. Clayton (Sheffield)
Professor J. Gilbert (Sheffield)
Professor E. V. Morgan (Manchester)
Professor D. Laidler (Manchester)
Professor M. Fleming (Bristol)
Professor C. M. Kennedy (Kent)
Professor A. A. Walters (L.S.E.)
Mr. R. Alford (L.S.E.)
Dr. M. Miller (L.S.E.)
Mr. B. Griffiths (L.S.E.)
Professor D. Rowan (Southampton)
Mr. M. Townsend (Southampton)
Professor J. S. G. Wilson (Hull)
Mr. M. Parkin (Essex)
Professor D. Fisher (Essex)
Professor P. Davidson (Rutgers, New Jersey, U.S.A.)
Dr. A. B. Cramp (Cambridge)

Dr. R. Smethurst (Oxford)
Dr. P. Oppenheimer (Oxford)
Mr. C. Barrett (Birmingham)
Dr. D. K. Sheppard (Birmingham)

Sir D. MacDougall (H.M. Treasury)
Mr. R. Armstrong (H.M. Treasury)
Mr. A. Lovell (H.M. Treasury)
Mr. M. V. Posner (H.M. Treasury)
Mr. R. Sheppard (H.M. Treasury)

Mr. C. Mcmahon (Bank of England)
Mr. M. Thornton (Bank of England)
Mr. L. Dicks-Mireaux (Bank of England)
Dr. C. Goodhart (Bank of England)

Mr. M. J. Artis (National Institute of Economic and Social Research)
Mr. A. R. Nobay (N.I.E.S.R.)

Mr. T. C. Maynard (National Westminster Bank Ltd.)
Mr. J. E. Maycock (Midland Bank)
Mr. P. K. Marks (Midland Bank)
Mr. A. H. Milton (Barclays Bank)
Mr. R. H. Everett (Barclays Bank)
Mr. R. J. Clark (Westminster Bank)
Mr. P. W. Wilkinson (Westminster Bank)
Mr. J. E. Wadsworth (Midland Bank)
Mr. T. M. Rybczynski (Lazard Brothers)
Mrs. H. Thompson (The Standard Bank)
Mr. J. C. Hunt (B.O.L.S.A.)
Mr. D. E. Fair (National Commercial Bank)
Mr. J. R. Winton (Lloyds Bank)
Mr. E. S. Tibbetts (Lloyds Bank Europe)
Mr. A. Peters (Shell Ltd.)
Mr. D. Andrew (Shell Ltd.)

INDEX

(Entries printed in italics are references to particular authors or their works)